A CLEAR VIEW OF THE LAW

洞悉法门

理解法律的复杂性

MAKING SENSE OF
LEGAL COMPLEXITY

Low Kee Yang

| 汉英对照 |

[新加坡] 刘启扬 | 著

张 巍 翁 磊 李嘉宝 | 译

中国法制出版社
CHINA LEGAL PUBLISHING HOUSE

作者简介　刘启扬（Low Kee Yang），毕业于新加坡国立大学及英国伦敦大学国王学院，新加坡管理大学杨邦孝法学院副教授，院长特别顾问，新加坡管理大学创校团队成员，负责领导法学院的组建，曾任法学院执行院长。刘启扬博士执教三十余年，讲授公司法、侵权法、合同法、金融顾问法等一系列课程，专长于商法，著有公司法、担保法及商法等专著，并发表众多相关论文。

译者简介

张　巍，毕业于复旦大学、早稻田大学、哈佛大学及加州大学伯克利分校，获得法律与公共政策学博士学位，现任新加坡管理大学杨邦孝法学院副院长、副教授。主要从事民商法研究，著有《资本的规则》及《资本的规则 II》，发表中英文论文数十篇。

翁　磊，江苏南京人，新加坡执业律师，拥有新加坡、英国（事务律师）以及美国纽约州三地律师执业资格，担任新加坡瑞信德亚洲律师事务所（RHTLaw Asia LLP）中国国际业务部高级律师，擅长涉及中国企业、海外中资企业以及有中国背景的企业或个人的国际（大宗）贸易、建筑工程、投资并购、公司治理、知识产权等复杂跨境商事纠纷争议解决业务。在国内外多个仲裁委担任仲裁员，多个国际调解机构担任调解员，同时还在国内外多个著名大学担任客座或兼职讲师。

李嘉宝，四川德阳人，获得新加坡政府奖学金赴新加坡留学，2021年获得新加坡管理大学法学院学士（优等）学位，是新加坡最年轻的认证调解员之一，现从事法律行业相关工作。

愿汉语法学枝繁叶茂

FOREWORD

Why do people obey the law? Lawmakers know the key to effective laws is their ability to make laws that have general acceptance and will be observed. An instrumentalist approach presupposes that people model their behaviour in response to tangible incentives and consequences. Often, policymakers adopt this approach. On the other hand, the normative approach focuses on the compliance of what is considered to be necessary, just and moral rather than observance based purely on self-interest. The importance of this approach cannot be overstated. After all, acceptance and voluntary compliance requires less oversight and reinforces legitimacy. Notions of legitimacy are particularly critical when discretionary powers are being exercised.

The publication of this book is timely. There is growing interest in how laws are made and applied in modern society. This is a positive development as laws impact all of us in every facet of our lives. Why laws are in place and how they are applied do really matter. All of us have an interest in ensuring that laws are applied fairly, equally and consistently.

What are the sources of our laws? How do policies affect the content, crafting and application of our laws? What are legal principles and how is their hierarchy determined? How do the legislature and the judiciary interact? How

序言

人们为什么遵守法律？立法者知道，能够被大众接受并遵守的立法才是确保法律效力的关键。工具主义认为，人们会根据真实的激励和后果来规范调整自己的行为。通常政策制定者采取的也是这种思路。另一方面，规范性方法论则侧重于遵守被认为是必要的、公正的和道德的规则，而不是纯粹为了自我利益而遵守。规范性方法论的重要性怎么强调都不为过。毕竟，接受和自愿遵守需要更少的监督，也更显示其合法性。合法性的观念在行使自由裁量权的时候尤为关键。

本书出版得正当其时。人们对现代社会中法律如何制定并适用这个问题的兴趣日增。这是一种积极的进展，毕竟法律在生活的方方面面影响着我们每个人。为什么要制定法律以及如何适用这些法律确实很重要。确保法律适用的公正、平等和一致与我们每个人都息息相关。

我们的法律渊源是什么？政策是如何影响我们法律的内容、制定和适用的？法律原则是什么，其效力层级是如何确定的？立法机关和司法机关是如何互动的？法律是如何被解释的？自由裁量权是如何行使和受到限制的？为什么正义观念和法律有时会发生冲突？法律是如何跨越国界运作的，是否有明

are laws interpreted? How are discretions exercised and circumscribed? Why do notions of justice and the law sometimes conflict? How does the law operate across international borders and is there a clear hierarchy of application? These are just some of the big and important questions raised and addressed in this book.

While the internet and its myriad sources provide a rich trove of information and are easily accessible, they are neither invariably accurate nor reliable wells to draw upon. Professor Low draws upon his four decades of rich experience and unique personal insights as a practitioner, academic and administrator to distil a compelling compendium on law within a common law system. There is no other overview quite like this. Ambitious in intent, comprehensive in scope and, ultimately, satisfying in content. The book ticks all the right boxes as a primer. It is a stimulating and engaging introduction to legal systems and their operating software.

Books like this help to shed light on technical concepts, demystify the fog of legal jargon, give insights into legal decision making and promote active citizenry. They make a difference. Professor Low, therefore, deserves our gratitude for making the workings of the law more accessible to the wider public.

VK Rajah SC

Managing Partner, Rajah & Tann (1987–2003)

Judge of the Supreme Court, Singapore (2004–2007)

Judge of Appeal of the Supreme Court, Singapore (2007–2014)

Attorney–General of Singapore (2014–2017)

确的适用层级？这些只是本书中提出并阐述的部分重大问题。

虽然互联网及其浩瀚的资料构成了一个丰富且易于访问的信息库，但这些信息既不一定准确，也不一定可靠。刘教授根据他四十多年来作为律师、学者和管理者的丰富经验和独特的个人见解，提炼出这样一本引人注目的关于普通法体系的汇编书籍。这是首次有此类文献问世。本书立意高远，讨论全面，内容详尽。作为一本入门书，本书符合一本好书需要具有的所有属性，它深入浅出地介绍了法律制度及其运作方式。

本书有助于阐明技术性概念，揭秘法律术语，使人深入了解法律决策的方方面面，提升公民意识，这些绝非无足轻重。通过本书，刘教授使更多的公众能够了解法律的运作，在此，我们应当表达对刘教授的诚挚谢意。

维·库·拉贾资深大律师

立杰律师事务所管理合伙人（1987—2003）

新加坡最高法院法官（2004—2007）

新加坡最高法院上诉庭法官（2007—2014）

新加坡总检察长（2014—2017）

PREFACE

As a young man pondering career choices, I considered literature, medicine, architecture, psychotherapy and law, amongst others. In the end, mainly out of pragmatism, I chose law.

Now, after over three decades of teaching, researching and writing on law, what do I observe? Well, foremost, law is intensely logical; the study of law involves deep analysis. Next, it requires a mastery of words. This is especially important when delicate nuancing is required to achieve a just result. Finally, a keen appreciation of the real world is needed. Legal principles must relate to the contexts to which they apply.

I also observe, regrettably, that law is often very complicated and complex. And, at times, the law is unfair and, dare I say, incorrect. Whether it be a new court decision or a novel piece of legislation, much analysis is needed to figure out what the decision or legislation is saying, how it changes the existing law, and what the implications and imperfections are.

Likewise, legal agreements are often difficult to digest. The non–lawyer, as well as the beginner law student, is perplexed. There is a chasm, almost, between him or her and an understanding of the law.

This book seeks to help the reader cross the chasm. It explains the broad

前 言

年轻的时候，我在做事业选择时曾举棋不定，考虑过文学、医学、建筑、心理治疗、法律等方向。最终出于现实的考虑，我选择了法律。

时至今日，在积累了三十多年的法律教学、研究和写作经验之后，我都有些什么体会呢？首先，法律有严密的逻辑性，学习法律需要进行深层的分析。其次，法律需要对语言的精通，这在需要通过把握微妙的差别才能实现正义时显得尤其重要。最后，法律需要对现实世界有敏锐的洞察力，法律原则的适用必须与其相关的场景相结合。

遗憾的是，我也注意到了法律的复杂性。有时法律并不公平，甚至我敢说，法律是不正确的。无论是新的判决还是新的立法，都需要进行大量的分析，弄清楚判决或立法想表达的意思，知道它们将如何改变现行法律，以及它们造成的影响和不完善之处。

同样地，法律协议通常理解消化起来也很困难。非律师人员，甚至包括那些初入法学院的学生，常常会感到困惑。在他们与对法律的理解之间似乎存在着一道巨大的鸿沟。

本书意在帮助读者跨越这一鸿沟。本书解释了制定法律时

challenge of crafting law and the detailed aspects involved in configuring a legal principle. It examines the many ways in which legal complexity arises and helps the reader make sense of the complexity. It grapples with error and unfairness within the law and the reasons for these blemishes.

In other words, to help you understand the design and fabric of the law, know whether it is in harmony with logic and justice, and discern, when the law errs, what the correct position should be.

I must say I found it challenging trying to simplify, explain and demystify the law, and to do so in an accurate yet interesting way. But it was enjoyable too.

May you have a clear view of the law.

需要面对的各种挑战和配置法律原则所涉及的多种细节，研究了产生法律复杂性的各种成因，以便帮助读者理解这种复杂性，同时也剖析了法律中的错误和不公及其形成的原因。

换句话说，这本书会帮助你理解法律的设计和结构，知道它是否符合逻辑和正义，并在法律出现错误时辨明正确的立场。

我必须说，试图以准确且有趣的方式对法律进行简化、解释和揭秘，这是一件具有挑战性的工作。但我乐在其中。

愿你能洞悉法律的门径。

ACKNOWLEDGEMENTS

This book was written over a period of three years and with the help of many people. I am very grateful to each of them.

I owe an enormous debt to Leong Kwong Sin, my good friend and university colleague, for the many discussions we had over versions of the draft. A brilliant accountant who is extremely knowledgeable, he gave me very valuable views and insights.

I am very thankful for my research assistant, Gerome Goh, who explored many legal facets with me, discussed the drafts and researched various aspects of the book. His acuity, responsiveness and optimism brightened my journey.

I am extremely grateful to VK Rajah, a long-time friend and a superb lawyer and judge, for taking time to read the manuscript and penning the kind Foreword.

At the conception stage, I benefitted from discussions with Henry Chan, Iqbal Jummabhoy and Leonora Leow. Their time and thoughts are much appreciated.

When the manuscript was completed, I approached two groups of people at the School of Law of the Singapore Management University. They were very kind to spend time reading and commenting on the draft.

致谢

本书的写作历时三年，得到了许多人的帮助。我在此对他们每个人表示感谢。

我欠了我的好朋友兼大学同事 Leong Kwong Sin 一大份人情。我们就书稿的版本进行了多次讨论。他是一位出色的会计师，且知识渊博，他给了我非常宝贵的意见和见解。

我非常感谢我的研究助理 Gerome Goh，他和我一起探讨了许多法律方面的问题，我们也一起讨论并研究了本书涉及的各个方面。他的敏锐和乐观为我的前行提供了指引。

我非常感谢我的老友 VK Rajah，他也是一位出色的律师和法官，他抽出时间来阅读书稿并慷慨地为本书撰写了序言。

在构思阶段，我受益于与 Henry Chan、Iqbal Jummabhoy 和 Leonora Leow 的讨论。我非常感谢他们的想法和为此付出的时间。

书稿完成后，我联络了新加坡管理大学法学院的两个团队。他们非常热心地花时间阅读并提出意见和建议。

第一个团队是我优秀的同事 Basil Bitas、Tan Seow Hon、Dorcas Quek-Anderson 和 Nicholas Liu。第二个团队是我具有洞察力的学生 Ian Mah、Darien The、Aaron Lim Chor Yin 和 Lai Siang

The first are my wonderful colleagues Basil Bitas, Tan Seow Hon, Dorcas Quek-Anderson and Nicholas Liu. The second are my perceptive students Ian Mah, Darien The, Aaron Lim Chor Yin and Lai Siang Ping. The final product is much better because of their comments.

I am also much indebted to Rosa Dwisanty and Ian Lim, who provided the perspective of young adults who, though not legally trained, have to grapple with law in the course of their work.

Many thanks to my publisher Candid Creation Publishing for bringing this project to fruition. I am grateful, in particular, to Phoon Kok Hwa for his enthusiasm and guidance, to Patricia Ng for her felicitous editorial pointers, to Ryanne Ng for the cover design and Corrine Teng for the page layout.

My sincere thanks to each and every one of you.

Ping。他们的建议大大提升了作品最终的质量。

我也非常感谢 Rosa Dwisanty 和 Ian Lim，他们虽然没有受过法律训练，但在工作过程中必须与法律打交道，他们为我提供了年轻人的视角。

我非常感谢出版商 Candid Creation Publishing，是他们使这个项目圆满完成。我特别感谢 Phoon Kok Hwa 的热情和指导，感谢 Patricia Ng 娴熟的编辑指导，也感谢 Ryanne Ng 的封面设计和 Corrine Teng 的内文设计。

我真诚地感谢你们每一个人。

INTRODUCTION

A place for everything and everything in its place.

——Benjamin Franklin

The law is like an ocean, deep as it is wide. Parts of its waters are clear and calm; other parts are murky; still others are tumultuous.

Each of us, in his or her journey in life, encounters the law in personal and in professional or business capacities. As we do so, we may find the law to be unwieldy and incomprehensible. Sometimes, we feel the law is unfair. Law perplexes and exasperates us.

The objective of this book is to help the layperson, the professional and the novice law student better understand the law, complex as it is. The aim is to bridge the gulf between law and the comprehension of the law. For sure, the goal is an ambitious one.

Law is about what you can and cannot do, in relation to others. The law sets boundaries in a society, conferring rights and imposing obligations. It comprises diverse and detailed sets of principles and rules.

The reason for law? Law is needed to provide order, harmony and justice in society.

导 言

地适其物，物得其所。

——本杰明·富兰克林

法律就像一片海洋，广阔且深邃。它有清澈和平静的部分；也有混浊的部分；还有动荡的部分。

我们每个人在人生旅途中，都会遇到涉及个人、职业或商务领域的法律问题。每每至此，我们会发现法律冗繁且难以理解。有时我们觉得法律不甚公平，并因此感到困惑和气愤。

本书的目的在于帮助普通人、专业人士和新晋法科学生更好地理解复杂的法律，希望能够跨越法律和对法律的理解之间的鸿沟。毫无疑问，这是一个雄心勃勃的目标。

法律说的是关于你能做什么和不能做什么，以及与其他人的关系。法律规定了社会的界限，赋予权利并规定义务。法律包括各种详细的原则和规则。

为什么要有法律？因为需要法律为社会提供秩序、和谐和正义。

普通人希望法律是清晰、简明、连贯、全面和公平的。人们也希望法律是有效且实用的。

The layman expects the law to be clear, concise, coherent, comprehensive and fair. He also expects it to be effective and practical.

Much of the law does satisfy the above wish list. Regrettably, some of it falls short of the ideal.

The reality is that, quite often, the law on a particular subject is complex or controversial. Sometimes, the law is even wrong or unfair.

Why is this so, you may protest. There are three main reasons.

First, the world is a complicated place. Many scenarios the law has to address are complex, involving diverse interests, perspectives and challenges. If the scenario is complex, it should not surprise that the law is complex as well.

Secondly, fairness, like beauty, is in the eye of the beholder. In a dispute, each party has his or her own interest and perspective and it is rare to find a party who can be objective about what fairness in the dispute requires. It seems fair when you win a dispute, but not when you lose. Further, there is the interest of society to consider. It is hard for the law to appear fair from all these perspectives.

Finally, the law is only as good as the lawmaker. The lawmaker, whether legislator or judge, is a person — finite and imperfect. It may surprise the reader to know how often the lawmaker, in his reasoning process, falls prey to biases, fallacies and misconceptions. Hence, the resulting error or unfairness.

The key to making sense of law, especially complex, controversial or unfair law, is to understand what is involved in the crafting of law and how it is done. There is also a need to appreciate the limitations of lawmaking and recognise when and why law goes awry.

Whether we like them or not, and whether we are aware of them or not, myriad laws apply to and affect us. We have no choice but to seek to understand

很多法律确实满足了上述愿望。遗憾的是，有一些法律没有达到理想的状态。

现实情况是，关于某个特定问题的法律往往复杂或有争议。有时法律甚至是错误的或不公平的。

你可能会质疑说：为什么会这样呢？这主要有三个原因。

首先，世界很复杂。许多法律必须处理的情景也很复杂，涉及不同的利益、观点和挑战。在复杂的情境中，复杂的法律也就不足为奇了。

其次，就像对“美”的定义一样，“公平”也取决于看客的角度。在纠纷中，每一方都有自己的利益和观点，很少有一方能客观地看待纠纷中所需的公平。当你打赢官司时，公平似乎就实现了，但当你打输时，你就不会这样想。此外，还有社会的整体利益需要考虑。法律很难做到从所有这些角度看都显得公平。

最后，法律的好坏受到法律制定者能力的限制。法律制定者，无论是立法者还是法官，都是人——都有其局限性和不完美性。读者可能会惊讶地发现，立法者在其说理的过程中经常陷入偏见、谬误和误解之中。因此，也就产生了错误或不公平。

理解法律，尤其是理解复杂的、有争议的或不公平的法律，关键在于了解法律的制定过程中涉及的步骤，以及这些步骤如何得以完成。此外，还需要了解制定法律的局限性，并认识到法律何时以及为何出错。

无论我们喜欢与否，也无论我们是否意识到，海量的法律都会对我们适用，它们影响着我们。我们别无选择，只能设法理解法律、遵守法律，并利用法律来保护自己，尽量让我们的

the law, to comply with it and to leverage upon it to protect ourselves, minimise our liabilities and optimise our rights.

This book aims to explain law in a clear, concise and interesting manner in five parts.

Part Ⅰ introduces the world of law, explains where law is found and gives an overview of the areas of law.

Part Ⅱ deals with the dynamics of crafting law, such as contextual objectives, policies, morality and notions of justice.

Part Ⅲ delves deeper into the exercise of crafting law and considers, with illustrations from case law, legislation and regulatory law, how a principle of law is assembled.

Part Ⅳ, a substantial portion of the book, grapples with complexities and controversies. Here, we deal with an array of circumstances and reasons for complications and intrigue in the law.

Part Ⅴ explains why there are errors in the law and why there is often unfairness.

The book ends with some concluding thoughts.

Law is necessary for an orderly society. Yet, it can be daunting and impenetrable. May this book help you to have a clear view of the law.

责任最小化，让我们的权利最优化。

本书共分为五个部分，旨在以清晰、简明和有趣的方式解释法律。

第一部分介绍法律的世界，解释法律的来源，并概述法律的各个领域。

第二部分论述制定法律的各个方面，如背景、政策、道德与法律和正义的理念等。

第三部分深入探讨法律制定的过程，并以案例法、成文法和行政法规为例，讨论法律原则是如何形成的。

第四部分是本书的一个重要部分，致力于剖析具有复杂性和争议性的问题。在这一部分，我们讨论法律显得复杂和吊诡的各种背景和原因。

第五部分解释为什么法律中会有错误，以及为什么经常会有不公平。

本书的末尾提供了一些总结性的想法。

法律是维持社会秩序的必要前提。然而，法律可能令人望而生畏，难以捉摸。愿这本书能帮助你洞悉法律的门径。

目录

CONTENTS

It is tempting to say that this book demystifies the law as the title A Clear View suggests; but it actually does something more than that. It captures the law's majesty, its relevance, and its immediacy in an accessible and intellectually rigorous manner.

——Basil Bitas (Attorney and author)

一看《洞悉法门》这个题目，我们不禁会说这是一本为法律揭秘的书；其实，不止如此，这本书深入浅出地揭示了法律的壮丽炫美、无所不在，更与我们近在咫尺。

——贝索·比特斯（律师、作家）

Part I

The World of Law

This country is planted thick with laws from coast to coast.

——Robert Bolt

A Man for All Seasons

第一部分

法律的世界

这个国家，从一侧海岸到另一侧海岸，法律丛生。

——罗伯特·博尔特

《良相佐国》

The world of law is as vast, detailed and complicated as many other realms and disciplines. And we have to find it and understand it.

In seeking legal information and knowledge, it is not surprising that one resorts to the internet. There, we encounter a whole array of material, some reliable and some not, some digestible and others incomprehensible. What is important to know is that, legally, there are secondary sources and primary sources. Helpful as secondary sources may be, it is the primary sources — statute and case law — that are authoritative. Chapter 1 explains the distinctions as to the sources of law.

As one finds the law and tries to understand it, one is amazed by the sheer number of areas or types of law, much like how medicine, engineering and many other fields of study splinter into a myriad subdivisions.

Fortunately, for law, there is a fundamental core of three areas — crime, tort and contract — and this reasonably distinct subdivision helps greatly as one seeks to understand the law. Chapter 2 explains this categorisation of law.

法律的世界就像其他许多领域和学科一样，庞大、细致而复杂。而我们必须去发现它、理解它。

在寻找法律信息和法律知识的时候，人们会求助于互联网，这毫不奇怪。在那儿，我们将遇到各式各样的材料——有些可靠，有些不可靠；有些我们能够理解，有些则显得不知所云。然而，重要的是要知道，法律资料的来源可以分为衍生性来源和基础性来源。尽管出自衍生性来源的资料可能很有帮助，但出自基础性来源的资料——成文法和判例法——才具有权威性。第一章将解释法律资料来源的区别。

当我们找到法律并试图理解它之时，又会惊讶于法律领域、类型的纷繁，就像医学、工程学和许多其他学科一样，法律被分割成数不胜数的分支。

幸运的是，对于法律来说，其基本核心只包含三个领域——犯罪、侵权和合同。在我们试图理解法律的时候，把握住这三个不同分支将大有助益，能帮助我们理出头绪。第 2 章将介绍法律的这种基本分类。

Chapter 1
Where to Find the Law

He was searching for something and, like everyone else, he had no idea where to find it.

——Nick Burd

Today, the fastest and most common way to find information is to search the internet. There is an astonishing amount of material on the web. Whether you are looking for a product, a story, a song or a video, and whether the search relates to architecture, climate, economics, history, politics or zoology, you can find a mountain of material on the internet. Just google it. (The name Google was well chosen by Larry Page; "googol" — one, followed by a hundred zeroes.)

If one googles the law on a particular topic or issue, the search unearths a huge mass of results, such as Wikipedia notes, comments from law firms (including blogs and podcasts), articles and books.

Of course, the more reliable way to know the law on a particular matter is to consult a lawyer, either on a friendly or a professional basis. Professional advice,

第 1 章
法律应向何处觅?

他在找寻着什么，然而，就像其他人一样，他不知在哪里才能找到。

——尼克·博德

今天，最快捷和最常见的找寻信息的方法是搜索互联网。网络上的信息资料数量惊人，无论你是在寻找一个产品、一个故事、一首歌曲，或者一段视频，也无论搜索的内容是关于建筑、气候、经济、历史、政治，还是动物学，你都可以在互联网上找到堆积如山的材料。谷歌一下，应有尽有。[“谷歌”这个名字是拉里·佩奇精心挑选的，“古戈尔”（googol）原本就是一个计数单位——数字一，后面跟着一百个零]。

如果人们在谷歌上搜索关于某个特定主题或争议的法律，就会搜索出一大堆结果，比如维基百科的条目、律师事务所的评论（包括博客和播客），还有专门的文章和书籍。

当然，要了解关于某个特定事项的法律问题，更加可靠的

however, can be expensive.

Short of taking legal advice, an internet search may be the next most realistic way to get a simplistic and tentative idea of the law on the matter. Of course, as this book seeks to explain, there are many challenges in trying to understand law. Wikipedia is a rich and reasonably accurate source of legal information. Notes from law firms vary in terms of usefulness; some are very brief whilst others go beyond a summary to provide some insight and analysis. If you want comprehensive analysis from law firms, you will have to pay for it.

Articles by academics can provide detailed analysis but you usually have to subscribe to the journal. One challenge is that such articles may be impenetrable because of legal jargon and, at times, verbose language.

And, of course, there are books, physical or electronic. There are two main categories of law books — those for law students and law teachers, and those for practitioners. Apart from these two, there are books for non- law students and books for the general public.

Just as the right note or article is useful for finding out the law on a particular issue or topic, the right book can also give you a good understanding of an area of law, such as criminal law, banking law or intellectual property (IP) law.

What is particularly important to know, in the context of this chapter, is that the authoritative law is not any of the above-mentioned resources. Lawyers term them "secondary" materials. The actual law is found in the "primary" materials.

What are the primary materials? Basically, they are the statutes (or legislation) and case reports (reports of judgments). Let me elaborate.

Legislation may be primary or subsidiary. Primary legislation refers to the

办法是咨询律师——无论是友情点拨，还是专业意见。不过，专业的咨询可能会十分昂贵。

假如不专门谋求法律意见，那么，要想简单地针对某个问题获得一些初步的法律概念，在互联网上搜索也许是最为现实的办法。当然，正如本书要说明的那样，在你希望理解法律的时候，会遇到诸多挑战。维基百科是一个丰富，而且有相当准确性的法律信息来源。律师事务所写的综述类文章，其实用性各不相同，有的非常简短，而有的不光是一篇摘要，还会提供一定的见解与分析。不过，假使你想从律师事务所获得全面的法律分析，那就不得不为之付费了。

学者们写的论文会有详尽的分析，但你通常必须订阅相关的学术杂志。而且，还有一个挑战是，这类文章可能因为专业术语，以及时而繁冗的语言而让人不明就里。

除此之外，当然还有书籍——实物书或电子书。法律书主要有两大类，一类是写给法学院的学生和教师看的，另一类则是写给法律实务工作者看的。此外，还有面向非法律专业的学生，以及普通公众的法律书籍。

正如合适的综述或论文有助于了解有关特定问题的法律规则，合适的法律书籍也可以让你很好地了解某个法律部门，如刑法、银行法或知识产权法。

就本章讨论的内容而言，特别需要理解的是，以上所有材料都不是具有效力的法律，法律专业人士把它们称为“衍生性”资料。而要找实际适用的法律，则要去搜索“基础性”资料。

那么，什么是基础性资料呢？概而言之，它们是成文法（即立法机构批准的法律）和案例记录（即对法院判决的记录）。

Acts (statutes) passed by parliament. Subsidiary legislation refers to legislation which parliament has delegated to someone else (usually the relevant minister) to bring to pass. For example, in companies legislation, it is common to find a Companies Act, which is supplemented by Companies Rules and Companies Orders. If there is ambiguity or inconsistency between the primary and the subsidiary legislation, naturally the former prevails.

The authority or basis for the law on the crime of killing is not some famous textbook writer but a statutory provision. In Commonwealth countries (see Chapter 31 for an explanation of legal systems), there is typically a Penal Code, which contains a section with wording such as — "Whoever causes death by doing an act with the intention of causing death... commits the offence of culpable homicide." If a writer of an article or a book wants to state a legal proposition (that is, a principle or rule) on this offence, he needs to give or quote an authority. Thus, he may write: "It is an offence for a person to intentionally kill another person: section 299, Penal Code" .

Besides a statutory provision, the authority for a legal principle may originate from case law — a case report of a judgment — instead. For example, on the question of what a defamatory statement is, a lawyer from a common law country (practically, countries which are/were part of the British Commonwealth; see Chapter 31) would give a response such as: "A defamatory statement is one which injures the reputation of another by exposing him to hatred, contempt or ridicule, or which tends to lower the claimant in the estimation of right-thinking members of society generally: *Sim v. Stretch*" .

Basically, in this landmark decision of *Sim v. Stretch*, the English court, and more specifically Lord Atkin, defined defamation in that way.

下面我就来详细说明。

立法机构批准的法律有基础性立法和辅助性立法之分。基础性立法指由立法机构直接制定的法案（即成文法），辅助性立法指的是立法机构委托授权给其他人（通常是行政机构的主管部长）来制定的法规。例如，在有关公司的立法中，最常见到的是《公司法》，而《公司条例》及《公司律令》则可以是《公司法》的补充。如果基础性立法和辅助性立法之间出现歧义或者不一致，那自然是以前者为准。

规定杀人罪的法律依据不是哪本有名的教科书，而是一条成文法的条款。英联邦国家（有关法系，参见第 31 章）通常有一部《刑法典》，其中会有类似这样的条文：“任何人通过意图造成死亡的行为，导致他人死亡的……构成杀人罪。”如果哪篇论文或哪本书的作者想要说明关于这一罪行的法律立场（即原则或规则），就需要引述一项法律依据。于是，他可以这样写：“故意杀害他人构成犯罪：《刑法》第 299 条。”

除了成文法的条款之外，判例法——对法院判决的记录——也可以成为法律原则所依据的正式权威。例如，对于什么是名誉毁损性言论，来自普通法国家（基本就是目前或曾经属于英联邦的国家，参见第 31 章）的律师会这样来解释：“名誉毁损性言论是指通过令他人遭受仇恨、蔑视、嘲弄，或者普遍降低思维正常的社会成员对其评价的言论，致使他人名誉遭受伤害的言论：*Sim v. Stretch* 案。”

实际上，在 *Sim v. Stretch* 案这个具有里程碑意义的判决中，英国法院——更具体地说是法官 Atkin 勋爵——以这种方式对名誉毁损作出了定义。

The above statement of the law may look simple but, in substance, it is not. A lot goes into the crafting of legal propositions, as we shall see in Part II. Because the *Sim v. Stretch* statement was so well–crafted, it continues to be cited as authority today, some 80 years later.

In common law countries, the case law which a court refers to is not confined to decisions from its own courts. Judges often refer to decisions from other common law countries, especially those of higher level and apex courts (apex courts are the highest courts, such as the Supreme Court in the UK and the Court of Appeal in Singapore). These decisions are of persuasive authority and, for courts in some countries, even binding authority. Singapore courts, for example, often refer to decisions from the UK, Australia, Canada, Malaysia and Hong Kong SAR, amongst others.

It should be noted that in countries with a federal system of government, such as the US, Canada, Australia and Brazil, there are laws at the state level as well as at the federal or national level. Sometimes, the state may even be broken into municipalities (towns and districts) with power to make laws as well. Hence, in these countries, one has to adhere to two (or more) sets of laws, along with the complications which that might bring.

Although the primary materials are the authoritative source, the practical thing to do is to go to secondary sources first. A good secondary source, be it an article or a book, gives the enquirer a good introduction to the subject. It sets out the legal principle (s) and the relevant authorities, and may discuss and analyse the controversies.

So, basically, in the search for law, one begins with the secondary sources, which leads one to the authoritative primary sources.

上述对法律的宣示也许看起来很简单，但其实并非如此。正如我们将在第二部分看到的那样，设计法律规范会牵涉方方面面。而正是由于 *Sim v. Stretch* 案的表述设计得如此精巧，才使得它在 80 余年后的今天，依然被当作法律依据来引用。

在普通法国家，法院参考的判例法并不局限于本国法院的判决，法官也经常参考其他普通法国家的判决，特别是那些级别更高的或者终审法院的判决（终审法院即审判级别最高的法院，如英国的最高法院、新加坡的上诉法院）。这些判决具有非正式的说服性效力，在某些国家甚至还具有正式的约束力。例如，新加坡法院经常参考英国、澳大利亚、加拿大、马来西亚和中国香港特别行政区等地的法院的裁判。

值得注意的是，在实行联邦制的国家，如美国、加拿大、澳大利亚和巴西，除了联邦或国家层面的法律外，还有州一级的法律。有时，州还会被进一步分解成拥有立法权的市（或镇、区）。因此，在这些国家，人们必须遵守两套（或更多）法律，而这也可能带来一些复杂的问题。

虽然，基础性资料是正式的法律渊源，不过，实践中，我们往往先去找衍生性资料。因为一个好的衍生性资料——无论是文章还是书籍，都能给查询法律者提供一个针对相关法律问题的有用指引，它会阐述法律原则及其依据，也许还会讨论和分析相关的争议。

整体而言，在寻找法律的过程中，我们通常会从衍生性资料入手，并由此得到线索，进而找到基础性资料。

Chapter 2
Areas of Law

We categorise as we do because we have the brains and bodies we have and because we interact in the world as we do.

——George Lakoff

Every discipline or field has a kaleidoscope of categories and subcategories.

In music, for instance, there is classical, pop, jazz, rock, country, blues and countless other genres. In fields of study, be it architecture, engineering, medicine or psychology, one spends three or more years in the university, learning some 30 to 40 subjects in that field. And so on.

Likewise, in law, there is a whole compendium of areas or subjects. The full list exceeds a hundred and, as in other fields, the list just keeps expanding. Quite intimidating.

Fortunately, as in all disciplines, it is possible to identify fundamental or basic categories. The wide field of science, for example, can as a start be categorised into biology, chemistry and physics.

第 2 章
法律领域

我们选择如此分类，是因为我们有着这样的头脑和身体，也因为我们就在这个世界里这样互动着。

——乔治·拉科夫

每个学科和领域都有纷繁复杂的分类体系。

例如，音乐领域可以划分古典、流行、爵士、摇滚、乡村、蓝调，以及其他数不胜数的流派。学科领域也分成建筑学、工程学、医学、心理学等，一个人通常需要在大学里花上三年以上的时间学习专业领域内的 30 至 40 个科目。凡此种种，不胜枚举。

同样地，法律领域汇集了各式各样的部门和科目。整个分类列表超过 100 项，并且和别的领域一样，这个列表的长度还在不断地增加。听起来确实有些吓人。

幸运的是，正如在别的领域里那样，我们至少能确定基本的分类。就好像科学这个广域可以先分为生物、化学和物理三

In law, the three basic building blocks are crime, tort and contract (or criminal law, tort law and contract law) and, for that reason, these subjects are typically taught in the first year of studies in law schools.

Criminal law is something most of us can grasp, probably because of what we have seen or read on TV, in the cinemas, in the newspapers or on social media. Criminal law seeks to establish order in society. A crime is essentially a wrong done to society (and not just to the individual victim).

A crime carries the consequence of punishment, whether in the form of a death sentence (in some countries), a prison term or a fine. In criminal law, the state takes an active role in enforcing the law. Accused persons are prosecuted and courts mete out punishment that is proportional to the crime.

In each country, there is usually a key statute (Commonwealth countries typically have a Penal Code) setting out the more serious crimes, such as murder, rape, robbery, cheating, assault, etc. This statute is complemented with a Minor Offences Act (or Miscellaneous Offences Act), which sets out less serious crimes such as those relating to nuisances, vagrancy and disorderly conduct.

On top of that, there are myriad individual statutes focused on specific crimes, such as bribery, gambling, drug taking, money laundering and traffic offences, to name a few. The statute books of each country contain literally hundreds of crimes and offences.

Tort, a term of French origin, refers to a civil (as opposed to criminal) wrong other than a breach of contract. A tort is a wrong done to an individual (or an entity).

As you may suspect, some torts may be crimes and vice versa. For example, trespass into a person's home is both a crime and a tort. For the criminal

个类别。

在法律领域，这三个基本分类就是指犯罪、侵权与合同（或者刑法、侵权法和合同法），因而这几门课通常会在法学院的第一个学年中讲授。

我们大多数人都比较容易掌握刑法，这可能是由于我们通过电视、电影、新闻和社交媒体经常接触的缘故。刑法的目的在于建立社会秩序。犯罪本质上是对社会（而不仅仅对受害人）造成了危害。

犯罪行为将受到惩罚，惩罚形式可以是死刑（在某些国家）、监禁或罚金。在刑法领域，国家在执法方面发挥着积极作用。刑事被告人被提起公诉，法院则根据犯罪性质的严重程度进行量刑。

每个国家通常都有一部核心成文法（英联邦国家通常都有一部《刑法典》）规定诸如谋杀、强奸、抢劫、欺诈、伤害等严重犯罪，同时也会有一部《轻罪法令》（或称为《其他犯罪法令》）规定诸如与滋扰、流浪和扰乱秩序有关的各类轻罪。

除此之外，还有特定的成文法专门涉及某类特殊犯罪，例如贿赂、赌博、吸毒、洗钱以及交通犯罪等。各国的成文法中囊括了成百上千的犯罪和犯罪行为。

"侵权"一词源于法语，指除了合同违约以外的其他民事（而非刑事）不当行为。

侵权行为对个人（或法人）造成伤害。正如你所猜测的，有些侵权行为会构成犯罪，反之亦然。例如，侵入他人家中的行为既是犯罪也是侵权。在刑事领域，罪犯需要承担刑事责任，由国家对其提起公诉。在民事领域，业主可以侵占他人领地这

dimension, there is criminal liability and it is for the state to prosecute the wrongdoer. On the civil side, the homeowner may sue the intruder under the tort of trespass to land.

Unlike criminal law, which enforces the law through punishment, tort law aims primarily to compensate the victim. In some situations, an injunction (a court order telling someone not to do something; see Chapter 13) may be sought.

Tort law is a very substantial and complex area of law. In the main, there are some two dozen torts. The most prominent and prevalent of these is the tort of negligence. Negligence is essentially the failure to take reasonable care to avoid causing harm to others. Apart from negligence, the more common torts are nuisance, defamation and, increasingly, what are collectively called business torts, such as the tort of inducing a breach of contract and the tort of conspiracy.

The tort of inducing a breach of contract is where A intentionally causes B to break his contract with C. This situation allows C to sue A in tort. This is in addition to his right to sue B for breach of contract. In the tort of conspiracy, A and B conspire to harm C's business.

While the majority of torts require fault on the part of the defendant, either in terms of intention or negligence, some torts impose strict liability (liability even if there is no fault, in the sense of intentionally or negligently causing harm), such as the liability for keeping wild animals.

Contract law is the third major area. It deals with the legal relationship between two (or more) persons when they enter into a transaction or an agreement. Contract law concerns itself with the rights and liabilities between the contracting parties.

Like tort law, the main aim in suing in contract is to seek compensation,

一侵权行为为由对闯入者提起民事诉讼。

与刑法以惩罚的方式执法不同，侵权法的主要目的是向受害者赔偿。当然在某些情况下，也可以申请禁止令（告知某人不得做出某个行为的命令，参见第 13 章）。

侵权法是一部非常重要且复杂的部门法。光主流的侵权行为就有 20 多种。其中最突出也最普遍的是过失侵权。侵权本质上是指因为未能尽到合理注意而导致伤害他人。除了过失侵权以外，更常见的侵权行为有滋扰、名誉毁损以及日益增加的包括诱使他人违约和共谋侵权在内的所谓商业侵权。

诱使他人违约是指甲故意导致乙违反其与丙的合同约定。这时丙可以侵权为由起诉甲。这是在他能够起诉乙合同违约的权利之外的诉因。而根据共谋侵权，甲和乙可能被视为共谋损害丙的商业利益。

虽然大部分侵权都要求被告一方有过错，无论这种过错属于故意还是过失，但某些侵权推行严格责任（即使无过错，即并非因故意或过失造成伤害，也需要承担责任），例如饲养野生动物需要承担的责任。

第三个大类就是合同法。合同法处理当两个（或多个）当事人在达成交易或合约时产生的法律关系。合同法关注的是合同方之间的权利和责任。

与侵权法类似，根据合同法提起诉讼的主要目的也是获得赔偿，但有时也会寻求禁止令作为救济（例如，阻止员工离职并加入竞争对手）。除此之外，法庭也可签发强制执行令（指要求某合同方履行其合同义务的命令，参见第 13 章），而非要求其因未履行合同而支付赔偿。

although sometimes an injunction may be sought as well (for example, to prevent an employee from leaving to join a competitor). In addition, exceptionally, a court may give specific performance, that is, order a contracting party to perform his contractual obligation (see Chapter 13), rather than paying damages for not doing it.

Contract law performs three functions — facilitation, regulation and adjudication. It facilitates by setting out the requirements for a valid contract. It regulates by prohibiting parties from certain types of conduct or activities. It adjudicates by deciding, in a given dispute, what is just. Freedom of contract, the right of parties to enter into contracts and on such terms as they wish, is said to be the pillar of contract law and, consequently, contract clauses are generally upheld by the courts. Yet, courts do intervene to invalidate clauses which are inappropriate, such as a clause which unfairly excludes one party's liability towards the other. For example, if a clause states that one party will only pay a small percentage in damages should problems arise, and from the onset, it is already known that this small percentage will not cover even the basic costs of carrying out the contract. The difficulty is in discerning when courts will and will not intervene.

Criminal law, tort law and contract law form the foundational areas of law. It is not uncommon for countries in Continental Europe to organise their laws into three substantial bodies of law — the Criminal Code, the Civil Code and the Commercial Code. Many other areas of law are added to or built upon this foundation.

Beyond the three core areas, there are numerous important areas and the list includes constitutional law, administrative law, property law, family law, trust law and tax law. In the commercial realm, there is a host of relevant and often interrelated laws, the foremost of which are banking law, agency law (the law on

合同法发挥着三种功能——促进、监管和裁决。合同法的促进功能来自它明确了合同有效的条件；合同法的监管功能在于禁止各方实施某些行为；而合同法的裁决功能则体现在它对现实发生的争议给予公正评判。合同自由，即各方按照自己的意愿签订合同的权利，被认为是合同法的支柱，因此合同条款通常会得到法院的支持。然而，法院也确实会干预并排除一些不适当的条款，例如，不公平地排除一方对另一方责任的条款。再如，合同约定，一旦履行出现问题，一方将只赔偿极小比例的损害，这个比例小到双方明知它甚至无法涵盖履行合同的基本费用。这里的困难在于辨别法院何时应当介入，何时不应介入。

刑法、侵权法和合同法构成了法律的基础领域。欧洲大陆国家经常将其法律照此分为三个大类——刑法典、民法典和商法典。其他的法律领域则是在此基础上增加或者发展而来。

除了以上三个核心领域以外，还有诸如宪法、行政法、物权法、家事法、信托法以及税法等重要领域。在商业领域，有一系列互相关联的法律，其中主要的有银行法、代理法（规定一人如何授权另一人代表其采取行动的法律）、公司法、监管法、贸易法、知识产权法和破产法。培养一名好的商业律师需要通过很长时间的充分实践。

也许有人注意到，在法律分类中有一种方法是将公法和私法区分开来。公法处理的是社会中政府和个人之间的关系。公法包括刑法、宪法、行政法和税法。私法处理的是个人之间的关系。私法包括侵权法、合同法、公司法和家事法。顺便提一下，虽然刑法影响到个人，但它被归类为公法，理由是每一项

how a person can authorise another person to act on his behalf), corporate law, regulatory law, trade law, intellectual property law and insolvency law. A very substantial period of practice is required for the cultivation of a good commercial lawyer.

It may be noted that in the categorisation of law, one approach is to distinguish public law from private law. Public law deals with the relationship between the government and individuals in a society. Public law includes criminal law, constitutional law, administrative law and tax law. Private law deals with the relationship between individuals. Private law includes tort law, contract law, company law and family law. By the way, although criminal law affects individuals, it is categorised as public law because each crime is, in theory, a wrong done to society. Another distinction is that between substantive law and procedural law. Substantive law deals with rights and liabilities between the parties involved. For example, in both criminal law and tort law, an individual is entitled to be protected against bodily harm, and in contract, a contract party has the expectation that the obligations undertaken will be performed as promised. In contrast, procedural law governs the way legal action should proceed. The main procedural laws are the law of evidence and the rules of court procedure. One expects fairness in the content of the law as well as in the legal process.

There are dozens of areas of law and even a lifetime of practice is insufficient for a lawyer or judge to master all the areas. As such, it seems virtually impossible for a person in modern society not to fall foul of the law in some respect. However, a good grasp of the three core areas is an essential starting point for understanding the law.

犯罪在理论上都是对社会造成的危害。另一种分类方法是区分实体法和程序法。实体法涉及有关各方之间的权利和责任。例如，在刑法和侵权法中，个人有权得到保护，不受身体伤害；在合同中，当事人期望对方允诺承担的义务能够如约履行。与此相对，程序法对司法程序应该如何进行做出了规定。程序法主要包括证据法和法庭程序规则。人们期待法律的内容和程序都具有公平性。

法律有几十个领域，一个律师或法官即使毕其一生去实践，也无法掌握所有的领域。于是，似乎在现代社会中，一个人几乎不可能完全避免在某些方面触犯法律。然而，掌握这三个核心领域是开启理解法律之门必不可少的钥匙。

PART II

Making Law

Good laws lead to the making of better ones.

——Jean-Jacques Rousseau

第二部分

制定法律

善法为源，源清流自明。

——让－雅克·卢梭

The task of creating new law (or changing an aspect of existing law), whether in the form of legislation or case law, is a solemn undertaking and a complicated one.

In terms of process, briefly, legislation is drafted and then debated and finally passed in Parliament. The process sometimes involves a public consultation. As for case law, the written judgment issued by a court as it decides a case contains legal reasons and principles which may serve as precedents for future cases. If there is more than one judge hearing the case, they may confer and discuss.

In either process, the substantive dynamics (see Fig. 1) are essentially the same and should involve some or all of the following:

- examining the context of the subject matter and the policy concerns;
- applying notions of justice;
- considering the applicability of moral values;
- applying legal maxim;
- adopting established legal concepts; and
- crafting the legal principle and deciding its requisite elements.

The context must be the starting point of the exercise. Without a good appreciation of the scenario, its stakeholders and the problems and challenges, one cannot proceed meaningfully to lay down the law. The contextual inquiry helps the lawmaker identify the practicalities and the relevant policies and arrive at the key objectives of the relevant law. We explore these in Chapter 3.

要创立新的法律（或要改变某一方面的现行法律），无论是采用立法还是判例法的方式，这项任务都是庄严且复杂的。

程序上，简而言之，起草好的成文法会先拿到议会进行辩论，最后获得通过。这个过程有时涉及向公众咨询。至于判例法，法院在判决案件时发布的书面判决中包括法律理由和原则，可作为未来案件的先例。如果一个案件有多名法官审理，他们也可以进行商议和讨论。

无论是哪个程序，需要考虑的实质因素（见图 1）其实都是相同的，都包括了以下的全部或部分内容：

- 研究课题的背景和政策关注的角度；
- 应用正义的理念；
- 考虑道德价值的适用性；
- 适用法律原则；
- 采用既定的法律概念；以及
- 拟定法律原则并决定其必要的要素。

立法工作必须以了解背景为起点。如果不能很好地了解情况、利益相关者以及问题和挑战，就不能有意义地进行法律制定工作。对背景的调查有助于立法者确定实际情况和相关政策，并得出相关法律的关键目标。我们将在第 3 章中探讨这些问题。

The next step is instinctual to the lawmaker as relevant notions of justice surface in his mind. To clarify, a notion of justice is different from a desired quality of a legal framework. Notions of justice are not what people think justice should be, that the law is simple, coherent, consistent, predictable and comprehensible, or that the legal system is accessible, affordable and expeditious.

Rather, we are talking about the idea of justice itself. There are many notions of justice but there are a handful of fundamental ones, namely, fairness, reasonableness and honesty. Each of them figures prominently in many areas of law and will be discussed in Chapters 6 to 10.

As the boundaries of the law are being considered, there is also a delicate task of deciding the extent to which the law should encapsulate moral values. As a rough delineation, morality requires each of us to do good and not to do evil, whereas the law only requires us not to do evil. Beyond such generalisation, there are many situations of controversy. The relationship between morality and law is discussed in Chapter 5.

Another important part of the lawmaker's armoury is legal maxims. These are wise sayings of general application, such as "No one should be a judge in his own cause". We discuss legal maxims in Chapter 11.

In the process of crafting, the lawmaker may also utilise relevant established legal concepts and doctrines. As an example, so far as fault is concerned (see Chapter 12), a concept the law sometimes uses is constructive notice, which means notice or knowledge which a reasonable person would have. So, where this is thought appropriate for the matter at hand, the lawmaker may include constructive notice in crafting the principle of law.

The legal world abounds with concepts and doctrines.

接下来的一步对立法者来说是本能性的，因为相关的正义理念一定会浮现在他的脑海中。我需要在此澄清，正义的理念与法律框架的理想品质有所不同。正义的理念并非指人们认为正义应该是什么，诸如法律是简单的、连贯的、一致的、可预测的和容易理解的，或者法律系统是可利用的、可负担的和高效的。

相反，我们所谈论的是正义这个观念本身。正义的理念有很多，但有几个基本概念，即公平、合理和诚实。它们中的每一个都在许多法律领域中占有重要地位，并将在第 6 章至第 10 章中讨论。

在考虑法律的界限时，还有一项精细的工作要做，即需要决定法律应在多大程度上囊括道德价值。在此，我们做一个粗略的区分：道德要求我们每个人行善，不作恶，而法律只要求我们不作恶。当然在此基础之上，还有许多有争议的情况。第 5 章将讨论道德和法律之间的关系。

法律格言是法律制定者的另一件重要武器。这些都是普遍适用的明智之言，如“任何人都不应该审判自己”之类。我们在第 11 章讨论法律格言。

在制定法律的过程中，立法者也可以利用相关的既定法律概念和理论。例如，就过错而言（见第 12 章），法律有时使用“推定知悉”这一概念，指合理的人应当知道或知悉的事情。因此，如果认为推定通知可以适用于当前的问题，立法者就可以在制定法律原则时将其包括在内。

法律世界充满不同的概念和理论。

许多法律概念已经存在，因此在制定新的法律时，立法者

There are numerous legal concepts and in crafting new law, the lawmaker will naturally refer to and borrow from these concepts, just as he consciously (more often, subconsciously) applies the notions of justice and legal maxims. The notions, maxims and concepts are part of the armoury of law the lawmaker has at his disposal.

A good lawmaker understands fully the context that he is dealing with and the relevant policies, decides the extent to which ethics and morality should be imposed, and uses notions of justice, legal maxims as well as established legal concepts to craft the law. If he does so skillfully and wisely, the resultant legal principle will be robust and optimal.

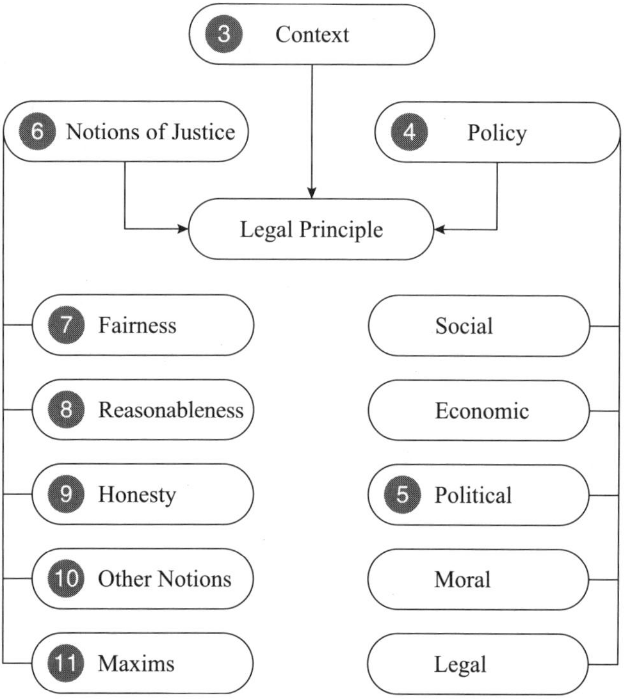

Fig. 1: Dynamics of Crafting Law
(numbers indicate the chapters in which the topic is covered)

自然会参考和借鉴这些概念，正如他有意识地（更多时候是下意识地）应用正义的理念和法律格言一样。这些理念、格言和概念都在立法者所掌握的法律武器库之中。

好的立法者会充分理解他所处理的背景和相关的政策，决定实施伦理和道德标准的程度，并使用正义的理念、法律格言以及既定的法律概念来制定法律。如果立法者的技术熟练并心存智慧，那么他就能创造出有力且最佳的法律原则来。

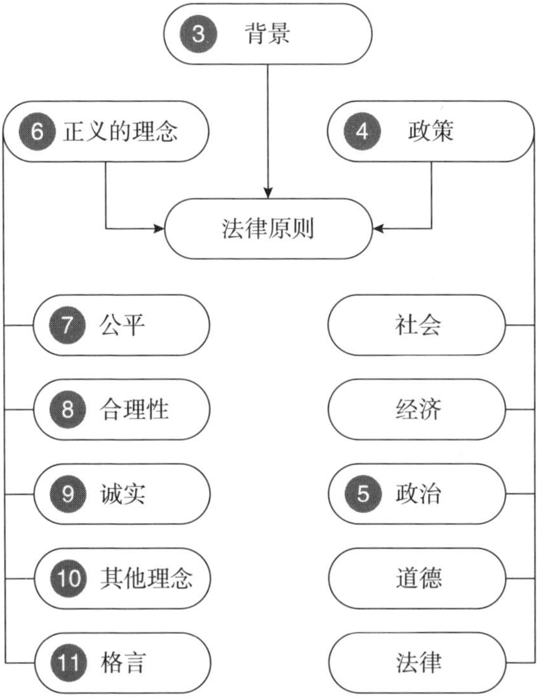

图 1：制定法律时考虑的因素
（数字代表讨论相关课题的章节号）

Chapter 3
Context

Justice can only be dispensed when you have all the facts in front of you.

——Julian Baggini

In any situation, before a lawmaker can decide what justice requires and what the law should be, the starting point must be to understand the underlying context. This enquiry into the context includes the following:

- Who are the parties involved?
- What is the dispute or matter about?
- Are there other stakeholders, such as the industry/profession and society at large?
- What are the problems, the challenges and the constraints?

With a good appreciation of the context, the lawmaker can proceed to the next step of deciding the overarching principles. Many different terms are used

第3章 背景

当你将所有的事实摆在面前时，才能伸张正义。

——朱利安·巴吉尼

无论如何，在立法者能够决定正义的要求和法律的内容之前，必须先了解其基本的背景。这种对背景的调查包括以下内容：

- 当事人都是谁？
- 争议是关于什么的？
- 是否有其他利益相关人，例如有没有牵涉到行业或社会利益？
- 有哪些问题、挑战和制约？

有了对背景的充分了解，立法者就可以进行下一步工作，决定总体原则。这些最高级别的指导原则可以用不同的术语

to describe these highest-level guides — cardinal principles, philosophies, key objectives, aims, goals, policies, pillars, tenets, approaches, desired outcomes and so on. Unfortunately, there is no uniform usage of terminology. Let us look at these overarching principles in a few areas of law.

In criminal law, a few overarching principles stand out. First, there is the presumption of innocence. Article 11 of the Universal Declaration of Human Rights (a document adopted by the United Nations General Assembly and subscribed to by most countries) states that everyone charged with a penal offence has the right to be presumed innocent.

Related to this, there must be "due process"; the accused is entitled to a fair hearing. Also, the general attitude is that a person should not be convicted unless he had a guilty mind (*mens rea*) . Further, the prosecution has the weighty burden of proving its case beyond reasonable doubt.

If the court concludes that the accused is guilty, there is the issue of sentencing. In meting out the consequences of committing a crime, the judge has to consider the applicable theories of punishment and arrive at the suitable form and extent of punishment for the wrongdoer. The reader is probably aware of some of the five key theories or objectives of punishment — retribution, deterrence, incapacitation, rehabilitation and restoration. Of course, one objective may clash with another and there is much controversy on this subject, both in theory and in its actual application.

Tort law, which seeks to allocate rights and liabilities in the civil (as opposed to criminal) realm and to compensate for harm suffered, subscribes primarily to the idea of corrective justice. This means simply that it is the wrongdoer (the "tortfeasor") who should be made to compensate the innocent victim.

来描述——基本原则、理念、关键目标、目的、意图、政策、支柱、信条、方法、预期结果等。不幸的是，这些术语的使用并不统一。让我们来看看这些总体原则在几个法律领域中的应用。

在刑法中，有几个总体原则非常突出。首先是无罪推定原则。《世界人权宣言》（由联合国大会通过并由大多数国家签署的文件）第 11 条规定，每个被指控刑事犯罪的人都有权被推定为无罪。

与此相关的是一定要有“正当程序”；被告有权获得公平的审判。同时，通常认为除非一个人有犯罪意识（*Mens Rea*），否则不应该被定罪。此外，检方在案件中的举证责任标准需要达到排除合理怀疑的程度。

如果法庭认定被告有罪，就会涉及量刑问题。在对犯罪处以惩戒时，法官必须斟酌适用的惩罚理论，确定何种惩戒形式和惩罚程度对该罪犯较为恰当。本书的读者可能已经完全或者部分知道惩戒的五个关键理论或目标——惩罚、震慑、遏制、改造和修复。当然，其中一个目标可能会与另一个目标发生冲突，针对这个问题，无论是在理论还是在实践层面都存在很多争议。

侵权法旨在认定民事（与刑事相对）领域的权利和责任，并对遭受的伤害进行赔偿，它主要遵循矫正正义的理念。简单说，就是应当让过错方（“侵权行为人”）对无辜受害者进行赔偿。

这里的问题在于矫正正义并不是唯一的依据。侵权法有时会诉诸分配正义。从本质上讲，分配正义关注的是对受害者进

The problem is that corrective justice is not the only basis. Tort law, at times, resorts to distributive justice. Essentially, the focus is on compensating the victim and, with that in mind, it may not matter if the burden falls wholly or partly on someone other than the party at fault. This may result in perceived injustice, as we shall see in later chapters.

And there is yet another subsidiary objective in tort law — deterrence. On rare occasions, a court may impose tortious liability on the defendant because it wishes to deter certain tortious conduct. For example, a court may hold a company liable for its employee's financial fraud so that in future, companies will exercise greater financial oversight.

So, in dealing with a problem at hand, including a new problem, tort law looks primarily to corrective justice. But, sometimes, it applies distributive justice or, even, deterrence.

In contract law, it is a continual refrain that freedom of contract is the cornerstone of a free market economy. Some even refer to the "sanctity" of the freedom of contract. There is a predisposition to uphold what the parties had agreed.

However, freedom of contract does not have unrestrained application. Courts do intervene when the conduct of a contracting party or the substance of a contractual clause is thought to be unfair, for instance, because of grossly unequal bargaining power. The big picture is that contract law balances freedom of contract with the need to intervene for good reason. The dividing line is unsteadily drawn and a Jekyll-and-Hyde attitude is periodically observed.

As a final illustration of objectives, let us look at the financial advisers law. In response to the 2009 Global Financial Crisis, regulators in many countries made changes to their legal and regulatory landscape and emphasised the

行赔偿，为达此目的，有时责任全部或部分落在没有过错的一方也无妨。我们将在后面的章节中看到，这可能会导致人们认为不公正。

另外，侵权法中还有另一个从目标——震慑。法庭偶尔会因为希望震慑某些侵权行为的发生而让被告承担侵权责任。例如，法庭可能判令公司对其雇员的财务欺诈行为承担责任，这样公司以后就会加强财务监督。

因此，在处理手头的问题时，无论问题新旧，侵权法主要还是着眼于矫正正义。但有时它也适用分配正义，甚至是震慑。

关于合同法，契约自由是长期以来支撑自由市场经济的基石，有些人甚至称之为契约自由的“神圣性”。维护当事人约定的内容已成为一种预设立场。

然而，契约自由并非不受约束。假如合同方的行为或合同条款被认为不公平，例如，由于双方议价能力严重不等而导致不公平的时候，法庭确实也会干预。从宏观角度看，合同法旨在平衡契约自由与理由充分时进行司法干预。这条界线的划定并不稳定，且经常出现反复。

作为对立法目的的最后一个示例，让我们看一下金融顾问法。为了应对 2009 年的全球金融危机，许多国家的监管机构对其法律和监管环境进行了修改，并强调了公平交易的重要性。为此，他们公布了他们认为的公平交易的预期目标。其中比较突出的两个预期目标是知情决策权和产品适当性。

为了实现这些目标，立法者和监管者颁布了新法或加强了现有法律，例如，银行的高级管理层现在被要求必须对每一个

importance of fair dealing. To this end, they declared what they perceived as the desired outcomes of fair dealing. Two of the more prominent desired outcomes are informed decision and product suitability.

To achieve these outcomes, the lawmakers and regulators introduced laws or enhanced existing ones, such as that the senior management of a bank must deliberate upon and approve every new financial product.

In summary, in crafting law, understanding the context is critical. The examination of the context enables the lawmaker to lay down the fundamental aims or objectives. From these flow the detailed principles and rules and the ability to calibrate the law to the context at hand. Context is certainly the starting point.

新的金融产品进行审议和批准。

总之，在制定法律时，了解其立法背景是至关重要的。对立法背景的研究使立法者能够确定根本目的。从这些目的中能得出具体的原则和规则，也能根据当前环境调整法律。当然，了解背景只是制定法律的起点。

Chapter 4
Policy

This is a legal question that has to be answered in the context ...
and it's a social policy question.

——Paul Levy

The world of law is primarily about legal doctrines, concepts and principles. It is steeped in logic and analysis. However, principles, although vital to law, often have to work in tandem with policy. Sometimes, they have to give way to policy.

What is policy? It is a set of ideas or plans agreed upon by a group of persons or an organisation. Policy is an important part of the context which the lawmaker has to understand.

There are different types of policy. The two most common are social policy and economic policy. (Another is moral policy, and we discuss this important subject in the next chapter.)

Social policy is concerned with how society looks after the needs and well–

第4章
政　策

这是一个法律问题，必须结合背景回答……并且这是一个社会政策问题。

——保罗·莱维

法律的世界主要涉及法律学说、概念和原则。它沉浸在逻辑和分析之中。然而，尽管原则对法律至关重要，但往往必须与政策协同工作。有时，它们必须为政策让路。

什么是政策？它是由一群人或一个组织商定的一套想法或计划。政策是立法者必须了解的背景中的重要部分。

政策分不同类型。最常见的两种是社会政策和经济政策（还有一种道德政策，我们将在下一章讨论这一重要议题）。

社会政策涉及社会如何照顾其成员的需求和福祉。社会政策首先关注的领域包括安全、住房、教育和健康。

经济政策涉及政府在国家金融、商业和就业方面的措施和战略。传统上，经济政策有三个分支——财政政策、货币政策

being of its members. The foremost areas of social policy include safety, housing, education and health.

Economic policy relates to a government's measures and strategies on the financial, business and employment aspects of a country. Conventionally, there are three branches of economic policy — fiscal policy, monetary policy and "supply-side" policy.

In terms of economics, countries are broadly categorised as capitalist and socialist. Capitalist countries believe in a free market and permit the means of production to be owned by private individuals and companies. In contrast, in a socialist country, the state owns the means of production and subscribes to the equal distribution of wealth.

The social, economic and political policies of a country are closely related and they shift over time. Naturally, the changes in law will be influenced by changes in social, economic and political thinking.

Apart from these categories of policy, there is also moral policy. Whilst considerations of social, economic and political policy may involve questions of morality, the subject of morality is of great importance and deserves separate treatment. We discuss morality in Chapter 5.

There is also a species of policy called legal policy. Legal policy is about legal system considerations of judges as they seek to administer justice. The most prominent example of this is the "floodgates" argument for not imposing legal liability. Basically, if you allow one claimant to succeed, there will be a flood of claims. So if this is undesirable, then do not open the floodgates; do not allow even one plaintiff to succeed in his claim.

There are significant variations in policy inclinations from country to

和“供给侧”政策。

就经济而言，国家大致可分为资本主义和社会主义。资本主义国家相信自由市场，允许生产资料由私人和公司拥有。相反，在社会主义国家，国家拥有生产资料，并赞同财富的平等分配。

一个国家的社会、经济和政治政策密切相关，它们随着时间的推移而转变。自然而然地，法律的变化也会受到社会、经济和政治思想变化的影响。

除了以上提到的政策类别之外，还有道德政策。虽然对社会、经济和政治政策的考虑可能涉及道德问题，但道德问题非常重要，值得单列出来。我们在第 5 章讨论道德问题。

还有一种政策称为法律政策。法律政策是关于法官在实现正义时的法律制度考量。这方面最突出的例子是用于决定不施加某类法律责任的“水闸”说。其主要观点是，如果你允许一个人成功索赔，将会产生大量的其他人跟风索赔的情况。因此，如果不希望这种情况发生，那么就不要“打开水闸”，也就是从开始就不允许任何一名原告成功索赔。

各国的政策倾向根据本国不同的文化传统会有很大不同。例如，一个国家可能强调言论自由，另一个国家可能强调隐私的重要性。同样地，对就业、医疗保健或教育权利也可能有不同的态度。而这些文化差异将反映在影响法律制定的政策中。

（应该注意的是，“公共政策”一词经常被用来代替“政策”一词。广义上讲，它们是可以互换的。）

政策和法律之间的关系是一个复杂的问题。

法律的三个核心领域——犯罪、侵权和合同——落实了当

country, reflecting their diverse cultural traditions. For example, whereas one country may emphasise free speech, another may stress the importance of privacy. Likewise, there may be different attitudes towards the right to employment, healthcare or education. And these cultural differences will be reflected in the policies which influence the making of the law.

(It should be noted that the term "public policy" is often used in place of the term "policy". Broadly speaking, they are interchangeable.)

The relationship between policy and law is a complicated matter.

The three core areas of law — crime, tort and contract — give effect to the social, economic and political policies of the day. Together, they cater to the needs and well-being of the members of society.

Criminal law implements the social policies of safeguarding the members of a community and their rights. Hence, the criminal law should protect the body, property and other rights of a person. Criminal law also implements the government's policies as it regulates societies and business. Wrongs against society and against the state or the state's policies are also rectified or remedied.

Tort law also responds to the policies of the day. In the tort of negligence, the most prominent of all torts, there is a three-stage test for whether there is a duty to take care (see Chapter 19). This test requires the court to consider whether, as a matter of policy, there should be such a duty. The economic torts, such as inducing breach of contract and conspiracy, are influenced by the economic ideas of desirable competition. Defamation law balances one person's right to his reputation against another's freedom to express as well as the listener's right to know.

Contract law sets its foundations on the basic economic subscriptions of the

时的社会、经济和政治政策。它们共同满足了社会成员的需求和福祉。

刑法贯彻了保障社会成员及其权利的社会政策。因此，刑法应该保护人的身体、财产和其他权利。刑法也通过管理社会和商业活动执行政府的政策。针对社会、国家或国家政策的错误行为也通过刑法得到纠正或补救。

侵权法也回应了现时的政策。在所有侵权行为中最突出的过失侵权行为中，有一个关于是否有注意义务的三阶段检验法（见第 19 章）。该检验法要求法院考虑，认定相关责任是否符合政策。经济侵权行为，如诱导违约和共谋，受到理想竞争的经济理念的影响。诽谤法则用于平衡一个人的名誉权和另一个人的表达自由以及听众的知情权。

合同法以社区或国家的基本经济模式为基础。古典合同法理论相信自由市场的重要性，并尊重有权利和自由选择的人所签订的合同关系。因此，法律应尽可能少地进行干预。但是，法律也会对例如标准格式合同的出现和垄断的兴起这类基本经济现实的变化做出反应（见第 7 章）。

法律也用来实施政策的重大变化。例如，当英国在 20 世纪中叶作出为每个人提供免费的优质医疗服务的激进决策时，便以《国家卫生服务法》的形式进行了立法。

同样，每年在宣布税率、税前抵扣额度和税务优惠措施的变化之后，都会对相关的税收法规进行修订。

同样，如果国家认为应该更多地关注工作中的健康和安全问题，那么就会有相应的立法或加强立法。事实上，在过去 20 年中，许多国家加强立法，以提高工作场所的安全条件。

community or country. Classical contract law theory believes in the importance of a free market and respects contractual relationships entered into by people who have the right and freedom to choose. Hence, the law should interfere as little as possible. But the law also responds to changes in the underlying economic realities, such as the advent of standard form contracts and the rise of monopolies (see Chapter 7) .

Law is also used to implement major changes in policy. For example, when the UK made the radical decision in the mid–twentieth century to provide everyone with free, good quality medical treatment, legislation was introduced in the form of the National Health Service Act.

Likewise, every year, announcements on changes to tax rates, deductibles and incentives are followed by amendments to the relevant tax statutes.

Similarly, if more attention should be given to the matter of health and safety at work, then legislation or enhanced legislation will be brought to pass. Indeed, in the past two decades, many countries have strengthened their laws to raise the level of workplace protection.

While policy obviously shapes legislation, the exact relationship between policy and case law is far from clear. The perception of judges is not uniform or consistent. While some judges regard policy as an "unruly horse"' and hence, best left to parliament, others believe they can and should consider policy as they decide on the legal outcome. Further, where the matter involves substantial controversy, it is thought that parliament, being elected by the people, is the more appropriate body to decide. There is no clear delineation as to when policy is a matter best left to parliament (see Chapter 23) .

虽然，政策显然会影响立法，但政策和判例法之间的确切关系还远未明确。法官们的看法并不相同或一致。一些法官认为政策是一匹“不羁的奔马”，因此最好留给议会处理，而另一些法官则认为他们在决定法律结果时可以而且应当考虑政策因素。此外，如果问题涉及实质性的争议，人们往往认为议会由人民选举产生，因此更适合作出决定。但在政策何时最好留给议会解决的问题上，则没有明确的划分（见第 23 章）。

Chapter 5
Morality and Law

In civilised life, law floats in a sea of ethics.

——Earl Warren

There is an intricate relationship between law and morality. For sure, they overlap. The question is: When do they not overlap? When does law enforce morals and when does it not?

In the first place, what is morality? Morality refers to principles or values to discern if conduct is right or wrong, good or bad (or evil). The contrasting terms virtue and vice are sometimes mentioned in definitions. Let us say morality is concerned with values of good and evil.

Another preliminary question is, whose moral values does the law enforce? A spontaneous answer — that of the majority. In general, the minority has to abide by the will of the majority. That is how any grouping of persons works.

As regards legislation, on a proposed piece of law, the members of parliament will debate its pros and cons, including the moral aspects. The

第 5 章
道德与法律

在文明人的生活中，法律漂浮在道德的海洋中。

——厄尔·沃伦

法律和道德之间存在着错综复杂的关系。可以肯定的是，它们会重叠。问题是：它们何时不重叠？法律何时执行道德，何时不执行道德？

首先，什么是道德？道德指的是辨别行为是对是错、是好是坏（或邪恶）的原则或价值观。在定义中，有时会提到美德和恶习这两个对比鲜明的术语。我们可以说，道德关注的是善与恶的价值。

另一个前提问题是，法律执行的是谁的道德价值观？一个脱口而出的答案是——执行多数人的道德价值观。一般来说，少数人必须遵守多数人的意愿。任何由人组成的团体都是这样运作的。

在立法方面，对于一项拟议的法律，议会成员将辩论其利

members of parliament represent their constituents, including the values shared by the latter.

Morality may be enforced by the courts. For example, in a negligence case, a judge may have to grapple with whether moral policy dictates that the claim should be disallowed. For instance, in a claim by a mother for an unwanted baby (doctor being negligent in performing ligation or vasectomy), the judge may reject such a claim on the moral ground that it goes against the sanctity of life.

In the contractual realm, a judge may have to decide if a particular contract is invalid because it tends to corrupt public morals, such as a contract involving child pornography. A point to note is that while the judge should objectively ascertain what society's stand on the particular moral issue is, sometimes, he may be subconsciously asserting his personal position on the matter instead.

The majority view should generally prevail. But where diversity should be encouraged or tolerated, or where it is unjust to impose the will of the majority on the minority, the will of the latter should be respected. An interesting example is the exempting, in some countries, of male Sikh motorcyclists from the requirement of wearing helmets on religious grounds.

Next, it should be pointed out that in countries governed by a religious system, such as Islamic countries, there is unity of religion and law. The religious (and moral) principles become and are the law.

In secular society, however, the law at times enforces morals and at times, it does not. As regards the former, there is an expectation that law is not too far removed from morality. In the latter situation, it is thought sufficient or desirable to leave the influencing of behavior to the religious or cultural workings of society.

So how and when does the law draw the line between legally enforceable

弊，包括道德方面的利弊。议员们代表他们的选民，也代表后者所认同的价值观。

道德可以由法院强制执行。例如，在一个过失案件中，法官可能要努力解决道德政策是否决定了索赔应该被拒绝的问题。例如，在一个母亲为她不想生育的孩子提出的索赔案件中（医生在进行结扎或输精管切除术时发生疏忽），法官可能以违背生命的神圣性的道德理由拒绝这种索赔。

在合同领域，法官可能要决定某项合同是否因其倾向于败坏公共道德而无效，例如涉及儿童色情的合同。需要注意的是，虽然法官理应客观地确定社会对特定道德问题的立场，但有时他可能会下意识地主张他个人对这个问题的立场。

通常来说，多数人的观点应该占上风。但在应该鼓励或接纳多样性的场合，或者在把多数人的意愿强加给少数人会导致不公正时，后者的意愿也应该得到尊重。其中的一个有趣的例子是，在某些国家，男性锡克族摩托车骑手因宗教原因可以免除佩戴头盔的要求。

接下来应该指出的是，在由宗教制度管理的国家，如伊斯兰国家，宗教和法律是统一的。宗教（和道德）原则就是法律。

然而，在世俗社会中，法律有时会执行道德标准，有时则不会。对于前者，人们期望法律不会与道德相差太远。对于后者，人们则认为将影响行为的方式留给社会的宗教或文化工作就足够了。

那么，法律如何以及何时在可依法执行的道德和不可依法执行的道德之间划清界限？这里我们讨论几个衡量标准或区别。

morals and morals which are not? There are several yardsticks or distinctions.

First, a rough line is drawn between doing good and not doing evil. Morality encourages a person both to do good as well as not to do evil. In general, the law only commands a person not to do evil or not to cause harm (such as to kill or to steal). So, a person who is unforgiving, ungenerous or unkind may earn the rebuke or chastisement of his religious leader but he gets no reproof from the law. Quite simply, the law does not require from each of us love or good deeds.

Secondly, the law may in fact permit what the majority in society agree is undesirable and evil. An example is legalised gambling. Each country typically has laws which make gambling an offence and yet provides for licensed gambling, often run by the state. Other situations include prostitution and alcohol consumption. It seems the law, as a matter of practicability (and even revenue generation), tolerates certain unavoidable evils.

Thirdly, the law is concerned with wrongful conduct that results in outward or external harm. In general, a crime requires both the mental element (*mens rea*) and the physical element (*actus reus*). Evil thoughts and intentions alone do not attract legal liability. In tort and contract, damage is usually required. In contrast, under moral norms, an evil thought itself may be a wrong. For example, in New Testament Christian teaching, a man who has adulterous thoughts towards a woman is guilty of sin. In this regard, morality has a much wider ambit than law.

Broadly speaking, we see three categories in the interaction of morality and law. First, there are moral wrongs which the law clearly frowns upon and proscribes. These include killing, kidnapping, robbery, cheating, assault and a host of other wrongs. At the other end, there are shortfalls the law does not deal with, like the failure to be noble, merciful or sacrificial. In the middle, there is

第一，应当在行善和不作恶之间划出一条粗略的界限。道德既鼓励一个人行善，也鼓励他不作恶。但通常法律只要求一个人不做坏事或不造成伤害（如杀人或偷窃）。因此，一个不宽容、不慷慨或不仁慈的人可能受到他的宗教领袖的责备或责罚，但他不会受到法律的责备。简而言之，法律并不要求我们每个人都要有爱或善行。

第二，法律事实上可能允许社会上大多数人认为不可取的邪恶行为。一个例子是合法的赌博。每个国家通常都有法律规定赌博为犯罪行为，但有些又允许持照经营，通常是由国家统一管理的赌博业务。其他情况包括卖淫和饮酒。这反映出法律可能出于实用性（甚至是创收）的考量而容忍了某些不可避免的恶行。

第三，法律关注的是导致外在或外部伤害的不法行为。一般来说，犯罪需要具有心理要素（犯罪意图）和身体要素（犯罪行为）。仅仅是邪恶的想法和意图并不会导致法律责任。在侵权行为和合同中，通常需要有损害。相反，根据道德规范，邪恶的想法本身可能是一种错误。例如，在新约基督教教义中，一个男人如果对一个女人有通奸的想法，就是有罪的。在这方面，道德的范围要比法律广得多。

大体上，我们可以看到，道德和法律之间有三类互动。首先，有一些道德上的错误，是法律明确反对和禁止的。这些包括杀戮、绑架、抢劫、欺骗、攻击和其他一系列的错误行为。其次，有一些法律未予涉及的部分，例如未做到高尚、仁慈或牺牲。最后，在两者之间，有一个中间或灰色地带，在那里，法律是否应该执行道德标准饱受争议。

an intermediate or grey zone where it is very debatable whether the law should enforce morals.

Good Samaritan laws are an interesting example of this grey zone. A Good Samaritan law requires a person to go to the aid of another who is in danger of grave physical harm, so long as there is little or no risk of injury to the rescuer. The existence and extent of such a law varies from country to country. For example, whilst English law, in general, does not impose a duty to rescue, such an obligation is clearly established under French law.

Other areas of controversy include abortion, euthanasia, drug consumption, gender issues, genetic engineering and a host of other issues. Countries differ widely in their treatment of these controversial areas. Further, the societal views on these issues change over time.

It should be noted that morality plays a large part in the codes of conduct of professions. Doctors, for example, are expected to ensure beneficence and non-maleficence. In short — do good and do not do evil. In keeping with such high aspirations, the ethical codes of doctors often require doctors to uphold the patient's welfare and best interests as the "highest consideration". Such a position is, in fact, loftier than what the law generally requires.

Moral considerations often factor in the law-making process. The line between morality which law enforces and morality which law does not enforce is not easy to draw. It shifts from time to time and varies from place to place. The boundaries are unclear, but the importance and relevance of morality are undeniable.

灰色地带中的一个有趣的例子是“好撒玛利亚人法”（“好心人法”）。“好撒玛利亚人法”要求在救援者受伤风险较低或不存在的情况下，需要帮助面临遭受严重身体伤害风险的他人。这种法律是否存在及其程度因国家而异。例如，虽然英国法律一般不规定救助义务，但法国法律却明确规定了这种救助义务。

其他有争议的领域包括堕胎、安乐死、毒品消费、性别问题、基因工程和一系列其他问题。各国在对待这些有争议的领域方面存在很大差异。此外，社会对这些问题的看法也随着时间的推移而变化。

应该指出的是，道德在职业的行为准则中起着很大的作用。例如，对医生提出的期望是确保有益和无害原则，简而言之——行善不作恶。为了与这种崇高的愿望保持一致，医生的道德准则通常要求医生把维护病人的福利和最佳权益作为“最高级别的考量”。事实上，这样的立场比法律通常要求的高得多。

在法律制定过程中往往会涉及道德方面的考量。法律执行的道德标准和法律不执行的道德标准之间的界限不容易划定。它因时而变，因地而异。尽管两者之间的界限不明确，但道德的重要性和相关性是不可否认的。

Chapter 6
Notions of Justice

The arc of the moral universe is long and it bends towards justice.

——Dr Martin Luther King, Jr

Human beings are drawn to justice. Instinctively, we feel that justice should prevail. As children, we were in awe of the superheroes in DC Comics' Justice League — Superman, Batman, Wonder Woman and others.

But what does justice really mean? In a given scenario or dispute, what does justice require? If we analyse and dissect the concept of justice, what are its essential parts and what are the constituent facets?

I suggest there are three basic notions of justice. As explained in the introduction for Part II, we are not talking about desirable characteristics of the law, such as clarity or comprehensibility; neither are we discussing the expectations of a good legal system, like affordability or expeditiousness.

Rather, the question is: When faced with a new scenario, what are the essential ideas to refer to as a lawmaker crafts law in the endeavour to administer justice?

第 6 章 正义的理念

道德宇宙的弧线漫长并向正义倾斜。

——小马丁·路德·金博士

人类总是被正义所吸引。我们本能地觉得正义应该获胜。作为孩子，我们对 DC 漫画中的超级英雄——超人、蝙蝠侠、神奇女侠和其他人充满敬畏。

但正义的真正含义是什么？在一个特定的场景或争端中，如何才算正义？如果我们分析和剖析正义的概念，它的基础是什么，构成面又是什么？

我认为基本正义理念有三个。正如在第二部分的引言中所解释的，我们并不是在讨论法律的理想特性，如清晰性或可理解性；我们也不是在讨论对好的法律体系的期望，如可负担性或快速性。

我们真正需要思考的问题是：当面对一个新的环境时，作为一个法律制定者在努力实施司法的过程中，需要参考哪些基

Amongst the dozen or so notions, the following are the most fundamental: fairness, reasonableness and honesty. We shall consider each of the three basic notions as well as other notions in the following chapters.

Before that, a few points should be noted.

First, whilst each of the three notions has its own definition and central subscription (s), they tend to overlap. An aspect of a notion may be found in the list of descriptive terms in another notion. For example, honesty may overlap with fairness, just as reasonableness may overlap with fairness.

Indeed, in the widest sense, it may be said that fairness is the cornerstone of justice.

Secondly, out of a basic notion, there may spring subsidiary or associated notions. Fairness leads to other notions such as freedom and equality. Proportionality is associated with reasonableness. And honesty encompasses the notions of good faith and loyalty. And so on.

Thirdly, in grappling with a particular scenario, the law may combine more than one notion. Instances include "fair and reasonable" (exemption clauses in contracts), "free and fair" (as in elections), "true and fair" (as in financial accounts) and "honestly and reasonably" (as in a director's defence for a breach of duty).

As one stands underneath the whole panoply of the law — its dozen or so notions of justice, its scores of legal concepts and maxims and its hundreds and thousands of constituent pieces of law — it is reassuring that they have a common core. For one thing, it facilitates understanding. For another, it facilitates compliance.

Be fair, be reasonable and be honest. In so doing, by and large, you should be fine.

本理念？

在这十几个概念中，以下是最基本的理念：公平、合理和诚实。我们将在下面的章节中分别考虑这三个基本理念以及其他理念。

在此之前，有几点需要注意。

第一，虽然这三个理念中每个理念都有自己的定义和核心模式，但它们往往会发生重叠。一个概念的其中一个方面可能也会包括在描述另一个概念的术语之中。例如，诚实可能与公平重叠，正如合理也可能与公平重叠一样。

事实上，从最广泛的意义上来说，公平是正义的基石。

第二，从一个基本理念中，可能会产生一些附属的或相关的理念。公平导致了其他理念，如自由、和平等。“相应”则与合理相关。而诚实则包含了诚信和忠诚的概念。凡此种种，不一而足。

第三，在处理一个特定情况时，法律可能会结合一个以上的理念。相关的例子包括“公平合理”（合同中的豁免条款）、“自由公平”（如选举）、“真实公平”（如财务账目）和“诚实合理”（如董事对违反其职责的辩护）。

当站在整个法律的全景之下时，人们会欣慰地发现——无论是十几个正义的理念，几十个法律概念和格言，还是成百上千的法律条文——它们拥有一个共同的核心。这既有助于理解，也有利于遵守。

要公平，要合理，要诚实。只要你这样做了，那么，你大可安枕无忧。

Chapter 7
Fairness

When truth and fairness are different from what is law, better it is to follow truth and fairness.

——Bandamanna Saga, Chapter 6

Fairness, a fundamental notion, is something which human beings instinctively understand. It is also something they expect and passionately speak up and fight for.

Whether it is in a children's playground, a corporate battlefield or an international territorial dispute, one expects dealings to be fair.

What does the word "fair" mean? Definitions typically talk about treating people equally, and without favouritism or discrimination. Some mention "right", "just" and "equitable" .

In my view, the three words "fair", "just" and "equitable", so far as law is concerned, can be used interchangeably. A small caveat is that "equitable" is sometimes used in connection with where the law came from. Historically, in

第7章 公 平

当真理和公平与法律发生分歧时，最好是遵循真理和公平。

——《班达曼娜传奇》第6章

公平是一个基本理念，是人类凭本能理解的东西。这也是他们所期望，并为之热情地大声疾呼和奋斗的东西。

无论是在儿童游乐场、公司战场还是国际领土争端中，人们都期望交易是公平的。

“公平”这个词是什么意思？大家给出的定义中通常谈到平等对待人们，没有偏袒或歧视。有些人提到“权利”“公正”“衡平”。

在我看来，就法律而言，“公平”“公正”“衡平”这三个词可以互换使用。一个小小的注意事项是，“衡平”有时会与法律的来源联系起来使用。历史上，在英国，判例法来自普通法法院。后来，衡平法法院（以前称为大法官法院）开始提供

England, case law came from the common law courts. Later, courts of equity (previously called the courts of chancery) were started to provide remedies not available in the common law courts (e.g. requiring that a specific act be performed instead of awarding damages), and these courts also made law. A legal principle coming from the courts of equity is called an equitable principle. For instance, in contract law, compensation is a common law remedy (originating from the common law courts) while specific performance is an equitable remedy (emanating from the courts of equity).

Some definitions of "fair" even include the terms "honest" or "reasonable". As mentioned in the earlier chapter, there is an overlap of the three basic notions of fair, reasonable and honest.

So it seems fairness is a concept we all understand but struggle to define precisely. But it is a handy concept and a yardstick which is often used.

The 2008 Global Financial Crisis seems a memory away, but at the time, the effect was devastating. The regulatory response in the UK (and several other countries) was the declaration of a philosophy or culture of TCF — Treat Customers Fairly. Based on the idea of fairness, the regulators identified Desired Outcomes such as informed decision and product suitability, and elaborated upon them through detailed guidelines.

In the arena of professional football (or soccer), smaller clubs often complain of the uphill challenge of competing against clubs with huge financial resources. In Europe, the UEFA (Union of European Football Associations) response was to lay down Financial Fair Play Regulations, which seek, among other things, to curb excessive expenditure in buying players. The NBA (National Basketball Association in the US) has an interesting system of selecting new

普通法法院无法提供的救济措施（例如，要求实施特定行为，而非判决经济赔偿），这些法院同样负责制定法律。来自衡平法院的法律原则被称为衡平法原则。例如，在合同法中，经济赔偿是普通法的补救措施（源于普通法法院），而强制履行是衡平的补救措施（源于衡平法法院）。

一些关于“公平”的定义甚至包括“诚实”或“合理”。如前一章所述，公平、合理和诚实这三个基本概念是重叠的。

因此，公平似乎是一个我们都能理解的概念，却很难准确定义。但它是一个便捷的概念，也是一个经常被使用的评判尺度。

2008 年的全球金融危机似乎已成为过去时，但在当时其影响是毁灭性的。英国（和其他几个国家）监管机构的反应是宣告了“TCF”这一理念或文化——公平对待客户。基于公平的理念，监管机构规定了若干“期望的结果”，如知情决策权和产品适用性，并通过详细的指导方针对其进行了阐述。

在职业足球（或足球）领域，较小的俱乐部经常抱怨在与拥有巨大财政资源的俱乐部竞争时面临艰难的挑战。在欧洲，UEFA（欧洲足球协会联盟）的反应是制定了金融公平竞争条例，该条例的目的之一是遏制购买球员的过度支出。NBA（美国国家篮球协会）有一个有趣的挑选大学毕业的新球员的系统。选拔的优先权给予（表现）较弱的球队，这听起来相当开明和公平。（当然，NBA 方面可能有一些自利因素——更均衡的球队使比赛更有观赏性。）

在消费者保护领域，许多国家都有专门的立法，针对企业的不良行为，称为“不公平手段”。不公平手段关注到消费者

players coming out of college. Priority of selection is based on the weakness (of performance) of the teams, which sounds rather enlightened and inherently fair. (Of course, there might be some self-interest on the part of NBA — more even teams make the games more enjoyable to watch.)

In the field of consumer protection, many countries have specific legislation which target undesirable conduct by businesses, calling it "unfair practice" . Unfair practice concerns the vulnerability of the consumer, in that he is unable to protect himself or is unable to understand the transaction or its terms. Conceptually as well as practically, this is serious protection indeed.

In Chapter 6, I mentioned that notions of justice are often used in combination. The inclusion of another notion may or may not add any substance to the legal principle. To illustrate, in the tort of negligence, a duty to take care will not be imposed if it is not "fair, just and reasonable" to do so. As mentioned earlier, fair and just mean the same thing and so, frankly, one of the terms is extra or unnecessary. Reasonable, in contrast, introduces a different concept — that of doing what other people would do (see Chapter 8) .

In a similar vein, the validity of an exclusion clause (a contract clause whereby one party seeks to exclude his liability when he does not perform or when he breaks a term of the contract) is subject to the controls of fairness as well as reasonableness. An exclusion clause is valid only if it is fair and reasonable.

The addition of a second notion may also be an elaboration. For example, in the expression "free and fair election", the idea is that for an election to be fair, it is critical that the voters are free to vote as they wish. If voters were being coerced or inappropriately enticed, then they were not free to choose and the election would not be fair.

的弱势地位，理解消费者无法保护自己或无法理解交易或交易条款。无论是从概念上还是从实践上，这确实是一种大力度的保护。

在第 6 章中，我提到正义的各种理念经常结合使用。加入另一个理念不一定会为法律原则增加任何实质内容。举例来说，在过失侵权中，如果不“公平、公正和合理”，就不会施加注意义务。如前所述，公平和公正的意思是一样的，因此坦率地说，其中一个术语是多余的或不必要的。相比之下，合理则引入了一个不同的概念——做别人会做的事（见第 8 章）。

同样地，免责条款（一方当事人在不履行合同或违反合同条款时寻求免除其责任的合同条款）的有效性也要受到公平和合理的控制。只有在公平和合理的情况下，免责条款才是有效的。

增加第二个理念也可能是一种解说方式。例如，在“自由和公平的选举”这一表述中，其理念是，要使选举公平，关键是选民可以按照自己的意愿自由投票。如果选民受到胁迫或不当诱惑，那么他们就不能自由选择，选举也就不公平。

还有另一个例子是关于被称为“公平评论”的有趣的诽谤抗辩理由。最初，制定法律时同时要求公平和诚实——公平的评论是一个有公平心态的评论员可以诚实地做出的评论。评论者既要公平，也要诚实。在一些国家，法律已经发展到只要求诚实。例如在英国，这种抗辩理由现在被称为“诚实的意见”。

将“真实和公平的观点”这一表述运用在财务账目的审计中，更值得商榷。在这里，我们是将不同的概念结合起来，还是用两个类似的概念中的一个是对另一个进行解说？有一种观

Yet another example is the interesting defence to defamation called "fair comment". Originally, the law was crafted so as to require both fairness and honesty — a fair comment is one which a fair-minded commentator could honestly make. There is a need for the commentator to be fair as well as to be honest. In some countries, the law has evolved to requiring honesty alone. In the UK, for example, the defence is now known as "honest opinion".

The expression "true and fair view", which is used in relation to the auditing of financial accounts, is more debatable. Do we have here a combination of different concepts or are they similar concepts, with one elaborating upon the other? On one view, the primary notion is truth, or freedom from error, and the addition of fairness is necessary because in some situations, it is a matter of judgment whether it is permissible to present a matter in a certain way. For example, whether a particular purchase can be recognised as an expense rather than an asset. In this situation, the issue is not so much about truth but about fairness or, more loosely, appropriateness.

Law is established so that there may be order and justice in society.

And justice is, above all else, about fairness.

点认为，主要的理念是真实，或者说是没有错误。而增加公平性是必要的，因为在某些情况下，是否允许以某种方式呈现某个事件是一个判断问题。例如，某项收购是否可以被确认为费用而非资产。在这种情况下，问题不在于真相，而在于公平性，或者更宽泛地说，在于适当性。

法律的建立是为了让社会有秩序和正义。

而正义首先在于公平。

Chapter 8
Reasonableness

In contrast to logic, there is common sense, or still better, the spirit of reasonableness.

——Lin Yutang

If one searches for the meaning of the word "reasonableness", the most common results are "sensible" and "of sound judgment". The terms "fair", "appropriate" and "moderate" also appear.

To be reasonable is to be sensible and to exercise sound judgment.

A critical aspect of reasonableness, certainly so far as law is concerned, is objectivity. A person is judged not by his own standard or expectation. A person does not act reasonably simply because as he does an act, he exercises his judgment and thinks that his conduct is right, prudent or appropriate.

Instead, the measure is an objective one — would a hypothetical sensible and rational person in his position have done the act and in the manner that it was done? Reasonableness judges a person by what others would have done.

第 8 章
合理性

> 和逻辑相对的有常识，或更好一些的说法：还有近情的精神。
>
> ——林语堂

如果搜索“合理性”一词的含义，最常见的结果是“明智的”和“合理的”判断。同时还会出现“公平”“适当”“适度”等词语。

合理就是理智，并作出正确的判断。

合理性的一个重要方面，当然是就法律而言，就是客观性。对一个人的评判不是根据他自己的标准或期望。一个人的合理行为并不只是因为他在做某一行为时，行使了他的判断力，认为他的行为是正确的、谨慎的或适当的。

相反，合理性的衡量标准是客观的——一个假设的理智和理性的人在他的位置上是否会以这样的方式做出该行为？合理性是根据别人会怎么做来判断一个人。

It should be pointed out that reasonableness may not mean doing what the majority would do. It is possible that the majority are careless. For example, on a highway where the maximum speed limit is 80 kmph, it is possible that the great majority of drivers are driving at speeds of 90 kmph and beyond. But that does not mean it is reasonable to drive at 90 kmph. Rather, the question is at what speed the hypothetical sensible and careful driver would drive. The answer, it seems, is 80 kmph, or lower.

The most prominent application of reasonableness in law is in the tort of negligence. Negligence is the failure to do what a reasonable or reasonably careful person would have done. This duty to take care applies to each person in his personal capacity as well as in his professional or business capacity.

In contract law, reasonableness is often the measure for deciding whether a clause should be upheld. For example, "non-compete" clauses (in legal terms — restraint of trade clauses), which seek to restrict an employee or the seller of a business from working in competition against the employer/buyer, are subject to this test. In a nutshell, the law says that the clause is valid only if it is reasonable in terms of duration, geographical boundary and scope of work or business activity. For example, if an employee works only in France, it may be unreasonable to restrict him, upon leaving the company, from working anywhere in the European Union (EU).

In company law, a director is expected to exercise care, skill and diligence as he carries out his duties. In so doing, the law requires him to rise to the standard of a reasonably competent director.

In administrative law (law relating to the regulation of governmental agencies), while decisions of a public body are, in general, not subject to

需要指出的是，合理性可能并不意味着做大多数人都会做的事。大多数人有可能是不小心的。例如，在一条最高限速为 80 公里 / 小时的高速公路上，绝大多数司机有可能以 90 公里 / 小时以上的速度行驶。但这并不意味着以 90 公里 / 小时的速度行驶是合理的。相反，问题是假设的明智和谨慎的司机会以什么速度驾驶。答案恐怕是 80 公里 / 小时或者更低。

合理性在法律中最突出的应用是在过失侵权中。疏忽是指没有做一个合理或谨慎的人应该做的事情。这种谨慎的责任适用于每个人的个人身份、专业身份或商业身份。

在合同法中，合理性往往是决定一个条款是否应该得到支持的尺度。例如，旨在限制雇员或企业的卖主在工作中与雇主 / 买主产生竞争的“竞业”条款（用法律术语来说也可称之为交易限制条款）就需要适用这一衡量标准。简而言之，法律规定只有当该条款在竞业期限、竞业地理范围以及工作或商业活动范围方面合理，该条款才有效。例如，如果一个雇员只在法国工作，那么限制他离开公司后不能在欧盟（EU）范围内任何地方工作是不合理的。

在公司法中，董事在履行其职责时应保持谨慎、熟练和勤勉。在此过程中，法律要求他达到合理、合格的董事标准。

在行政法（与政府机构监管有关的法律）中，虽然公共机构的决定一般不受司法审查，但可以以所谓的“温斯伯里”不合理性（英国法院在 *Associated Provincial Picture Houses v. Wednesbury* 案中规定的原则）为由对决定提出疑问。根据这一原则，如果一项行政决定非常离谱，以至于任何明智的人都不可能做出这样的决定，例如允许在一个住宅区内修建赛车场，

judicial scrutiny, a decision may be challenged on the ground of what is known as Wednesbury unreasonableness (a principle laid down by an English court in *Associated Provincial Picture Houses v. Wednesbury*). According to this principle, an administrative decision may be subject to judicial review if it is so outrageous that no sensible person could have arrived at it, such as allowing a motor racing track to be built in a residential estate.

Finally, reasonableness is often stated as a possible defence to liability, both in the criminal and civil realms. For example, it is common to find a provision in companies legislation providing that in proceedings against a director for breach of duty, the court can grant him full or partial relief if he had acted honestly and reasonably, and ought fairly to be excused (e.g. section 391 of the Singapore Companies Act). (The astute reader will observe that all the three basic notions of justice are employed here.)

The notion of reasonableness is an important one and is often resorted to for setting norms of behaviour in society and in business.

那么该决定就可能受到司法审查。

最后，在刑事和民事领域，合理性经常被认为是针对责任的抗辩事由。例如，在公司立法中经常可以看到这样的规定：在针对董事违反职责的诉讼中，如果他诚实合理地进行工作，应该基于公平原则获得谅解，法院可以给予他全部或部分的责任免除（例如新加坡《公司法》第 391 条）。（精明的读者会发现，这里采用了所有三个基本的正义理念。）

合理性理念非常重要，其经常被用来制定社会上和商业中的行为准则。

Chapter 9
Honesty

Honesty is the best policy, in love as in law.

——Louisa May Alcott

Honesty. A very desirable human trait. Abraham Lincoln, for example, was so legendary in his honesty that he earned the nickname "Honest Abe". Does the law require a person to be honest? Definitely.

Honesty has two facets. The first is truthfulness. An honest person is one who tells the truth. He is candid, sincere and straightforward. He is free of deception.

But honesty has another important facet. This second facet is variously described as integrity, honour and uprightness. An honest person is virtuous — he does not do things which are morally wrong. The law sometimes focuses on the first facet and at other times, the second.

Whilst reasonableness is an objective concept, honesty, as it relates to truth, is generally subjective. To illustrate, if we say someone has an honest

第9章
诚　实

诚实是最好的策略，无论是在爱情还是在法律中，都是如此。

——路易莎·梅·奥尔科特

诚实，一个非常令人向往的人类特质。例如，亚伯拉罕·林肯在诚实方面如此具有传奇色彩，以至于他赢得了“诚实的亚伯”的绰号。法律是否要求一个人要诚实？这是肯定的。

诚实有两个方面。首先是真实性。一个诚实的人是说真话的人。他是坦率的、真诚的、直截了当的。他没有欺骗行为。

但诚实还有另一个重要方面。对于第二个方面有不同的描述，即诚信、荣誉和正直。一个诚实的人是有美德的——他不做道德上错误的事情。法律有时会关注第一个方面，有时会关注第二个方面。

合理性是一个客观的概念，而诚实因为它与真实有关，通常是主观的。举例来说，如果我们说某人对某事有一个诚实的

belief regarding something, we mean that he actually held that belief. In contrast, a person has reasonable belief only if a hypothetical sensible person in his position would have held that belief.

For example, on the issue of whether a landlord believed his tenant to be a lawful migrant, honest belief would enquire if the landlord actually believed that the tenant was lawfully present in the country. However, because of the seriousness of the matter of illegal immigrants, the law is usually framed objectively — did the landlord have reasonable belief? For example, did he ask the tenant for documentary proof?

Honesty applies in all the three core areas of crime, tort and contract, albeit in descending order of applicability or prevalence.

Criminal law has a whole catalogue of crimes and offences dealing with dishonesty and the long list includes theft, robbery, cheating, criminal breach of trust (CBT), bribery, smuggling, counterfeiting and money laundering, to name a few. Note that criminal law, and law in general, is more concerned with dishonesty as it relates to property and things of monetary value than as it relates to emotions.

Tort law also frowns upon dishonesty and, here, the key tort is the tort of fraud or deceit. Although deceit is a well-established tort, it typically occupies a tiny fraction of a textbook on torts. The explanation is probably that although dishonesty and fraud are rampant in society and in business, there are relatively few civil suits because quite often the wrongdoer is unable to pay or cannot be found.

In relation to statements, one makes a fraudulent statement if one makes a false statement knowingly, recklessly or without belief of its truth (*Derry v.*

信念，我们的意思是他确实持有这个信念。相比之下，只有当一个假设的明智的人在他的位置上会持有这种信念时，一个人才有合理的信念。

例如，在一个房东是否相信他的租户是合法移民的问题上，“诚实地相信”需要确定房东是否确实相信该租户是合法在该国居留。然而由于非法移民问题的严重性，法律规定的通常是客观标准——房东是否有合理理由相信？例如，他是否要求租户提供文件证明？

诚实适用于犯罪、侵权和合同这三个核心领域，不过，它在此三个领域的适用性或普遍性依次递减。

刑法有一整套涉及不诚实的犯罪和违法行为的名单，其中包括盗窃、抢劫、欺骗、刑事失信罪（CBT）、贿赂、走私、伪造和洗钱，谨此举例若干。请注意，刑法和一般法律更关注与财产和具有货币价值的东西有关的不诚实行为，而非与情感有关的不诚实行为。

侵权法也反对不诚实，这里的关键侵权是欺诈或欺骗的侵权行为。尽管欺骗是一种公认的侵权行为，但它通常在侵权行为的教科书中只占很小的一部分。其原因可能是，尽管不诚实和欺诈在社会和商业中很猖獗，但民事诉讼相对较少，因为不法行为人往往无法支付或无法找到。

在言论方面，如果一个人在明知、鲁莽或不相信其真实性的情况下做出虚假的言论，就构成欺诈性声明（*Derry v. Peek*案）。所有这三种心理状态都被视为欺诈行为，但罪责的程度是递减的。

不诚实也可能是其他侵权行为的一个组成部分，如恶意损

Peek）. There is a descending degree of culpability, but all three states of mind are regarded as fraudulent.

Dishonesty may also be an ingredient in other torts, such as malicious falsehood, passing off (misrepresenting goods/services as that of another person) and conspiracy.

Honesty has some application in contract law. For example, if a fraudulent misrepresentation (a false statement made by the seller before the contract was entered into) of a material fact induced a person to enter into a contract, the innocent party is entitled to avoid (cancel) the contract.

However, it must be pointed out that the starting point in contract law is *caveat emptor* or buyer beware. In essence, a seller does not have the obligation to disclose material facts to a buyer; it is for the buyer to ascertain the relevant information about the product or service he intends to purchase and to satisfy himself as to its suitability.

In short, a seller must not misrepresent but he generally does not have the duty to disclose material facts.

Honesty is also required of persons such as trustees, agents and directors. A director, for example, is required to act *bona fide* (or honestly) in the interests of his company. He should not put himself in a position where his personal interest conflicts with the interest of the company. If he is interested in a proposed transaction, he should disclose his interest. Needless to say, he should not make any secret profits.

Law encapsulates, in many of its realms, the notion of honesty. As a guide, it is true that honesty is the best policy.

害名誉、假冒（将货物/服务误称为他人的货物/服务）和通谋。

诚实在合同法中也有一些应用。例如，如果对某一重要事实的欺诈性虚假陈述（卖方在签订合同前的虚假陈述）诱使某人签订合同，则无过错方有权撤销（取消）该合同。

然而，必须指出的是，合同法的默认原则是“买方注意”。原则上卖方没有义务向买方披露重要的事实；应该由买方来确定他打算购买的产品或服务的相关信息，而且，对相关商品或服务是否合适、满意，也是买家的自身体验。

简而言之，卖家不得作虚假陈述，但他一般也没有披露重要事实的义务。

法律对受托人、代理人和董事等人也有诚实的要求。例如，一名董事被要求为其公司的利益诚信（或诚实）行事。他不应该使自己处于个人利益与公司利益相冲突的位置。如果他对一项拟议的交易感兴趣，他应该披露他的相关利益。毋庸置疑的是，他不应该赚取任何秘密利润。

法律在其许多领域都包含了诚实的概念。作为指导原则，诚实是最好的策略，这一点确凿无疑。

Chapter 10
Other Notions

The virtue of justice consists in moderation, as regulated by wisdom.

——Aristotle

Fairness, reasonableness and honesty form a trinity of fundamental notions of justice. In addition, there are a dozen or more other notions of justice, some of which overlap with or spring from one of the three. In this chapter, we look at the more prominent ones.

Proportionality is probably the most important notion after the trinity. The concept surfaces frequently. In criminal law, punishment is required to be proportional to the gravity of the crime. In tort law, the concept of contributory negligence reduces the amount of a claim to the extent to which the claimant's fault contributed to the damage. As a counterpart, in contract law, the innocent party is required to take reasonable steps to mitigate his loss, and his claim is to be reduced to the extent that he could have mitigated but did not do so. Culpability

第 10 章
其他理念

正义的美德在于智慧的节制。

——亚里士多德

公平、合理和诚实构成了三位一体的基本正义理念。此外，还有十几种其他的正义理念，其中一些与这三个理念中的一个重叠或从中产生。在这一章中，我们将探讨比较突出的几个理念。

相应性可能是三位一体的正义理念以外最重要的理念。这个理念经常出现。在刑法中，惩罚措施要求与犯罪的严重程度相应。在侵权法中，共同过失的概念将索赔金额降低到索赔人的过失造成损害的程度。与此相对应，在合同法中，无过错方被要求采取合理措施减轻其损失，其获得的索赔额可能会根据其可以减轻但没有减轻的程度予以下调。罪责也考虑了相称性。

自由常常被作为正义的旗帜。自由有很多形式或方面——说

takes into account proportionality.

Freedom is often raised as a banner of justice. There are so many forms or aspects of freedom — freedom to speak, to work, to contract, to marry, to vote and so on. In some countries, the law catalogues a list of "fundamental liberties". The European Convention of Human Rights (ECHR) lays down more than a dozen human rights and political freedoms, such as the right to life, the right to a fair trial and the freedom of expression.

Different species of freedom surface in different contexts. It should be noted that there is often a clash of freedoms. A simple example is that a homeowner's freedom and right to enjoy music may impinge upon his neighbour's freedom to enjoy peace and quiet.

Equality is another much-touted notion and is famously found in the French motto "Liberty, Equality, Fraternity". As you may recall from Chapter 7, fairness is often defined in terms of equality. In a modern and free society, it is expected that there should be equal treatment, regardless of race, language, religion and, increasingly, gender.

In some contexts, the idea of neutrality or impartiality is emphasised. Administrative law has its twin pillars of "natural justice", one of which is *nemo judex in causa sua*, meaning no man should be a judge in his own cause or case. So, for example, a judge would recuse (disqualify) himself if he has a close association with one of the disputants. The other is *audi alteram partem*, or listen to the other side.

Mutuality, and its close cousin reciprocity, may also be relevant. Contract law requires for a binding contract that there be mutuality of promises. So, A promises B something and B promises something in return; typically, one party

话、工作、签约、结婚、投票等自由权利。在一些国家，法律列出了一份“基本自由权利”清单。《欧洲人权公约》（ECHR）规定了十几种人权以及政治自由，如生命权、公平审判权和言论自由。

不同种类的自由会在不同的背景下出现。应该指出的是，自由之间往往存在冲突。一个简单的例子是，一个业主享受音乐的自由和权利可能会影响到他的邻居享受和平安静的自由。

平等是另一个被大肆宣扬的概念，在法国著名的国家座右铭“自由、平等、博爱”中就可以找到。你可能还记得第 7 章中提到，公平往往是以平等来定义的。在一个现代的自由社会中，人们期望能够不分种族、语言、宗教，以及（最近越来越多见的）性别，而得到平等的待遇。

某些情况下会强调中立性或公正性的概念。行政法中有“自然正义”的双重支柱，其一是“无人得自断其案”（*nemo judex in causa sua*），意思是任何人都不应成为自己争议或案件中的法官。因此举例来说，如果一个法官与其中一方当事人有密切联系，他就应当回避（取消继续担任法官的资格）。其二是“兼听则明”（*audi alteram partem*），或同时听取另一方的意见。

相互性及其意思相近的互惠性也可能相关。合同法规定，有约束力的合同必须有相互的承诺。因此，A 向 B 承诺了什么，B 也承诺了什么作为回报；通常情况下，一方承诺履约，另一方承诺为该履约行为付费。在执行外国判决方面互惠原则的意思是，如果 B 国会执行 A 国的判决，那么 A 国就会执行 B 国

promises to perform and the other promises to pay for that performance. In the area of enforcement of foreign judgments, the reciprocity approach is that country A will enforce a judgment from country B if country B would likewise enforce a judgment from country A. The notion of good faith, an offshoot of honesty, deserves special mention, not least because it occupies a central place in the civil law system (a system originating from Continental Europe, where the core principles of the law are found in substantial codes). In civil law countries, contracting parties are expected to transact with each other in good faith. Good faith connotes honesty, openness and, importantly, consideration of the interests of the other party to the transaction or relationship. Good faith stands in sharp contrast to opportunism. The concept of good faith is of limited importance in the common law world. The exact ambit of good faith is a matter of substantial controversy in both common law and civil law countries. The concept of good faith figures prominently in public international law (the law between nations).

Another notion is vulnerability — the inability to protect oneself. The idea is that a person may be particularly weak or susceptible to abuse and hence requires special protection. We see traces of the notion of vulnerability in the grounds for invalidating a contract, such as duress, undue influence and unconscionability. In tort law, we see that courts are inclined to impose a non-delegable duty (meaning the responsibility remains even though the task has been delegated) when there is a vulnerable victim, such as a child in an orphanage.

The final three notions to consider are not strictly notions but are more like considerations. It was mentioned in the introduction to Part II that in crafting law, logic is of great importance. Law is intensely logical and analytical. But, at times, logic may not necessarily prevail. One should bear in mind the following:

的判决。诚信的概念是诚实的一个分支，特别值得一提的是因为它在大陆法体系（源自欧洲大陆的体系，其法律的核心原则见于实质性法典）中占据了核心地位。在大陆法系国家，缔约各方被期望以诚信进行交易。诚信意味着诚实、公开，重要的是，需要考虑交易或关系中相对方的利益。诚信与机会主义形成鲜明对比。诚信的概念在普通法世界中的重要性比较有限。诚信的确切范围在普通法和大陆法国家都有很大争议。诚信的概念在国际公法（国家间的法律）中则占有重要地位。

另一个概念是脆弱性——无力保护自己。这个概念是指，一个人可能特别脆弱或容易受到欺负，因此需要特别保护。我们在合同无效的理由中看到了脆弱性概念的痕迹，如胁迫、不正当影响和不合情理。在侵权法中，我们看到法院倾向于在对待脆弱的受害者，如孤儿院的儿童时，施加不可推卸的责任（意味着即使工作任务被委任他人完成，委任者的责任仍然存在）。

最后要考虑的三个理念不是严格意义上的理念，而更像是考量因素。在第二部分的介绍中曾经提到，在制定法律时，逻辑是非常重要的。法律具有强烈的逻辑性和分析性。但是，有时候逻辑不一定占主导地位。大家应该牢记以下几点：常识、务实和现实。

美国法官威廉·道格拉斯简明扼要地指出："好的法律由常识制造。"托马斯·杰斐逊则以更夸张的方式宣称，常识是"所有权威的基础，是法律本身的基础，也是法律建设的基础"。常识对严格的逻辑起到了制衡作用。英国法官有时为了阐述新

common sense, practicality and reality.

American judge William Douglas put it succinctly when he said: "Common sense often makes good law". In somewhat more hyperbolic fashion, Thomas Jefferson declared common sense to be "the foundation of all authorities, of the law themselves, and of their construction". Common sense acts as a counterbalance to strict logic. English judges sometimes justify a new legal position by stating that law must make sense to the "man on the Clapham omnibus" or, more recently, "the man on the Underground [train]". Basically, law must make sense to the common man.

Similarly, it is often emphasised that law must be pragmatic. Compliance with the law must not only be practicable (possible), it must also be practical. Law should not be unduly burdensome. As such, workplace legislation typically require employers to do what is "reasonably practicable" to safeguard health and safety of employees and others at the workplace. For example, in an open construction site where there is a lot of dust, it is reasonable and practicable to require the employer to provide employees with masks but it may be too expensive to require dust extraction units to be deployed.

Another notion is reality. Law must reflect reality. In contracts, a common problem is that sellers tend to misrepresent and yet seek to hide behind a contract clause which says that the buyer is not relying on any representation made by the seller. A solution is that the clause will be upheld if it reflects reality (see, for example, *Raiffeisen v. RBS*, where the defendant bank tried unsuccessfully to rely on such a clause).

All three notions of common sense, practicality and reality are in fact closely related. A quotation from Scott Segrest captures it well: "The essence of

的法律立场的正确性，会说法律必须对“乘坐克拉珀姆巴士的人”或（最近更流行的说法）“乘坐地铁的人”有意义。就是说，法律必须对普通人有意义。

同样，人们经常强调，法律必须务实。遵守法律不仅要切实可行（可能遵守），还必须是实际的。法律不应成为不适当的负担。因此，工作场所立法通常要求雇主采取“合理可行”的措施，保障雇员和其他人在工作场所的健康和安全。例如在一个有大量粉尘的露天建筑工地，要求雇主为雇员提供口罩是合理可行的，但要求部署除尘装置就可能太过昂贵。

另一个概念是现实。法律必须反映现实。在合同中，一个常见的问题是，卖方倾向于虚假陈述，却试图躲在合同条款后面，说买方不依赖卖方的任何陈述。一个解决方案是，如果该条款反映了现实，它将得到支持（例如，*Raiffeisen v. RBS* 案中，被告银行试图依据这样一个条款，但没有成功）。

常识、务实和现实这三个概念实际上是密切相关的。Scott Segrest 的一句话很好地抓住了这一点：“常识的本质是与我们的生活保持密切联系。”

除了本章前面所说的，应该注意的是，法律在创造概念时经常会使用一系列的描述词。其中最重要的包括：

- “合法”（legal），如合法所有权；
- “正当”（due），如正当程序和尽职调查；
- “合法”（lawful），如合法终止和合法进入者；
- “合法”（legitimate），如合法利益和合法期望；以及
- “正当的”（justifiable），如正当的借口和正当的理由。

common sense is to stay in close contact with life as it is lived".

In addition to all that has been said previously in this chapter, it should be noted that the law often resorts to a range of descriptors when coining concepts. The foremost of these include:

- "legal", as in legal title;
- "due", as in due process and due diligence;
- "lawful", as in lawful termination and lawful entrant;
- "legitimate", as in legitimate interest and legitimate expectation; and
- "justifiable", as in justifiable excuse and justifiable cause.

Conversely, the antonyms of undue, unlawful, illegal, undue, illegitimate and unjustifiable are also used. Frankly, the descriptors may not mean very much, except that the crafter of the law, as arbiter, has decided what is acceptable and what is not acceptable. So, there may be less magic (or substance) than meets the eye.

The notions of justice are many. They are tools in the hands of the lawmaker, who uses them, it is hoped, skilfully and wisely in crafting law.

反之，不正当、不合法、非法、不当等反义词也经常被使用。坦率地说，这些描述性词汇可能意义并不大，只是法律的制定者作为仲裁者，决定了什么是可接受的，什么是不可接受的。因此，这些词汇可能没有想象中那么神奇（或具有实质性意义）。

正义的理念有很多。它们是立法者手中的工具，希望立法者在制定法律时能熟练而明智地使用它们。

Chapter 11
Maxims

Maxims are the condensed good sense of nations.

——James Mackintosh

We hear maxims all the time — "Prevention is better than cure", "A soft answer turns away wrath", "The unexamined life is not worth living" and so on.

But what is a maxim? For one thing, it should not be confused with slogans, mottos or mantras, like "Just do it", "The customer is always right" or "Cash is king". These catchphrases have their purpose within their contexts. But they are not really maxims.

Maxims are wise sayings to guide us through life. They are succinct formulations of truths. These truths are generally applicable and widely known. They are proverbs, adages, axioms.

The Greeks have a set of 147 maxims inscribed on a tomb (dated 300–250 BC) in Delphi, a town in Greece. Perhaps the most famous of these is "know yourself" (*nosce te ipsum*, maxim number 8). The maxims are credited to seven

第 11 章
格　言

格言是一个国家浓缩的良识。

——詹姆斯·麦金托什

我们经常听到格言——“预防胜于治疗”“婉言释怨”“浑浑噩噩的生活不值得过”等。

但什么是格言呢？首先，它不应与口号、座右铭或咒语相混淆，如“只管做就对了”“客户永远是对的”“现金为王”。虽然这些口号在其背景下有其目的，但它们并不是真正的格言。

格言是指导我们生活的至理名言。它们是真理的简明表述。这些真理普遍适用，广为人知。它们是谚语、警句、公理。

希腊人有一套 147 条格言，刻在希腊德尔斐镇的一座坟墓上（日期为公元前 300 年—公元前 250 年）。其中最著名的也许是“了解自己”（*nosce te ipsum*，格言第 8 条）。这些格言归功于七位圣人，其中苏格拉底是最著名的一位。

法律也有其格言。例如，“一个人被推定为对其行为的自

sages, of whom Socrates is the most famous.

Law has its maxims too. For example, "A man is presumed to intend the natural consequences of his action". Hence, a defendant may not have specifically thought of a consequence and may argue that he had no intention to cause the particular harm. The maxim may be called in to reason that he should be held liable nevertheless.

Take another maxim "He who seeks equity must do equity". This adage is crisp and concise — if you seek fairness, you must have acted fairly. So, a judge may cite this maxim in formulating a principle for the case before him.

There is a complication to legal maxims — many of them are in Latin. Naturally, this stumps readers who are unfamiliar with the language. Why Latin? Well, many states in medieval Europe used Latin as their legal language. The judges refer to Latin maxims from time to time as they reason and formulate legal principles. Over time, the adulation for Latin maxims has moderated to a healthy respect for them.

The uninitiated reader's apprehension towards a Latin maxim is natural. Be comforted that after translation, the maxim is easily understood. Let us look at several well-known ones.

Ignorantia juris non excusat.

This maxim translates to "ignorance of the law is no excuse". The philosophy is that each of us has the responsibility to know the law; and ignorance does not excuse us. Sounds right. But, upon further reflection, this is a huge imposition and expectation, for the full body of law is vast and complex.

Expressio unius est exclusio alterius.

This mean that the express mention on one thing excludes all others within the class. So, for example, if a rule says "No selling of food on Saturdays and

然后果有故意”。因此，被告可能没有具体想到某个后果，可以辩称他没有意图造成特定的伤害，但是，这句格言可能被用来推理，认为他还是应该承担责任。

以另一条格言为例，“寻求衡平的人必须做到衡平”。这句格言言简意赅——如果你寻求公平，你首先必须做到公平。因此，法官在为他面前的案件制定原则时可以引用这条格言。

法律格言有一个复杂的问题——许多格言是用拉丁文写的。自然，这让不熟悉这种语言的读者感到困惑。为什么是拉丁文？嗯，中世纪欧洲的许多国家把拉丁语作为他们的法律语言。法官们在推理和制定法律原则时，不时地参考拉丁文格言。随着时间的推移，对拉丁文格言的膜拜已经适当地蜕变为对它们正常的尊重。

不了解情况的读者自然会对拉丁文格言产生忧虑。令人欣慰的是，经过翻译，格言很容易理解。让我们来看看几条著名的格言。

不知法律不免责。（*Ignorantia juris non excusat.*）

这句格言被翻译为“对法律的无知不是借口”。其理念是，我们每个人都有责任了解法律；而无知并不是我们的借口。听起来很对。但是，经过进一步思考，你会发现，由于整个法律体系的庞大而复杂，这其实是一个巨大的负担与期望。

明示其一即排除其他。（*Expressio unius est exclusio alterius.*）

这句话的意思是说，对某一事物的明确提及即排除该类别中的所有其他事物。因此，举例来说，如果一条规则说“周六和周日不得出售食品”，那么，由这条格言就可以推论，在一周里的其他日子允许出售食品。

Sundays", the maxim suggests that sale on other days of the week is permissible.

Ex turpi causa non oritur actio.

This maxim means, "from a dishonourable cause, no legal claim arises". For example, if a person places a bet with an unlicensed bookie and wins, he cannot claim his prize by an action in a court of law. The law will not assist illegal transactions. The *ex turpi* maxim applies in tort law, contract law, property law and several others.

Nemo dat quod non habet.

This is a useful rule for deciding competing claims to items of property. The maxim (also discussed in Chapter 17) literally means "No one can give what he does not have". So, if A stole a portrait from B and sold it to C, in a claim by B against C, the application of the maxim will result in B recovering the portrait. The reason is that C's title (or legal ownership) is only as good as A's, and A has no right to ownership at all.

Western civilisations have tended to apply Latin maxims. But other civilisations have their legal maxims too. For example, the following (translated) Chinese maxim makes quite a lot of sense:

Pardon inadvertent faults, however great;

and punish deliberate ones, however small.

(Shun, 2317 BC)

Indeed, there are maxims from Indian, Persian, Egyptian and other great civilisations of the past. Perhaps, in time, there may result in a greater diversity of legal maxims.

Legal maxims are an important component in the lawmaker's toolbox as they enshrine deep value and logic. The reader needs to understand them and their place in the making of law.

违法行为不产生诉因。（*Ex turpi causa non oritur actio.*）

这句格言的意思是“从不光彩的原因中不会产生法律诉由”。例如，如果一个人在无执照的地下博彩公司下注并赢了钱，他不能通过法院的诉讼要求获得奖金。法律不会帮助非法交易。侵权行为法、合同法、财产法和其他一些法律中都适用 *ex turpi* 这条格言的原则。

自己所没有的就不能给予。（*Nemo dat quod non habet.*）

这个规则在用于决定财产索赔竞争时很有用。这条格言（也会在第 17 章中讨论）的字面意思是“任何人都不能给予他没有的东西”。因此，如果 A 从 B 那里偷了一幅肖像画，并把它卖给了 C，在 B 对 C 的索赔中，适用该格言将导致 B 收回肖像画。原因是，C 的所有权（或合法所有权）最多只与 A 的所有权一样，而 A 根本没有所有权。

西方文明倾向于适用拉丁格言。但其他文明也有其法律格言。例如，以下（翻译）的中国格言就很有意义。

眚灾肆赦，怙终贼刑。（无心之过，再大可赦；有意作恶，再小必惩。）

——《尚书·舜典（二）》（舜，公元前 2317 年）

事实上，（古）印度、（古）波斯、（古）埃及和其他过去的伟大文明中都有自己的格言。也许，随着时间的推移，法律格言可能会因此产生更大的多样性。

法律格言是立法者工具箱中的一个重要组成部分，它们体现了深刻的价值和逻辑。读者需要了解它们以及它们在法律制定过程中的地位。

PART III

Elements of a Legal Principle

Intuition and concepts constitute ... the elements of all our knowledge.

——Immanuel Kant

第三部分

法律原则的要素

直觉和概念构成……我们所有知识的要素。

——伊曼努尔·康德

In Part II, we looked at the dynamics of crafting law — how the context needs to be studied in order to arrive at the key objectives, how notions and maxims of law are applied and how established concepts are borrowed or adapted.

The lawmaker should do all this as he sets out to craft and configure the principle of law (see Fig. 2) for the matter at hand. I should point out that, in the realm of law, a distinction is sometimes drawn between a principle and a rule. A principle is like a general idea whereas a rule goes into details or the application of the principle to given situations. For example, in workplace safety, the law could set forth a general principle that an employer should take "reasonably practicable steps" to safeguard the interests of the employee and then proceed to set out rules outlining the application of the principle to specific situations, like the precautions required when the employee is working at heights.

It is important to know that every legal principle has "elements" or "ingredients" . In general, a legal principle can easily have four to six (or more) elements. What are these elements?

First, there is the conduct or physical act. In theft, it is the taking of another's money or property. In defamation, it is the publication of a statement, such as by posting on a chat site. In trespass, it is the entering or remaining on someone else's premises. The conduct could be an act; it could also be an omission, such as the failure to turn a switch off.

Secondly, there is fault or the mental element. The act could have been done intentionally, recklessly or carelessly, and intention involves some degree

在第二部分中，我们探讨了制定法律的机制——如何研究背景以达到关键目标，如何应用法律的概念和格言，以及如何借用或调整既定的概念。

法律制定者在着手为手头的事务制定和配置法律原则（见图 2）时，应该做到以上提到的每一件事。在此应当指出，在法律领域，有时会对原则和规则进行区分。原则就像一个一般性的想法，而规则则涉及细节或原则在特定情景下的应用。例如，在工作场所安全方面，法律可以规定一个一般原则，即雇主应采取“合理可行的步骤”来保障雇员的权益，然后再制定规则，阐述该原则在具体情形下的应用，如雇员在高处工作时需要采取的预防措施。

重要的是需要知道，每个法律原则都有“要素”或“成分”。一般来说，一个法律原则可以很容易地有四到六个（或更多）要素。这些要素是什么？

第一，有行为或物理性的行动。在盗窃案中，这个行为是获取他人的金钱或财产。在诽谤案中，这个行为是发表声明，例如在聊天网站上发帖。在非法侵入案中，这个行为是进入或停留在别人的场地。该行为可以是作为，也可以是不作为，例如没有关闭开关。

第二，有过错或心理要素。该行为可能是故意的、鲁莽的或不小心的，而主观故意涉及某种程度的知晓。由于过错是一个复杂的问题，我们将在第 12 章详细考虑。

of knowledge. As fault is a complicated subject, we will consider it in some detail in Chapter 12.

Thirdly, there is the harm resulting from the act, such as physical injury, emotional harm, damage to property or economic loss. Usually, the claim is for damages (monetary compensation) in respect of the harm that is done.

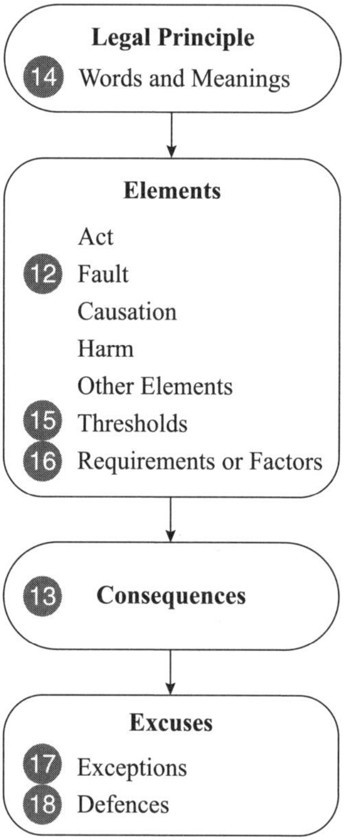

Fig. 2: Configuring a Legal principle
(numbers indicate the chapters in which the topic is covered)

Fourthly, there is the element of causation. The question is, did the wrongful act cause harm to someone thus prompting this person to complain?

第三，该行为造成了伤害，如身体伤害、精神伤害、财产损害或经济损失。通常情况下，法律请求的内容是对所造成的伤害进行赔偿（经济补偿）。

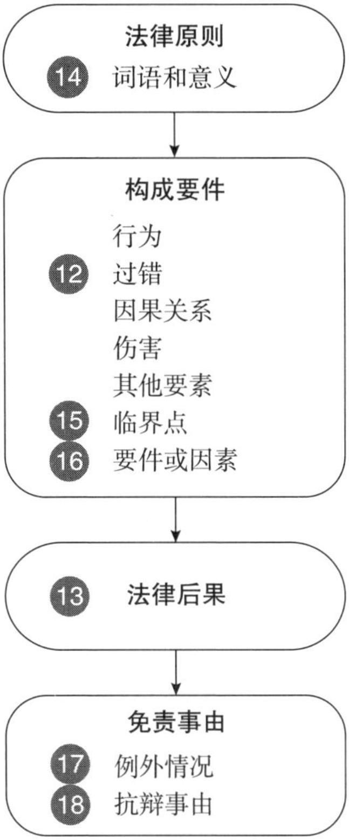

图 2：配置法律原则

（数字代表讨论相关课题的章节号）

第四，存在因果关系。需要回答的问题是：不法行为是否对某人造成了伤害，从而导致此人投诉？有时，不法行为并不造成伤害。例如，销售员可能就产品的某一特征向买方撒谎，

Sometimes, the wrongful conduct did not cause the harm. For example, the salesman may have lied to the buyer about a feature of a product but the buyer did not believe him anyway. In the language of the law on misrepresentation, the analysis is that there was no inducement. The particular challenges of causality are considered in Chapter 36.

In addition to these four, there may be one or two other elements, as well as the final element of legal consequences of infringing the legal principle (see Chapter 13). Together, all these form the conceptual elements of a legal principle.

In crafting the legal principle, several linguistic tools are used. In the first place, the maker of law plays with words, meanings and nuances, as we shall see in Chapter 14. Then, there is the important question of threshold. What degree or extent of a particular element is required in order to attract legal liability? When does the defendant cross the line? We consider thresholds in Chapter 15.

Another aspect is that although the elements of a legal principle are often set out as requirements, sometimes they are expressed as factors instead. The subject of requirements and factors is discussed in Chapter 16. To complete the legal framework for a particular principle, one has also to consider if there are situations where the law might excuse a person from the application of the legal principle. Sometimes, as is necessary, the law creates exceptions to the rule, as we shall see in Chapter 17. Quite similarly, the law may also create defences which may excuse the defendant either fully or partly, and this subject is dealt with in Chapter 18.

So, in any given scenario, when asked what the law is on the subject, we have to ascertain the elements, note the tools being used and be aware of exceptions and defences, if any. Whenever approached regarding a legal dispute,

但买方还是不相信他。那么在关于虚假陈述的法律分析中，就会认为诱导行为不存在。对于因果关系的特殊挑战将在第 36 章考虑。

除了这四个要素之外，还可能有一两个其他要素，以及违反法律原则的法律后果这一最终要素（见第 13 章）。所有这些共同构成了法律原则的概念性要素。

在制定法律原则时需要适用几种语言工具。首先，正如我们将在第 14 章中看到的那样，法律的制定者需要处理文字、意义和弦外之音。然后还有临界点这一个重要问题。某个特定要素需要达到什么程度或范围才会形成法律责任？被告何时会越界？我们将在第 15 章考虑临界点问题。

另外，尽管法律原则要素经常被设定为要件，但有时它们以因素的形式进行表述。第 16 章将讨论要件和因素的问题。为了完成特定原则的法律框架，我们还必须考虑是否存在法律可以免除某人适用该法律原则的情况。有时，正如我们在第 17 章中所看到的，法律为规则创造了一些例外。同样地，法律也可能创造出一些抗辩理由，这些抗辩理由可以完全或部分地免除被告的责任，这个问题将在第 18 章中论述。

因此，无论在什么情况下，当被问及有关该问题的法律是什么时，我们必须确定其要素，注意所使用的工具，并且，如果存在例外情况和抗辩理由，也要对此加以了解。每当涉及法律纠纷时，律师总会问：“争议焦点是什么？”假如我们用问题的形式作答，那么，答案可能包括：

the lawyer asks; "What are the issues?" The answer (in the form of questions) could include:

- Did the defendant do the act intentionally?
- What type of harm did the claimant suffer?
- Was the harm caused by the defendant and did the claimant contribute to it?
- Is the relevant threshold crossed?
- What remedy does the claimant want? and
- Can the defendant plead the defence of consent (meaning, the plaintiff knowingly and willingly agreed to the act)?

Understanding the configuration of a legal principle is key to a good appreciation of the law.

- 被告是否故意做出该行为?
- 原告遭受了什么类型的伤害?
- 伤害是否由被告造成，原告是否也有部分过错?
- 是否越过了相关的临界点?
- 原告想要什么救济类型? 以及
- 被告能否以同意为抗辩理由（意思是说，原告在知情的情况下自愿同意该行为发生）?

了解一项法律原则的构造是能够深入理解法律的关键。

Chapter 12
Fault

The woman you put here with me — she gave me some fruit from the tree, and I ate it.

——Genesis 3: 12

Dictionaries define fault as error, mistake or responsibility. But when is a person said to have made an error or mistake, and when should he be held responsible for his action? When is his conduct culpable?

In law, a critical aspect of fault is the mental element. More specifically, the law considers two related concepts — intention and knowledge.

A person is said to intend something when it is his purpose, goal or aim to do an act and to bring about certain results. A high degree of intention is indicated in words such as premeditated, calculated and deliberate. In comparison, words such as motivated and influenced indicate a lower level of intentionality.

Intentional acts stand in contrast to negligent acts. Negligence, as we have seen in Chapter 8, is the failure to take care. For some legal wrongs, the level of

第12章
过　错

你放在我这里的那个女人——她从树上摘了些果子给我，我就吃了。

——《圣经·创世记》3：12

字典将过错定义为“错误、失误或责任”。但是，什么时候可以说一个人犯了错误或失误，什么时候他应该为自己的行为负责？什么时候他的行为应受到谴责？

在法律上，心理因素是构成过错的关键方面。更具体地说，法律考虑两个相关的概念——意图和知晓。

当一个人的目的、目标或宗旨是实施一个行为并带来某些结果时，他就被说成是有意为之。高度的意图体现在诸如“预谋的”“有计划的”“故意的”这类词汇中。相比之下，诸如“有动机的”和“受他人影响的”等词则表示较低程度的主观故意。

故意行为与过失行为形成对比。正如我们在第8章中所看到的，过失是指未予以注意。对于一些法律上的错误，过错

fault is pegged at intention; for others, negligence is sufficient for liability.

A state of mind which straddles intention and negligence is recklessness. Recklessness is a disregard for danger. For example, it is reckless to drive a car at extremely high speeds. The law tends to equate recklessness with intentionality.

Usually, fault takes the form of either intention (including recklessness) or negligence. Exceptionally, a person may be liable even though his act was neither intentional nor negligent, such as the failure to file a tax return or the liability for the harm caused by keeping a wild animal. In such instances, the liability is said to be strict. The law tries to avoid imposing strict liability; when it does impose strict liability, this is usually clearly stated.

As mentioned earlier, intention and knowledge are related. Without some degree of knowledge, it cannot be said that the person had intention to cause harm. A person who intends to kill knows that his act will cause death.

In law, there is a broad spectrum of knowledge. It includes, in more or less descending order of intensity:

- actual knowledge;
- willful blindness;
- imputed knowledge;
- constructive knowledge;
- suspicion; and
- foresight.

A brief explanation of each category is in order here.

Actual knowledge, as the term suggests, is knowledge which the defendant

的程度需要与故意挂钩；而对于其他的错误，过失就足以构成责任。

故意和过失之间还有一种心理状态称为鲁莽。鲁莽是对危险的漠视。例如，以极高的速度驾驶汽车是鲁莽的。法律倾向于将鲁莽与故意等同视之。

通常情况下，过错的形式是故意（包括鲁莽）或疏忽。在特殊情况下，即使一个人的行为既非故意也非过失，也可能要承担责任，比如没有报税，或对饲养野生动物造成的伤害承担责任。这样的责任被称为严格责任。法律会试图避免规定严格责任；但若法律确实规定了严格责任时，通常会明确说明这一点。

如前所述，意图和知晓是相关的。没有一定程度的知晓，就不能说这个人有造成伤害的意图。一个打算杀人的人知道他的行为会导致他人死亡。

法律上对不同种类的知晓的范围定义非常广。粗略按强度降序排列，包括以下几种：

- 实际知晓；
- 故意视而不见；
- 推定知晓；
- 应当知晓；
- 怀疑；以及
- 预见。

这里需要对每一类进行简单的解释。

in fact had. For example, the person holding a gun may know the gun is loaded.

Willful blindness is also called Nelsonian knowledge. Famously, Admiral Nelson, when told by an assistant of signals that suggest they should retreat, brought the telescope to his blind eye and said, "I see no ships". Unsurprisingly, the law regards willful blindness as equivalent to actual knowledge. Willful blindness is also known as disregard of the obvious.

Imputed knowledge refers to knowledge which the court imputes to a defendant. The law says: "You must have known", in effect disbelieving the defendant's assertion that he did not know.

The next form of knowledge — an important and controversial one — is constructive knowledge. Here, the court is not concerned with whether it believes the defendant's assertion of innocence. Instead, it decides that in the circumstances, the defendant, like other reasonable persons, ought to have known.

Suspicion is a low-level form or type of knowledge. It is seldom used as a measure of fault.

Foresight is the idea that had the defendant thought about it, he would have known of the implications or consequences. Foresight, or foreseeability, as we shall see in Chapter 19, is an integral part of the tort of negligence.

Apart from the six mentioned, there are yet other expressions relating to knowledge and with differing nuances of mental element. They include realisation, perception, belief and guess.

Each of the different terms used to describe knowledge has a different meaning or shade of meaning. Depending on the actual word used for the element of a particular offence or legal principle, the defendant may or may not have the requisite mental element for legal liability.

实际知晓，正如该术语所暗示的，是指被告事实上知晓。例如，持枪的人可能知道枪已经上膛。

故意视而不见也被称为纳尔逊式知晓。这来自一个著名的故事，当年纳尔逊海军上将在助手告知有信号表明他们应该撤退时，故意将望远镜放到他的盲眼上并说："我没有看到船。"法律不出意外地认为故意视而不见等同于实际知晓。故意视而不见也被称为无视明显的事实。

应当知晓是指法院认定被告推定知晓。法律说："你肯定知道"，这实际上是不相信被告关于他不知道的说法。

下一种知晓形式非常重要但具有争议——应当知晓。在这里，法院并不关心它是否相信被告无辜。相反，法院决定在这种情形下，被告和其他合理的人一样，应该知道。

怀疑是一种低层次的知晓形式或类型，它很少被用来作为衡量过错的标准。

预见是指如果被告想到了这一点，他就会知道其影响或后果。正如我们将在第 19 章看到的，预见或可预见性是过失侵权行为的一个组成部分。

除了上述六种情况，还有其他与知识有关的表达方式，其心理要素也有细微差别。它们包括认识、感知、相信和猜测。

每一个用于描述知晓的术语都有其不同的含义或影射。根据特定罪行或法律原则的要素所使用的实际词汇，被告可能有，也可能没有承担法律责任所要求的心理要素。

过错可以是个复杂的问题。在特定情况下，法律必须决定被告必要的过错需要什么样的意图和知晓的组合。在极端情

Fault can be a complicated matter. In a given scenario, the law has to decide what combination of intention and knowledge is required for the requisite fault on the part of the defendant. In extreme circumstances, it may even decide that the mental element is not required. The defendant may be liable simply because he did an act and the act caused harm.

况下，法律甚至可能决定对心理要素不做要求。被告可能仅仅因为他做了某个行为，而这个行为造成了伤害，就需要承担责任。

Chapter 13
Legal Consequences

It is essential to the idea of a law that it be attended with a sanction.

——Alexander Hamilton

Legal rules and principles are put in place for a reason — to protect individuals and society at large. Rules and principles confer rights and impose responsibilities.

When rules are broken and rights infringed, there is legal recourse against the wrongdoer.

Where a crime has been committed, the state decides whether or not to prosecute the accused. If it does prosecute and the accused is found by the court to be guilty, he will be convicted and sentenced with the appropriate punishment, such as a fine or imprisonment.

If there is breach of civil laws as well, such as the tort of deceit or a breach of contract, the victim can bring a civil suit. The range of remedies is wide, and it includes:

第 13 章
法律后果

法律的概念里必须伴随着制裁。

——亚历山大·汉密尔顿

法律规则和原则的出台是有原因的——为了保护个人和整个社会。规则和原则赋予权利，也规定了责任。

当规则被破坏、权利被侵犯时，可以对不法分子进行法律追诉。

如果发生了犯罪，国家将决定是否对被告提起公诉。如果提起公诉且法院认定被告有罪，他将被定罪并被判处适当的惩罚，例如罚款或监禁。

如果发生了违反民事法律的行为，如欺骗或违反合同，受害者可以提起民事诉讼。民事救济措施的范围很广，包括：

- damages;
- injunction;
- specific performance; and
- self-help remedies.

In law, the term "damages" refers to monetary compensation. In tort law, the objective of awarding damages is to put the claimant in the position he would have been if no tort had been committed. In contract law, the aim is to put him in the position if the contract had been properly performed. Generally, the result is the same, but in some situations they differ. It should also be noted that, in general, punishment does not play a role in the awarding of compensation.

An injunction is a court order to the defendant not to do something. For example, if there is a valid non-compete clause, the court may order the defendant not to work for a competitor in violation of the clause. This is known as a prohibitory injunction. In contrast, in a mandatory injunction, the court orders the defendant to do something, such as to reinstate a fence that he had wrongfully dismantled.

Specific performance is a contract law remedy. It is given in rare instances where damages would be an inadequate remedy, such as in a contract to sell a rare painting or sculpture. In effect, it is much like a mandatory injunction.

The law allows a limited amount of self-help to redress civil wrongs. For example, a homeowner is allowed to cut off the overhanging branches of a neighbour's tree. He may also use a reasonable amount of force to evict a trespasser from his premises.

There are other civil remedies and they include an account of profits, an

- 损害赔偿；
- 禁止令；
- 强制履行；以及
- 自助救济措施。

在法律上，“损害赔偿”一词是指经济赔偿。在侵权法中，赔偿金的目的是使索赔人处于如同没有发生侵权行为情形下的位置。在合同法中，其目的是使被违约一方处于假设合同得到适当履行的状态。一般来说，这两种结果是相同的，但在某些情况下，它们也会有所不同。还应注意的是，一般来说，赔偿裁决中不包括惩罚的目的。

禁止令是法院对被告发出的不得做某事的命令。例如，根据有效的竞业条款，法院可以命令被告不得违反该条款，为竞争对手工作。这被称为禁止性禁令。相反，在强制性禁令中，法院命令被告做特定的事，例如恢复他错误拆除的围栏。

强制履行是一种合同法救济措施，在损害赔偿不足以提供适当救济的罕见情况下可以给予，例如在出售稀有绘画或雕塑的合同中。实际上它与强制性的禁止令类似。

法律允许适用有限的自助手段纠正民事不法行为。例如，法律允许房主砍掉邻居的树上悬垂的枝条。他也可以使用合理的武力，将入侵者赶出他的场所。

还有其他民事补救措施，其中包括披露利润、纠正令、撤销文件、宣布交易无效等和破产程序。

order of rectification, cancellation of documents, an order nullifying a transaction and bankruptcy proceedings.

The infringement of the law carries legal consequences and, all in all, there is a wide range of remedies by which the wrongdoer is brought to task and the wrong done to the innocent party is remedied as far as is possible and practical.

违法行为会产生法律后果，总而言之，法律设有一系列的救济措施，通过这些救济措施，不法分子会被追究责任，无辜的一方所受到的伤害也会尽可能地得到补救。

Chapter 14
Words and Meanings

'Twas brillig, and the slithy toves did gyre and gimble in the wabe.

——Lewis Caroll

Jabberwocky

Words are the means by which thoughts and ideas are captured and conveyed. They are the main mode of human communication. As the Bee Gees song goes, "It's only words, and words are all I have..." .

Words can be simple or complicated — one can argue, or one can expostulate. The choice of words can either assist or obstruct understanding. Sometimes, high-sounding words are used, and quite unnecessarily. For example, the writer or speaker may choose "disambiguate" or "discombobulate" when "clarify" and "confuse" could serve as well.

Words come in a cluster. For example, alternatives of the word "happy" include "glad", "pleased", "delighted", "elated" and "jubilant"; likewise, the word "sad" has its family of words, like "discouraged", "miserable",

第14章 词语和意义

滑菱鲆在缓慢扭动，时而翻转时而平衡。

——刘易斯·卡罗尔

《龙》

词语是捕捉和传达思想和观念的手段。它们是人类交流的主要模式。正如Bee Gees的歌所唱的那样，“It’s only words, and words are all I have…”。

词语可以简单，也可以复杂——人们可以争论，也可以争辩。词语的选择可以帮助理解，也可以阻碍理解。有时，使用一些听起来很“高大上”的词语是没有必要的。例如，当使用“澄清”和“混淆”能达到效果时，作者或演讲者选择“消除歧义”或“混淆视听”就显得毫无必要了。

词语会出现在近义词簇中。例如，“快乐”这个词可以用“高兴”“喜悦”“愉快”“欣快”“快乐”代替；同样地，“悲伤”这个词也有一系列的近义词，如“灰心”“悲惨”

"sorrowful", "depressed" and "devastated" . In each word cluster, there is depth and breadth in meaning and the choice of word conveys a different nuance of meaning.

Then, there is technical jargon. Every discipline or profession has its encyclopaedic armoury of technical terms. The doctor tells the patient he has non-Hodgkin's lymphoma and that the cancer has metastasised; in due course, he informs the patient's family that the patient is under palliative care. If clarification on the technical terms is not sought or given, the hearers are left confused and confounded.

Similarly, economists speak of the Gini coefficient, GDP per capita and PPP-adjusted, financial analysts talk about debt-equity ratio and a Goldilocks recovery and statisticians discuss null hypotheses and regression to the mean. Really, technicality and jargon are all around, despite the periodic responses to calls for the use of simple and ordinary language in making law.

To be fair, experts in their fields may have good reason for their jargon, such as that precision is required for distinct identification or that convenience or expeditiousness calls for the use of acronyms that only they undertand.

There are several things to note about the use of words in law.

First, as in all disciplines, the key to better understanding of a phrase is to analyse the meaning of the individual words. Take the concept "voluntary assumption of responsibility" . Looks quite intimidating. Essentially, it talks about a situation where the defendant freely undertook responsibility to another person. For example, a doctor who stops along a street to give assistance to an injured person may be said to have voluntarily assumed responsibility to that person.

“悲伤”“沮丧”“毁灭”等。在每一个词簇中，每个词的深度和广度都会有不同的含义，词汇的选择能够传达不同的细微含义。

然后，还有技术术语。每个学科或专业都有其百科全书式的技术术语。医生告诉病人他患有非何杰金氏淋巴瘤，而且癌症已经转移；在适当的时候，他通知病人的家人，病人正在接受安宁疗护。如果不对这些技术术语进行解释说明，听众就会感到困惑和迷茫。

同样地，经济学家谈论基尼系数、人均 GDP 和购买力平价调整，金融分析师谈论债务—资产比率和“金发女孩”复苏，统计学家讨论零假设和回归平均值。说实话，尽管对制定法律时使用简单和普通语言的呼吁定期不断地会有人附和回应，但技术性词汇和行话依然无处不在。

公平地说，各领域的专家可能有充分的理由使用他们的行话，例如，需要精确的识别，或者为了方便或快捷，需要使用只有他们才懂的缩写词。

关于法律中词语的使用，有几件事需要注意。

第一，和所有学科一样，更好地理解一个短语的关键是分析各个单词的含义。以“自愿承担责任”这一概念为例，它看起来有点吓人。但从本质上讲，它讲的是被告自主地对另一个人承担了责任的情况。例如，一个医生在街上停下来向一个受伤的人提供援助，可以说他是自愿承担了对这个人的责任。

再以另一个概念“实质性合法期望”为例，这个用法见于行政法（与挑战公共机构的决定有关的法律）。“实质性”一词

Take another concept "substantive legitimate expectations", which is used in administrative law (law relating to challenges of public bodies' decisions) . The word "substantive" is used in contrast to "procedural"; essentially, the idea is that apart from ensuring proper procedure, the merits of the decision are also important. The use of "expectation" refers to a situation where because the authority had made a representation, the recipient expects a certain outcome. Finally, the word "legitimate" simply indicates that the law decides that the expectation is an appropriate one to have.

Secondly, in seeking to understand complex legal terms and concepts, a certain degree of confidence and even boldness is required. Indeed, intimidating terms and expressions can be understood. More than that, sometimes beyond understanding the term, one needs to be bold enough to realise that the term, despite its apparent robustness and complexity, may not mean much at all. For example, whilst some judges pay high regard to the concept of voluntary assumption of responsibility, other judges are candid enough to admit that it is not much more than a label or tool for courts to use.

Thirdly, when there are related or associated concepts, it is important to ascertain the way and the extent to which they interact. A pertinent question to ask is whether two related concepts are overlapping circles or if one is a smaller circle within the other larger circle. For example, are intention and knowledge (see Chapter 12) overlapping circles or is knowledge a smaller circle within the larger circle of intention? The short answer is that they are overlapping, which leads to another question — when do they overlap and when do they not overlap?

Fourthly, legal terms often come with definitions. One will find, at the beginning of a statute, a list of definitions. For example, a company law statute

是与“程序性”相对应的；从本质上讲，其意思是除了确保适当的程序外，决定的优劣也很重要。使用“期望”指的是这样一种情况：由于当局已经做出了某种陈述，接受者期望得到某种结果。最后，“合法”一词只是表明，法律认为该期望是一种适当的期望。

第二，在寻求理解复杂的法律术语和概念时，需要一定程度的自信甚至是大胆。事实上，令人生畏的术语和表达方式是能够理解的。不仅如此，有时除了理解术语之外，还需要有足够的勇气来意识到，尽管该术语表面上很强大和复杂，但可能根本没有什么意义。例如，虽然一些法官高度重视自愿承担责任的概念，但其他法官却坦率地承认，这不过是法院使用的一个标签或工具。

第三，当存在相关或关联的概念时，重要的是要确定它们相互作用的方式和程度。与之相关的问题是，两个相关的概念是否相互重叠，还是一个被另外一个包含其中。例如，意图和知晓（见第 12 章）是重叠的圆圈，还是知晓是意图这个大圆中的一个小圆？简短的回答是，它们是重叠的，这又导致了另一个问题——它们何时重叠，何时不重叠？

第四，法律术语往往伴随着定义。我们会在法规的开头发现一个定义列表。例如，一项公司法法规可能将董事定义为“指导、控制或管理公司事务的个人”；一些法规还会补充说该术语“包括董事惯常按照其指示和指令行事的人”。后一类人也被称为“影子”董事。

同样，合同和协议的开头通常有一个定义列表。一份特许经营协议可以定义许多方面，如期限、地域和产品。协议中使

may define a director as "an individual who directs, controls or manages the affairs of the company"; some statutes add that the term "includes a person in accordance with whose directions and instructions the directors are accustomed to act". This latter category of directors is also referred to as "shadow" directors.

Similarly, contracts and agreements typically have a list of definitions at their beginning. A franchise agreement may define many aspects, such as: duration, territory and products. The terms used in agreements have to be interpreted in the way defined by the parties.

Fifthly, in the course of reading legal material, one will periodically come across Latin words and phrases, such as *prima facie* (based on first impression), a *fortiori* (with stronger reason, or all the more) and *causa sine qua non* (necessary or indispensable cause). In addition, as mentioned in Chapter 11, many maxims of law, such as *volenti non fit injuria* (to a willing person, no injury is done) are in Latin.

Finally, law sometimes makes use of metaphors, imageries and even parables, such as "palm tree justice", "thin skull rule" or "the mountaineer's knee". Metaphors are used because they help to explain a concept, especially a difficult one.

Let us take the third metaphor. Here, the judge (Justice Phillips, in *SAAMCO v. York Montague*) was explaining causation and responsibility. The scenario he gave was of a mountaineer consulting a doctor as to the condition of his knee prior to going for a climb. The doctor said the knee was fine when actually it was not. The mountaineer goes for his climb and is injured in an avalanche. The judge explained that although, in terms of chronology, the doctor's negligent diagnosis resulted in the mountaineer going for a climb and

用的术语必须按照各方定义的方式进行解释。

第五，在阅读法律材料的过程中，人们会不时地接触到一些拉丁语词和短语，如 *prima facie*（基于第一印象）、*a fortiori*（有更强的理由，或更多）和 *causa sine qua non*（必要或不可缺少的原因）。此外，如第 11 章所述，许多法律格言，如 *volenti non fit injuria*（对自愿的人不会造成伤害）是用拉丁文写的。

最后，法律有时会使用隐喻、联想甚至是寓言，如“棕榈树的正义”“薄头骨规则”“登山者的膝盖”等。隐喻的使用是因为它们有助于解释一个概念，特别是一个困难的概念。

让我们来看看第三个比喻。这里，法官（菲利普斯法官，在 *SAAMCO v. York Montague* 案中）这样解释因果关系和责任。他给出的情景是，一个登山者在去登山前向医生咨询他的膝盖状况。医生说他的膝盖挺好的，但实际上膝盖有问题。该登山者去登山并在雪崩中受了伤。法官解释说，虽然从时间顺序上看，医生的诊断失误导致了登山者去登山并受伤，但医生不应承担责任。原因是他没有对山坡的状况做出任何评估；他的职责范围只限于登山者的膝盖状况。

因此，联想在法律中的应用有时非常有效。例如，“登山者的膝盖”的比喻就很有帮助，并被法官在随后的几个案件中引用。每当使用一个形象的比喻时，读者必须顺着这个比喻来理解法官试图传达的想法。

法律的起草，特别是在进行巧妙的校准和精细的微调时，需要对文字有娴熟的掌握。正如我们所看到的，掌握文字有许多方面和维度。当读者遇到一项法律原则时，他必须非常

getting injured, the doctor should not be held liable. The reason is that he did not make any assessment as to the state of the mountain slope; the scope of his duty was confined to the condition of the climber's knee.

So, imagery is used in law, sometimes very effectively. The parable of the mountaineer's knee, for example, is helpful and has been quoted by judges in several subsequent cases. Whenever an image is used, the reader has to follow it and understand the idea the judge is trying to convey.

Crafting of law, particularly where skillful calibration and fine nuancing are needful, requires a mastery of words. As we have seen, there are so many facets and dimensions. When a reader comes across a legal principle, he has to examine the actual words used very closely to understand their meaning and to ascertain the elements of the legal principle.

仔细地检查实际使用的词语，以了解其含义并确定法律原则的要素。

Chapter 15
Thresholds

To measure is to know.

——Ernst von Siemens

If your systolic blood pressure exceeds 130 mmHg, you have hypertension. If the air quality hits 300 on the Pollutants Standards Index, the air is considered hazardous. If a bank's customer has US$30 million (of investible funds), he is categorised as an UHNWI — Ultra-High-Net-Worth individual.

In this world, almost anything and everything is measurable, and thresholds are set. What exactly is a threshold?

Simply defined, a threshold is a level which, when reached, triggers some phenomenon or change. So, at a systolic pressure of 140, the doctor diagnoses the patient as having hypertension and advises medication. At 300 PSI, the health authorities advise citizens to wear masks. And, when an investor is an UHNWI, the financial regulator regards him as having enough financial wherewithal to look after his own interests.

第 15 章
临界点

度量即认知。

——恩斯特·冯·西门子

如果你的收缩压超过 130 毫米汞柱，你就有高血压。如果空气质量在污染物标准指数（PSI）上达到 300，则空气被认为是有害的。如果一家银行的客户拥有 3000 万美元（可投资资金），他就被归类为超高净值人士（UHNWI）。

在这个世界上，几乎所有事情都是可以度量的，并且设定了临界点。究竟什么是临界点呢?

简单地说，临界点是一个水平，一旦达到这个水平，就会引发一些现象或变化。因此，当收缩压达到 140 毫米汞柱时，医生会诊断病人患有高血压，并建议用药。在 300 PSI 时，卫生当局建议公民戴口罩。而且，当一个投资者是超高净值人士时，金融监管机构认为他有足够的财力来照顾自己的利益。

临界点在法律上至关重要。当达到一定水平时，就会产生

Thresholds are of critical importance in law. When a certain level is reached, there are legal implications. Let us look at a few examples.

For civil proceedings, the standard of proof is a balance of probabilities. This means that after hearing all the evidence, the judge has to be persuaded that it is more likely than not that the claimant's side of the story is correct. In numerical terms, the claimant has to prove a >50% likelihood. If the threshold is not reached, the case is not proved. (Actually, if you think about it, this is not a very high threshold and it is debatable whether it is sufficient and acceptable to resolve a legal dispute based on such a measure.)

In a transaction, the law gives an innocent buyer the right to avoid a contract if the seller had made a misrepresentation provided that the false representation related a "material" (or significant) fact about the product. For example, when a person buys a second-hand car, it would be material to him that the car has not had a major accident and he may, therefore, ask the seller about this.

If the misrepresentation was about an immaterial fact, there is no legal recourse. A handphone, for example, has myriad features. Some of these would be material to the typical user, such as the calling, texting and photography and videoing functions. But other functions, such as the torchlight, calculator and games, may be material to some but immaterial to others.

The same term — "material" — is also used in relation to a doctor's duty of disclosure. The legal position in many countries is that a doctor is liable if he fails to disclose a risk which is material either to an average patient or to the particular patient. Non-disclosure of an immaterial risk does not attract legal liability.

Another common descriptor for legal threshold is "substantial" . In the performance of a contract, the general rule is that the performer has to render

法律影响。让我们看几个例子。

对于民事诉讼，证明的标准是可能性平衡。这意味着，在听取了所有的证据后，法官必须被说服，认为原告一方的说法更有可能是正确的。从数字上看，原告必须证明有大于 50% 的可能性。如果没有达到这个临界值，这个案子就没有被证明。（实际上，如果你仔细想想，这并不是一个很高的门槛，根据这样的措施来解决法律纠纷是否足够可以被接受，是值得商榷的。）

在交易中，如果卖方做出了虚假陈述，法律赋予无辜的买方撤销合同的权利，只要该虚假陈述与产品的"重大"（或重要）事实有关。例如，当一个人购买一辆二手车时，该车没有发生过重大事故对他来说是很重要的，因此，他可以向卖家询问这个问题。

如果虚假陈述是关于一个不重要的事实，则不涉及承担法律责任。例如，一部手机有无数的功能。其中有些功能对典型的用户来说是重要的，比如打电话、发短信、拍照和录像的功能。但其他功能，如手电筒、计算器和游戏，对一些人来说可能是重要的，但对另一些人来说却不重要。

同样的术语——"重要"——也被用于医生的披露义务。许多国家的法律规定，如果医生没有披露对普通病人或特定病人来说是重要的风险，那么他就要承担责任。而未披露不重要的风险则不会引起法律责任。

另一个常见的描述法律临界值的词是"实质性"。在履行合同的过程中，一般的规则是，履约者在有权获得任何付款之前必须完全和准确地履行合同。这一规则的一个例外是已经存

full and precise performance before he is entitled to any payment. One exception to this rule is where there has been substantial performance. A contracting party who has substantially performed is entitled to the contract price less the part of the contract which was not, or not properly, performed. In short, a substantial performer is entitled to proportional payment.

The law sets thresholds and uses different terms to describe the threshold. Apart from the terms already mentioned, there is a whole range of descriptors used, such as:

- "reasonable", as in proving a criminal case beyond reasonable doubt;
- "serious", as in UK defamation law, where there must be serious harm to the reputation of the claimant before a suit can be brought; and
- "radical", as in contract law, where a contract is "frustrated" and brought to an end if circumstances have changed and performance would be radically different from what the parties had expected.

There are several points to note about thresholds.

The first is that, on a particular subject, whether it is fault, risk, harm, damage or some other aspect, there is a range of extents. Fault, as we have seen in Chapter 12, for example, may range from deliberateness to recklessness to carelessness. Risk can be categorised into intolerable, high, substantial, significant and slight. Harm can be within a range of severe, serious, substantial and trifling. The point is that for a particular problem or issue, the law decides the appropriate threshold for liability.

The second point is that, in general, the descriptors are qualitative rather

在实质性履行。实质性履行的合同方有权获得合同价格减去合同中未履行或未适当履行的部分。简而言之，实质性履约者有权获得相应的付款。

法律规定了门槛，并使用不同的术语来描述临界点。除了已经提到的术语外，还使用了一系列的描述词，如：

- “合理”，如证明刑事案件无合理怀疑；
- “严重”，如在英国的诽谤法中，提起诉讼之前，必须对索赔人的声誉造成严重损害；以及
- “急剧”，如在合同法中，如果情况发生变化，合同的履行将与当事人的预期急剧不同，则合同将“落空”并终止。

关于临界点有几个需要注意之处。

第一，对每一个特定的对象，无论是过错、风险、伤害、损害还是其他方面，其程度都有一定范围。例如，正如我们在第 12 章中所看到的，过错的范围可以从故意到鲁莽、到粗心。风险可以分为不可容忍的、高度的、实质性的、重要的和轻微的。危害可以分为严重的、重大的、实质性的和微不足道的。关键是对于一个特定的问题或争议焦点，法律决定了当事人应当负责的适当临界点。

第二，一般来说，描述词是定性的而不是定量的。有些描述词，如“一致”“多数”“概率平衡”“同等机会”，有明确的数字或数学指示。但大多数描述词没有足够精确的水平或程度的指示。例如，在医疗建议的背景下，什么是实质性风险？在

than quantitative. Some descriptors, such as "unanimous", "majority", "balance of probabilities", "even chance" have a clear numerical or mathematical indication. But the majority of descriptors do not have a sufficiently precise indication of the level or extent. For example, in the context of medical advice, what is material risk? Is a 2% chance of heart failure or coma when under general anaesthesia a material risk? What kind of percentage does the word "significant" indicate to us? And what is the dividing line between harm that is serious and what is not serious or not so serious? It is noted that where qualitative terms are used, judges have greater discretion in administering justice.

The third point is that even for a particular word, the meaning may vary significantly, depending on the context. In substantial performance, the word envisages that the majority of the performance obligations have been completed. Yet, in company law, a substantial shareholder of a listed company is one who owns just 5% (or more) of the shares of the company. There is a final thing to note about thresholds — the law's response to extremes. Extreme situations, whether in terms of conduct or harm, tend to invoke a legal response.

Take the example of hazardous activities. At common law, there is strict liability for wild animals. Briefly, if you keep a wild animal on your premises, you will be liable for injury caused to others by your animal even if you had taken all the precautions to prevent injury, such as muzzling and chaining your animal.

Another example is in the area of damages. For civil proceedings, the main objective of awarding damages is to compensate the injured party. In general, the law does not award exemplary or punitive damages (damages which punish the defendant, in addition to compensating the claminant) . However, as an exception, courts may impose such damages if the defendant's conduct was

全身麻醉的情况下，2% 的心力衰竭或昏迷的可能性是实质性风险吗？“重大”这个词向我们表明了什么样的百分比？而严重的伤害与不严重或不太严重的伤害之间的分界线是什么？有人指出，在使用定性术语的情况下，法官在司法方面有更大的自由裁量权。

第三，即使是一个特定的词，其含义也可能有很大的不同，这取决于语境。在实质性履行中，“实质”考虑的是大部分履行义务已经完成。然而，在公司法中，上市公司的“实质性”股东是指拥有该公司 5%（或以上）股份的人。关于临界点，还有一件事需要注意——法律对极端情况的反应。无论是行为还是伤害方面的极端情况，都会引起法律的反应。

以危险活动为例。在普通法中，人们对野生动物有严格的责任。简而言之，如果你在你的个人场所饲养野生动物，即使你已经采取了所有的预防措施来防止伤害，例如给动物戴上口罩和链子，你仍然要对你的动物对他人造成的伤害负责。

另一个例子是在损害赔偿方面。对于民事诉讼，判给损害赔偿的主要目的是补偿受害方。一般来说，法律不会判处惩戒性或惩罚性的损害赔偿（这里指除了赔偿原告外，带有惩罚被告性质的损害赔偿）。然而一个例外情况是，如果被告的行为是恶意的、压迫性的或态度轻蔑的，法院可以判处这种损害赔偿。所谓极端的情况需要极端的措施。

相反，如果伤害是轻微的或微不足道的，法律就不愿意干预。律师们都知道“法律不理鸡毛蒜皮之事”（*de minimis non curat lex*）这一格言。这一拉丁语表达方式被翻译为“法律不为微不足道的事情提供救济”。这一原则或理念经常出现。侵

malicious, oppressive or scornful. Extreme situations call for extreme measures.

Conversely, where the harm is slight or trivial, the law is hesitant to intervene. The *maxim de minimis non curat lex* is well-known to lawyers. The Latin expression translates to "the law does not provide a remedy for a trifling matter" . This principle or philosophy surfaces from time to time. Tort law has a rather similar concept — vicissitudes of life. Some types of inconvenience or harm are perceived as part of the ups and downs of life, such as someone brushing past you in peak-hour pedestrian traffic or some insensitive remark made in a social media chat group.

Thresholds are vital in legal analysis. They are triggers or gateways to legal consequences. For every legal principle, the thresholds have to be scrutinised and applied to the situation at hand.

权法有一个类似的概念——生活琐事。某些类型的不便或伤害被认为是生活琐事的一部分，例如有人在上下班高峰时段的人行道上与你触碰，或在社交媒体的聊天群中说一些不适当的话，等等。

临界点在法律分析中是至关重要的。它们是法律后果的触发开关或门槛。每一个法律原则，都必须仔细审查其临界点并与相关事实进行对照适用。

Chapter 16
Requirements and Factors

You just have to get some idea of what matters and what doesn't, and how much.

——Lev Grossman

In explaining and delineating the ambit of a legal concept, the law sets out its aspects or features. These are laid out sometimes as requirements and sometimes as factors.

In the case of requirements, each and every aspect must be satisfied. Each is a necessary, but not sufficient, condition for the application of the legal concept. For example, in the area of liability for negligently-made statements (such as in the course of giving advice), the law is that in order for a duty to arise, there must be a "special relationship" between the maker and the recipient of the statement. According to the House of Lords in *Hedley Byrne v. Heller & Partners*, such a relationship exists if:

第 16 章
要件和因素

> 你只需了解什么是重要的，什么是不重要的，以及其重要的程度。
>
> ——列夫·格罗斯曼

在解释和划定一个法律概念的范围时，法律规定了它的各个方面或特征。这些内容有时是作为要件，有时是作为因素来规定的。

在要件的情况下，每个方面都必须得到满足。每个方面都是适用法律概念的必要条件，而非充分条件。例如，在因疏忽而作出的声明（如在提供建议的过程中）的责任方面，法律规定，为了使责任产生，声明的作出者和接受者之间必须有“特殊关系”。根据英国上议院在 *Hedley Byrne v. Heller & Partners* 案中的说法，这种关系存在的情况包括：

- the maker possesses or professes to possess skill or information;
- it is reasonable for the recipient to rely on this skill or information;
- the recipient relies on this skill or information; and
- the maker does not disclaim liability.

The maker is liable to the recipient for a negligently-made statement only if all four of the above are satisfied.

Factors, on the other hand, are relevant aspects of a total assessment where each aspect may not be a necessary condition. Take, for example, the question of the measures the authorities in charge of a public park should adopt, to prevent harm to visitors as a result of falling branches or falling trees.

In deciding the standard of care required to be taken, the law looks at a host of factors, including:

- the likelihood of harm;
- the seriousness of possible harm;
- the costs of avoiding the harm;
- the social utility of the activity; and
- industry practice.

In deciding the appropriate standard, the law considers all the relevant factors, some of which may call for a higher standard (such as, that the possible harm is very serious or very likely) and some may allow for a lower standard (such as the social utility and benefit of the public park, and the great expense which the maintenance of trees can involve).

- 声明者拥有或自称拥有相关技能或信息；
- 接受者依赖这种技能或信息系合理；
- 接受者确实依赖这种技能或信息；并且
- 声明者没有做无责声明。

只有满足上述全部四点，声明者才需要对接受者因过失而作出的声明负责。

另外，因素是整体评估的相关方面，其中每个方面都可能不是必要条件。例如，负责一个公共公园的当局应该采取什么措施，以防止树枝掉落对游客造成伤害的问题。

在决定需要采取的注意标准时，法律会考虑一系列的因素，包括：

- 造成伤害的可能性；
- 可能造成的伤害的严重性；
- 避免伤害需要支出的成本；
- 该活动的社会功能；以及
- 行业惯例。

在决定适当的标准时，法律会考虑所有的相关因素，其中一些因素可能需要更高的标准（例如，可能的伤害非常严重或非常可能），一些因素可能允许较低的标准（例如，公共公园的社会效用和利益，以及维护树木可能涉及的巨大费用）。

例如，在新加坡这个城市国家，道路两旁有超过 200 万棵树，国家公园委员会有一个 12 个至 18 个月的名册来检查这些

For instance, in the city-state of Singapore, where more than two million trees line the roads, the National Parks Board has a roster of 12 to 18 months to check the health of these trees. In determining whether this roster meets the legal standard of care, the relevant factors need to be considered. In this case, the high cost of maintenance and checking, as well as the benefits — physiological and aesthetic — of the trees are important practical factors to be weighed against the risks.

From time to time, there may be additions to the features in the legal framework. In the case of requirements, the additions will narrow the application of the concept. To illustrate, continuing with the "special relationship" discussed a few paragraphs before, the House of Lords, in another landmark decision *Caparo v. Dickman*, held that in order for the maker to be liable, the maker must have known the identity as well as the purpose of the recipient. Subsequently, yet another requirement was added — that the maker knew that the recipient would rely on the skill or information without seeking independent advice.

So, in the case of requirements, subsequent additions will narrow the scope of application of the particular concept. In contrast, adding new factors gives the judge greater leeway in deciding if the concept applies.

There is another aspect in the relationship between requirements and factors — sometimes, in the evolution of the law, requirements become factors. A good illustration of this is in the area of liability for negligently- caused psychiatric harm. A preliminary point to note is that this is an area where the law is very hesitant to award such a claim. This is so for various reasons, including the difficulty of verifying the authenticity of purported psychological harm (since diagnosis is principally based on the psychiatrist's interview of the victim) and the

树木的健康状况。在确定这个名册是否符合法律规定的护理标准时，需要考虑相关因素。在这种情况下，维护和检查的高成本，以及树木的——生理学的和审美的——益处是需要权衡风险的两个重要实际因素。

在法律框架中也可能会不时地增加一些特征。涉及要件时，内容的增加将缩小概念的适用范围。举例来说，继续前几段讨论的“特殊关系”，英国上议院在另一个具有里程碑意义的裁决 *Caparo v. Dickman* 案中认为，为了使声明者承担责任，声明者必须知道接受者的身份和目的。随后，又增加了另一项要求——声明者知道接受者会依赖相关技能或信息而放弃寻求独立意见。

所以，在涉及要件时，后期添加的内容会缩小特定概念的适用范围。相反，增加新的因素使法官在决定该概念是否适用时有更大的回旋余地。

要件和因素之间的关系还有另一个方面——有时，在法律的演变过程中，要件会变成因素。这方面的一个很好的例子是在过失造成的精神伤害的责任方面。首先需要注意的一点是，在这个领域，法律对承认这种索赔要求非常犹豫。这有多方面的原因，包括难以核实所谓的心理伤害的真实性（因为诊断主要是基于精神病学家对受害者的访谈），以及限制索赔者人数的挑战（例如，当事故发生在许多人面前时）。

为了限制索赔，法律最初要求索赔人满足“三接近”（或靠近）的要求——关系上的接近、身体上的接近和感知上的接近。首先，他必须证明他与事故的受害者有密切的关系（例如是受害者的配偶、父母或子女）。其次，他必须证明他在身体

challenge of limiting the number of claimants (for example, where an accident occurs in the presence of many persons).

To restrict claims, the law initially required the claimant to satisfy three requirements of proximity (or closeness) — relational, physical and perceptual. First, he must show that he had a close relationship with the victim of an accident (such as being a spouse, a parent or a child of the victim). Next, he must show that he was physically close to the scene of the accident. Finally, he must have witnessed the accident (perceptual proximity) and not have learnt of it indirectly.

Over time, judges realised that it was excessively demanding to require the claimant to satisfy all the three proximities. Instead, it came to be accepted that the three aspects should be factors, not requirements. They are all relevant and important, but not necessarily critical. One judge (Lord Keith in *Alcock v. Chief Constable*) acknowledged that a bystander who is totally unrelated to the victim but who witnessed a horrific accident may still be able to claim.

Essentially, the conversion of the aspects of a legal framework from requirements to factors broadens its applicability. The fact of the matter is that lawmaking is largely experimental and is a work in progress. A legal framework may start out being too liberal and hence needs to be narrowed down; conversely, a framework may begin cautiously and conservatively and become liberalised over time. And, within this dynamic, requirements and factors play their parts.

上接近事故现场。最后，他必须目睹了事故的发生（感知上的接近），而不是间接得知。

随着时间的推移，法官们意识到，要求索赔人满足所有三个接近的条件过于苛刻了。相反，人们开始接受，这三个方面应该是因素，而不是要求。它们都是相关和重要的，但不一定是关键。一位法官（Keith 勋爵在 *Alcock v. Chief Constable* 案中）承认，一个与受害人完全没有关系的旁观者，如果目睹了一场可怕的事故，仍然能够提出索赔。

本质上，将法律框架的各个方面从要件转换为因素，将扩大其适用性。事实上，法律的制定在很大程度上具有试验性，乃是一项持续进行的工作。一个法律框架开始时可能过于自由，因此需要缩小范围；反之，一个框架开始时可能比较谨慎保守，而随着时间的推移会变得自由。在这个动态过程中，各种要件和因素都在发挥作用。

Chapter 17
Exceptions

Only a Sith deals in absolutes.

——Obi-Wan Kenobi

Star Wars: Revenge of the Sith

The law is full of rules — principles and concepts to govern conduct in society and business. Hundreds of them. But, as the saying goes, every rule has its exceptions. Let us look at a few of them.

In the law of evidence, there is the parol evidence rule. According to this rule, where an agreement is in writing, no evidence outside of the agreement may be put forward to change or add to the terms of the agreement. The objective of this rule is to provide certainty in ascertaining the terms of an agreement.

But the parol evidence rule is subject to exceptions, and there are half a dozen of them. A notable exception is where a misrepresentation was made at or before the time of the contract. Hence, if a seller makes a false statement regarding a product prior to selling it, and the false statement induced the buyer to

第 17 章
例外情况

只有西斯族才会非黑即白。

——欧比旺·克诺比

《星球大战：西斯的复仇》

法律中充满了规则——管理社会和商业行为的原则和概念。这些规则数以百计。但是，正如俗话说的，每条规则都有其例外。让我们看看其中的几个。

在证据法中，有一个口头证据规则。根据这一规则，如果协议是书面的，就不能举出协议以外的证据来改变或补充协议本身的条款。这一规则的制定是为协议的条款提供确定性。

但是，口头证据规则也有例外，而且例外还不少。其中一个值得注意的例外情况是在合同签订时或签订前作出的虚假陈述。因此，如果卖方在出售产品之前对产品做了虚假陈述，并且该虚假陈述诱使买方购买该产品，那么，虚假陈述的例外

purchase the product, the misrepresentation exception allows the buyer, in a legal claim, to allege misrepresentation, even though the effect would be to add to the written terms of the agreement. Further, even if the contract contained a "non-reliance clause" — such as, "The buyer acknowledges that, in entering into the agreement, he is not relying on any oral statement made by the seller regarding the product" — the exception allows the buyer to allege the misrepresentation, even though doing that is attempting to contradict the above clause.

To take another example, in the sale of goods scenario, parties involved in a claim may be disputing who is the rightful owner of an item, such as a rare painting. The general common law rule is *nemo dat quod non habet* ("no one can give what he does not have", i.e., a person who does not have ownership cannot confer it to another); so, a person who buys from a thief gets no better title than the thief.

But the *nemo dat* rule is subject to several exceptions, such as where the buyer is a "bona fide purchaser for value without notice". In other words, the buyer acted in good faith, paid a proper price for the item and was not aware of the seller's defect in title. Hence, if the exception applies, he has good title to the rare painting as against the original owner.

Let's take a final example, this time, one which illustrates that the exception provides a legal remedy. In contract law as well as tort law, the primary objectives of awarding damages (monetary sums) for a breach of contract or for a tort is compensation. Punishment has little role to play in the civil realm.

However, as mentioned in Chapter 15, in exceptional cases, courts are prepared to award punitive damages — an additional sum beyond the compensatory sum — to punish the defendant. This is rarely done and only in circumstances where

情况允许买方在诉讼中指控虚假陈述，哪怕其效果是对协议的书面条款进行补充。此外，即使合同包含一个“否认依赖条款”——例如，“买方承认，在签订协议时，他不依赖卖方就产品所做的任何口头声明”——该例外依然允许买方主张虚假陈述，哪怕这样做会与上述条款产生矛盾。

再举一例，在货物销售中，参与索赔的各方可能会争辩一件物品——比如一幅罕见的画——的合法主人是谁。普通法的一般规则是 *nemo dat quod non habet*（“没有人可以给予他没有的东西”，即一个没有物品所有权的人不能把该物品赋予另一个人）；因此，从小偷那里购买的人不会比小偷获得该物品更多的所有权。

但是，“谁也不能以己所无予人”的规则有几种例外情况，例如，当买方是“未经通知并提供对价的善意购买者”。换句话说，买方是善意的，为物品支付了适当的价格，并且不知道卖方的所有权缺陷。因此，如果例外情况适用，他就对这幅稀有画作拥有完整的所有权，而不用理会原主人的权利。

让我们再举最后一例，说明例外情况如何提供法律救济措施。在合同法和侵权法中，对违约行为或侵权行为给予损害赔偿（货币金额）的主要目的是补偿。惩罚在民事领域的作用不大。

然而，如第 15 章所述，在特殊情况下，法院可以判决惩罚性赔偿金——赔偿金之外的额外金额，以惩罚被告。这种情况很少发生，只有在法院认为被告的行为很过分或具有蔑视性（轻蔑）的情况下才会这样做。

the court is of the view that the behaviour of the defendant was outrageous or contumelious (scornful) .

In fact, defences to a legal action (Chapter 18) operate as exceptions to liability, whether criminal or civil, imposed by a legal rule.

The reader may wonder: When and why does the law create exceptions to a legal rule? The answer: Where it is fair and reasonable for the lawmaker to do so. There are two ways whereby exceptions are created. The first is where the exceptions are laid down at the same time as the principle. The second is where exceptions are created along the way, as and when the need arises. In this latter situation, where too many exceptions are being created, judges often caution against letting the exception "eat up the rule" . The exceptions to the parol evidence rule illustrate both situations.

The Evidence Act in common law countries generally has a provision setting out the parol evidence rule. The provision would also list some six exceptions, of which the adducing of evidence of misrepresentation (as discussed in this chapter) is one. Further, over time, the courts created another exception — the collateral contract exception. Basically, the argument here is that the party seeking to adduce parol evidence is not trying to affect the written contract but rather seeking to prove that the parties had agreed to a separate oral contract which runs alongside the written contract. (The astute observer will note that this exception is in effect a device to sidestep the parol evidence rule.)

The world is a complicated place. There is so much diversity and variety in individuals and complexity in their interactions. Such reality cannot be perfectly accommodated by general statements of principle. If we look at the three examples provided, we find that in each case, the exception makes good sense. The

事实上，对法律诉讼的抗辩（第18章）也是一种对刑事或民事法定责任的例外。

读者可能想要知道：法律在什么时候以及为什么要为法律规则设置例外情况呢？答案是：当立法者这样做是公平和合理的时候。设置例外有两种方式：第一种是在规定原则的同时规定例外情况；第二种是在需要的时候，随时设置例外情况。在后一种情况下，由于创造了太多的例外，法官经常提醒不要让例外“吃掉规则”。口头证据规则的例外情况说明了这两种情况。

英美法系国家的《证据法》一般都有法条规定了口头证据规则。该条款通常还列出大约六种例外情况，其中，援引虚假陈述的证据（正如本章所讨论的）是其中之一。此外，随着时间的推移，法院还设置了另一种例外情况——附带合同例外。这里的观点主要是说，寻求援引旁证的一方并不是要对书面合同造成影响，而是要证明双方在书面合同以外还一并同意了另一项单独的口头合同。（精明的观察者会注意到，这种例外情况实际上是回避口头证据规则的一种手段。）

世界很复杂。每个人的多样性和差异性巨大，他们之间的相互作用也很复杂。这样的复杂世界不可能被一般的原则性声明完全容纳。如果看一下之前提供的三个例子，我们就会发现，在每一个例子中，例外都非常有意义。为了实现正义，这些例外都是必要的。

从另一个角度看，拥有规则及其例外的框架只是定义、过滤和划线工作的一部分。它是用以组织我们对世界的理解的一

exceptions were all necessary, in the interest of justice.

Seen from another perspective, the framework of having rules and their exceptions is just part of the exercise of defining, filtering and drawing lines. It is a logical way to organise our understanding of the world. It is also a sensible and useful way to organise the norms for behaviour in society and in business.

种逻辑方式，也是组织社会和商业行为规范的一种明智而有用的方式。

Chapter 18
Defences

Every vice has its excuse ready.

——Pubilius Syrus

In order to succeed, a claimant has to satisfy all the elements of the relevant legal principle. However, even if he manages to fulfill all the elements, the defendant may have a defence which negates his liability.

There is a wide range of defences and their availability differs from one legal area to another. Some defences apply to all the three core areas of crime, tort and contract. Some apply to crime and tort but not to contract; and some apply to tort and contract but not to crime.

The whole subject is complicated and is not as systematic and consistent as one would have hoped for or expected. Broadly speaking, defences fall into four categories:

- claimant's fault or responsibility;
- defendant's excuse or justification;

第 18 章
抗辩事由

每个恶习背后都有借口。

——普维利乌斯·赛勒斯

为了成功索赔，原告必须满足相关法律原则的全部要素。然而，即使他成功地满足了全部的要素，被告也可能有抗辩事由来否定其责任。

抗辩事由的范围很广，且因法律领域而异。有些抗辩理由适用于所有三个核心领域，即犯罪、侵权和合同。有些适用于犯罪和侵权行为，但不适用于合同；有些则适用于侵权行为和合同，但不适用于犯罪。

这个问题其实很复杂，并不像人们所希望或期待的那样具有系统性和一致性。概括地说，抗辩可分为四类：

- 原告的过错或责任；
- 被告的借口或正当理由；

- neither party's fault; and
- both parties' culpability.

In the first category, the two most commonly pleaded defences are consent and contributory negligence.

Consent involves the argument that the claimant or victim had agreed to the offending act and to the risk of the ensuing harm. The maxim (see Chapter 11) *volenti non fit injuria* (to a willing person, no injury is done) has general application and may absolve the defendant in crime, tort or contract. In contract, where the consent takes the form of a clause in the contract, there is an additional issue of whether the clause is an unfair exclusion of liability.

Contributory negligence is the idea that the claimant himself was partly at fault for the act or the injury (see Chapter 37). It is a partial rather than a full defence. For example, if a claimant in a car accident did not wear a seat belt, the court may decide the extent to which his negligence contributed to the harm and reduce his claim accordingly. There is a similar (but not identical) concept in contract law — a claimant who fails to take reasonable steps to mitigate his loss will have his claim reduced to the extent that he could have done so. Contributory negligence appears to have little or no relevance in criminal law, as well as in the law relating to fiduciaries.

In the second category, there are mainly two situations. The first is where there is total or partial excuse that affects the question of his fault. In criminal law, this includes defences such as mistake of fact, insanity, automatism (an involuntary action, without thought or intention) and duress. As regards insanity, there are two alternative situations — that the defendant did not know

- 双方均无过错；以及
- 双方都有可归责性。

在第一类抗辩中，两个最常见的抗辩理由是同意和与有过失。

同意的意思是，原告或受害人同意犯罪行为和随之而来的伤害的风险。法律格言（见第 11 章）*volenti non fit injuria*（对自愿的人不造成伤害）具有普遍的适用性，可以在犯罪、侵权或合同中免除被告的责任。在合同中，如果同意的形式是合同中的条款，那么还有一个问题就是该条款是否属于不公平的责任免除。

与有过失，是指索赔人自己对行为或伤害有部分过失的情况（见第 37 章）。它是一种部分而非全面的抗辩。例如，如果车祸中的原告没有系安全带，法院可以决定他的过失在多大程度上造成了伤害，并相应减少他的索赔。在合同法中也有类似（但不完全相同）的概念——原告人如果没有采取合理措施减轻损失，他的索赔将被减少到假定他减轻了损失以后的程度。在刑法以及与信义义务有关的法律中，与有过失似乎意义不大，甚至不相干。

在第二类抗辩中主要有两种情况。第一种情况是有某种完全或部分的借口，影响到被告的过错。在刑法中，这包括诸如事实错误、精神错乱、自动症（非自愿行为，没有思想或意图）和胁迫等抗辩事由。关于精神错乱，有两种可供选择的情况——被告不知道自己在做什么，或者他不知道自己在做的是错的（被称为 M'Naghten 规则）。以上强调的部分抗辩事由在

what he was doing, or he did not know what he was doing was wrong (known as the M' Naghten rule). Some of the defences highlighted so far have limited application in tort and contract, such as the defendant not having the fault element in tort or lacking capacity to enter into a contract.

The second situation is where the defence of necessity applies. Necessity can relate to protection from bodily harm — a defendant who hits another in order to protect himself from physical harm may have a good defence when sued for battery in crime or in tort. Necessity can also relate to the protection of property. For example, where the defendant entered another's property without permission in order to put out a fire, necessity may provide him a defence against a claim in trespass. The defence of necessity appears to have no application in contract.

The third category of defence is where neither the defendant nor the claimant/victim is at fault. The term Act of God, or its Latin counterpart *force majeure*, is a prime example in this category. So, if a freak storm uproots a tree in A's garden which then damages the property of his neighbour B, A may have a defence in crime and in tort. The concept of Act of God also applies in contract in the doctrine of frustration. Because of the frustrating event (such as an earthquake destroying the subject matter), both parties are released from their contractual obligations.

The final category is where both parties are culpable. The key example of this is illegality — where both parties are guilty of intentionally contravening the law, such as where both agreed to deal in smuggled goods. The *ex turpi causa* maxim (see Chapter 11) applies and neither party can claim against the other.

Above and beyond the complications and differentiations in defences, the overarching theme is that the law is able to give full or partial excuse to the defendant where it is just or appropriate to do so.

侵权行为和合同中也有有限的适用，例如被告不具备侵权行为中的过错要素或缺乏签订合同的能力。

第二种情况是适用正当防卫和紧急避险的抗辩事由。正当防卫与保护身体不受伤害有关——被告为了保护自己的身体不受伤害而打人，在被起诉为犯罪或侵权行为中的殴打时，可以成为很好的抗辩事由。紧急避险则也可以与保护财产有关。例如，如果被告为了救火而未经允许进入他人的领地，那么，紧急避险可以为他提供抗辩，使他不至于因侵入而被索赔。这项抗辩似乎在合同中并不适用。

第三类抗辩是被告和原告（受害人）都没有过错的情况。天灾一词，或其拉丁语对应的不可抗力，是这一类别中的主要示例。因此，如果一场怪异的风暴将 A 的花园里的一棵树连根拔起，然后损害了他的邻居 B 的财产，A 就可以在犯罪和侵权诉讼中进行抗辩。天灾的概念也适用于合同中的目的落空理论——由于发生了目的落空事件（如地震摧毁了标的物），双方当事人都解除了相应的合同义务。

第四类抗辩是双方都有过错的情况。这方面的关键例子是非法性——双方当事人都犯有故意违反法律的行为，例如双方都同意交易走私货物的情况。在此，“实施非法行为者无诉权”的法律格言（见第 11 章）不会令任何一方获得向另一方索赔的权利。

除了不同类型抗辩的复杂性和差异性之外，其最重要的共同特点是让法律能够在公正或适当的情况下给予被告全部或部分责任豁免。

Chapter 19
Crafting Case Law

Wisely and slowly, they stumble that run fast.

——William Shakespeare

We have been examining the complicated dynamics involved in the crafting of law. In this chapter, we look specifically at judicial lawmaking. Our example is a case known to virtually all law students in the common law world, *Donoghue v. Stevenson*. The case involved a suit by a consumer against the manufacturer on account of being poisoned by a contaminated substance (a decomposed snail!) in a bottle of ginger beer.

At the time (1932), the law was evolving and it was uncertain whether there existed, in civil as opposed to criminal law, a general principle that one should take care not to harm those around him. The related question was whether the principle would extend to making a manufacturer liable to the ultimate consumer. The appeal from the lower court's decision reached the House of Lords (which was reconstituted the Supreme Court in 2009), the highest court of

第 19 章
制定判例法

睿智而缓慢地走，脚程快的人容易跌倒。

——威廉·莎士比亚

我们一直在研究法律制定过程中涉及的复杂动态。在这一章中，我们将具体研究法官立法的问题。我们的例子是普通法世界中几乎所有法律学生都知道的一个案例，即 *Donoghue v. Stevenson* 案。该案涉及一名消费者因一瓶姜汁啤酒中的污染物质（腐烂的蜗牛！）中毒而对制造商提起诉讼。

当时（1932 年），法律正在不断发展，还不确定在民法和刑法中是否存在某种一般性原则，即一个人应该注意不要伤害他周围的人。相关的问题是，该原则是否会延伸到让制造商对最终消费者负责。针对下级法院判决的上诉到达了英国最高法院——上议院（2009 年改组为最高法院）。

上议院以 3 比 2 的多数决定，判决制造商确实负有注意义务。Atkin 勋爵的判决书中的以下文字很有启发性：

England.

The House, by a 3–2 majority, decided that the manufacturer did owe a duty of care. The following excerpt from the judgment of Lord Atkin is illuminating:

I do not think a more important problem has occupied your Lordships in your judicial capacity: important both because of its bearing on public health and because of the practical test which it applies to the system under which it arises....

At present I content myself with pointing out that in English law there must be, and is, some general conception of relations giving rise to a duty of care, of which the particular cases found in the books are but instances.

The liability for negligence, whether you style it such or treat it as in other systems as a species of "culpa", is no doubt based upon a general public sentiment of moral wrongdoing for which the offender must pay. But acts or omissions which any moral code would censure cannot, in a practical world, be treated so as to give a right to every person injured by them to demand relief. In this way rules of law arise which limit the range of complainants and the extent of their remedy.

The rule that you are to love your neighbour becomes in law, you must not injure your neighbour; and the lawyer's question, "Who is my neighbour?" receives a restricted reply. You must take reasonable care to avoid acts or omissions which you can reasonably foresee would be likely to injure your neighbour. Who, then, in law, is my neighbour? The answer seems to be — persons who are so closely and directly affected by my act that I ought reasonably to have them in contemplation as being so affected when I am directing my mind to the acts or omissions which are called in question.

我不认为各位法官在行使司法职权时对这个更加重要的问题给予了充分关注：说它重要既是因为它对公共健康的影响，也是因为它是适用于其涉及的法律问题的一项可行标准……

目前，我只想指出，在英国法律中，必须而且确实存在着某种会引发注意义务的关系的一般概念，而书中的特殊案例只是其中的实例。

对过失的责任，无论你是这样称呼它，还是像在其他制度中那样把它当作“过错”的一种，无疑都是基于公众对道德错误行为的普遍看法，认为过错方必须为此付出代价。但是，任何道德准则都会谴责的行为或不作为，在实际生活中并不都会让遭受其伤害的人获得请求救济的权利。这样一来，就出现了限制投诉人范围和救济范围的法律规则。

“你要爱你的邻居”的规则在法律上变成了“你不能伤害你的邻居”；而对于律师要问的问题——“谁是我的邻居？”答案也是有所限制的。你必须采取合理的谨慎措施，避免你可以合理预见的，可能会伤害你的邻居的行为或不作为。那么，在法律上，谁是我的邻居？答案似乎是——受我的行为密切和直接影响的人，以至于我在思考被质疑的行为或不作为时，我应该合理地考虑到他们会受到的影响。

在此，我们可以看到以下几点。

Atkin 勋爵首先指出该案背景——涉及公共健康问题的纠纷——是非常重要的。

然后，他说“必须而且确实”存在一个引起注意义务的关系的一般概念。Donoghue 案判决的效果是创造和确立了过失

Several observations may be made.

Lord Atkin began by observing that the context — a dispute over a matter which concerned public health — was of great importance.

He then said that there "must be and is" a general conception of relations giving rise to a duty of care. The effect of the *Donoghue* decision is to create and establish the tort of negligence.

Next, Lord Atkin alluded to the relationship between law and morality and the need to limit the extent to which moral values are imposed by the law. He referred to the Biblical commandment "love your neighbour" and explained that the principle then had to be modified for the purposes of framing a legal principle.

The question "Who is my neighbour?", the honourable judge remarked, receives a "restricted reply" . In the Biblical passage, the question led to Jesus telling the story of the good Samaritan. Essentially, the answer is that to love your neighbour is to help anyone, including a stranger who is in dire need. Loving your neighbour requires you to do good.

In contrast, the legal requirement is set at a much lower level. In Lord Atkin's reformulation, to love your neighbour means not to injure your neighbour. The legal principle put forward by the honourable judge is: You must take care not to injure your neighbour, and your neighbour is anyone who is so closely affected by your act.

As we look more closely at this "neighbour principle", we find it employs several concepts, the foremost of which are "care", "reasonableness" and "foreseeability" . Care, or taking care, is the idea of taking precautionary measures or doing due diligence to avoid causing harm.

As for the measure of care required, the concept of reasonableness is

侵权行为。

接下来，Atkin 勋爵提到了法律和道德之间的关系，以及需要限制法律强加的道德价值观的程度。他提到了《圣经》中“爱你的邻居”的诫命，并解释说，为了制定法律原则，必须对该原则进行修改。

尊敬的法官说道：“谁是我的邻居？”——对这个问题的回答“应有所限制”。在《圣经》中，这个问题引来了耶稣讲述的“好撒玛利亚人”的故事——从本质上讲，“爱你的邻居”就是帮助任何人，包括一个有迫切需要的陌生人，“爱你的邻居”需要你去行善。

相比之下，法律要求被设定在一个更低的水平。在 Atkin 勋爵的重新表述中，“爱你的邻居”意味着不伤害你的邻居。尊敬的法官所提出的法律原则是：“你必须注意不伤害你的邻居，而你的邻居是被你的任何行为所密切影响的人。”

当我们更仔细地研究这个“邻居原则”时，我们发现它采用了几个概念，其中最重要的是“注意”“合理性”“可预见性”。注意，或称小心，是指采取预防措施或尽职尽责以避免造成伤害的方式。

至于判断所需的注意程度，采用的是“合理”的概念。每个人都被期望以合理之人的行为方式行事。这个标准，或者说临界点，是一个客观标准。

至于对可能的伤害的了解，采用的是可预见性的概念。一个人承担责任不一定是因为他知道或预见到了危险，而是因为一个有理智的人在他的位置上会预见到它。请注意，在此，合理性再次被援用。

used. Each person is expected to behave in the way reasonable people conduct themselves. The standard, or threshold, is an objective one.

As for knowledge of possible harm, the idea of foreseeability is adopted. A person is liable not necessarily because he knew of or foresaw the danger but because a reasonable person in his position would have foreseen it. Observe that reasonableness is resorted to once again.

Essentially, the *Donoghue* principle requires one to take reasonable care to avoid causing harm to persons whom one can reasonably foresee would be affected by one's actions. The three essential elements of this principle are: taking care, reasonableness and foreseeability.

We observe that Lord Atkin's crafting of the law involved:

- a consideration of the context;
- an examination of policy, in particular moral policy;
- the application of a basic notion of justice — namely, reasonableness; and
- the application of legal concepts such as foreseeability and objectivity.

The duty of care also provides an excellent illustration of how novel legal principles evolve into frameworks. Essentially, the test for deciding the existence of a duty of care moved from a one-stage test to a two-stage test and finally to a three-stage test.

In *Donoghue*, the court laid down a single composite test of foreseeability — each person should take reasonable care to avoid foreseeable harm to others.

Over time, judges realised that it was necessary to have more control and added policy to the test. Basically, even if the foreseeability test was satisfied, the

从本质上讲，Donoghue 原则要求一个人采取合理的谨慎措施，以避免对他可以合理地预见会受到他的行为影响的人造成伤害。这一原则的三个基本要素是：注意、合理性和可预见性。

我们注意到，Atkin 勋爵对法律的精心设计涉及以下几点：

- 对背景的考虑；
- 对政策的审查，特别是道德政策；
- 应用一个基本的正义概念——合理性；以及
- 法律概念的应用，如可预见性和客观性。

注意义务也为说明新的法律原理是如何演变成法律规则提供了一个很好的例子。本质上，判断是否存在注意义务的测试从“一阶段标准”转向“两阶段标准”，最后转向“三阶段标准”。

在 Donoghue 案中，法院规定了一个单一的可预见性标准——每个人都应该采取合理的注意来避免对他人的可预见的伤害。

随着时间的推移，法官意识到有必要进行更多的控制，并在标准中加入了政策因素。于是，即使可预见性测试得到了满足，法院也会提出另一个问题：是否可以基于任何政策上的理由不施加注意义务？例如，虽然公园当局可以预见，在雨天树木或其树枝可能会掉落并伤害游客，但因此对他们施加沉重的负担可能是不可取的。人们可能会担心打开诉讼的闸门，或者担心公园当局会采取过度的防御行动（如在雨季关闭公园），

court asked another question: Is there any policy reason not to impose a duty of care? For example, whilst it may be foreseeable on the part of park authorities that on rainy days, trees or their branches may fall and injure visitors, it may not be desirable to impose a heavy burden on them. There may be the fear of opening the floodgates of litigation or that the park authorities may take excessively defensive action (such as closing the parks during the rainy seasons) to the detriment of park visitors.

The evolution of the law took a further step, prompted by the need to further limit the imposition of a duty of care. A good example is the area of psychiatric harm. In the case of a disastrous accident, there may be many persons who suffer psychiatric harm as a result — from the accident victim to his family members to passers-by and those who watched on the media. The courts decided to restrict the claimants by requiring proximity (or closeness) of relationship, physicality and manner of witnessing. Based on these factors, the court decides which claimants are sufficiently proximate and which are not. A duty is owed only to proximate claimants.

In the fullness of time (or rather the development of the law), a robust three-stage framework of foreseeability, proximity and policy was established to decide if there exists a duty of care.

As may be realised, the crafting of case law is a somewhat experimental exercise. A new or novel principle is a work in progress which needs time for refinement and recalibration. Only after a significant amount of revisitation and adjustment does a robust framework emerge.

从而损害公园游客的利益。

此后，法律的演变又向前迈进了一步，这是由进一步限制施加注意义务的需要所引发的，精神伤害是这方面很好的例子。在发生灾难性事故的情况下，可能会有很多人因此而受到精神伤害——从事故受害者到他的家人，再到路人和那些在媒体上观看的人。法院决定通过要求关系的接近程度（或亲密程度）、物理性距离和见证方式来限制索赔者。根据这些因素，法院决定哪些原告足够接近，哪些没有。被告只对足够接近的原告承担责任。

随着时间的推移（或者说法律的发展），法官们建立了一个强大的“三阶段”规则体系，即可预见性、接近性和政策，以决定是否存在注意义务。

正如我们可能会意识到的那样，制定判例法是一项具有一定程度的试验性质的工作。构建一项新的法律原则是一项持续进行的工作，需要时间来完善和重新调整。只有经过大量的重新审视和调整，才会形成一个强力稳定的法律框架。

Chapter 20
Understanding Legislation

> There are things known and ... things unknown, and in between are the doors of perception.
>
> ——Aldous Huxley

As compared with case law, law found in legislation is much easier to locate. There is no need to plough through a judgment to identify the relevant principle or principles of law, a task made more difficult where there are multiple judgments and each judge says something slightly or, sometimes radically, different.

Nonetheless, a statutory provision still needs to be understood and analysed. In particular, there is a need to ascertain the requisite elements of a legal principle contained in a statute.

We will consider the offence of bribery as we look at the following statutory provision:

第 20 章
了解立法

在已知的事物和……未知的事物两者之间是感知的大门。

——奥尔德斯·赫胥黎

与案例法相比，我们更容易分辨成文法中的法律规则，也不需要查阅判决来确定相关的法律原则——当出现多个判决，而每个法官的说法又略有不同，有时甚至完全不同时，查阅判决的就会更加困难。

尽管如此，成文法条款仍然需要理解和分析。特别是有必要确定成文法规中包含的法律原则的必要因素。

我们在此将论述贿赂罪，其法条如下：

任何人如果自己或与任何其他人一起——

（a）腐败地为自己或为任何其他人索取或接受，或同意接受；或

Any person who shall by himself or in conjunction with any other person —

(a) corruptly solicit or receive, or agree to receive for himself, or for any other person; or

(b) corruptly give, promise or offer to any person whether for the benefit of that person or of another person,

any gratification as an inducement to or reward for … any person doing or forbearing to do anything in respect of any matter or transaction … shall be guilty of an offence.

(Section 5, Prevention of Corruption Act, Singapore)

(You may wish to attempt to identify the elements in this provision on your own before reading what follows.)

Looking at the provision, we realise first that the offence can be committed with the aid of another person. For example, A may ask B to bribe C. A is also guilty of the offence of bribery. So, the hiring of a "consultant" to arrange for facilitation may not insulate the hirer from the law.

Next, the section uses the word "corruptly" to describe the fault or mental element. "Corruptly" is one of those words we understand intuitively but have difficulty defining. The closest synonym is "dishonestly" but that word does not capture the full meaning. To corrupt a person is to break, pervert or adulterate his purity or uprightness. It is to bend his will and make him do what he knows he should not do. A bribe perverts the purity of the giver or the recipient or both.

Thirdly, we come to the act or *actus reus*. Bribery has two facets — giving and receiving. Each of the facets can be an offence. The giver may commit an offence, and so may the receiver.

（b）腐败地向任何人提供、承诺或提议，不论是为了该人还是其他人的利益，

作为对……任何人就任何事项或交易做出或不做出任何事情的诱因或回报的满足……即为犯罪。

（新加坡《预防腐败法》第5条）

（在阅读下面的内容之前，你可能希望尝试自己识别这一条款中的要素。）

从条文来看，第一，我们意识到，该罪行可以在另一个人的帮助下实施。例如，A可以要求B贿赂C，A也犯有贿赂罪。因此，雇用“顾问”来安排提供便利并不会使雇人者免受法律制裁。

第二，该条使用“腐败地”一词来描述过错或心理因素。“腐败地”是我们可以凭直觉理解，却很难定义的一个词。最接近的同义词是“不诚实”，但这个词并没有抓住“腐败”的全部含义。让一个人腐败就是破坏、颠倒或干扰他的纯洁或正直，是扭曲他的意志，使他做他知道自己不应该做的事。贿赂扭曲了送礼者、受礼者或双方的纯洁。

第三，我们来看看犯罪行为。贿赂有两个方面——给予和接受。每个方面都可以是一种犯罪。给予者可以犯罪，接受者也可以犯罪。

在接受方面，该条明确规定，索取（要求）和同意接受均被禁止。在给予方面，犯罪的形式也可以是承诺给予，甚至是提议给予。

第四，我们看一下礼物。有趣的是，该条使用了“满足”

On the aspect of receiving, the provision makes it clear that soliciting (asking) and agreeing to receive are both prohibited as well. On the giving side, the offence can also take the form of promising to give and even offering to give.

Fourthly, we look at the gift. Interestingly, the section uses the term "gratification", not money or property, which we might have expected. Instead a broader term — gratification — is used. It includes money and property but goes further. Essentially, gratification is whatever makes the receiver happy, such as the conferment of a title or sexual satisfaction.

Fifthly, bribery has another element — the purpose of the gift. The section says that the gratification is given either as an inducement or a reward. Two scenarios are envisaged here. The first is where the bribe is given before the favour was done whilst the second is where bribing occurred after the favour was done. Both situations are reprehensible.

Finally, the section elaborates on the favour, which can take the form of an act, such as awarding a contract, or a forbearance. To forbear is to refrain from doing something that one should do, such as report an offender.

So, if we analyse this provision on bribery, there are basically six elements, namely:

- the defendant, by himself or together with another;
- corruptly;
- solicits, receives or agrees to receive, or gives, promises or offers to give;
- gratification for himself or another;
- as inducement or reward; and

一词，不是我们可能预期的金钱或财产。而是使用了一个更广泛的术语“满足”。它包括金钱和财产，但更进一步。从本质上讲，满足是指使接受者感到高兴的任何事情，如授予头衔或性满足。

第五，贿赂有另一个要素——礼物的目的。该条说，馈赠是作为一种诱因或奖励而给予的。这里设想了两种情况：第一种情况是，贿赂是在提供好处之前进行的；第二种情况是，贿赂发生在提供好处之后。这两种情况都应受到谴责。

最后，本条阐述了好处的形式，它可以是一种行为，如授予合同，也可以是一种忍让。忍让是指不做应该做的事情，比如举报罪犯。

因此，如果我们分析这个关于贿赂的条款，基本上有六个要素，即：

- 被告人本人或与他人一起；
- 腐败地；
- 索取、接受或同意接受，或给予、承诺或提议给予；
- 为自己或他人提供满足；
- 作为诱因或报酬；以及
- 实施某一行为或忍耐不做某一行为。

应该注意的是，如果任何术语，如“腐败”或“酬金”，在法规中被定义，在确定其确切含义时应参考该定义。

在阅读法律规定时，有一些解释规则，传统上，其中三个主要规则是字面规则（词语的普通含义）、黄金规则（如果导

- for an act or a forbearance.

It should be noted that if any term, such as “corruptly” or “gratification”, is defined in the statute, the definition should be referred to in ascertaining the precise meaning.

In reading a statutory provision, there are rules of interpretation of which, traditionally, the three main ones are the literal rule (the plain ordinary meaning of words), the golden rule (to avoid the literal meaning if this leads to absurdity) and the mischief rule (to find out the mischief which the statute aims to address and to advance the remedy).

The modern approach is to adopt a purposive interpretation, i.e. to construe a statutory provision within the purpose of that provision or, put another way, according to the intention of parliament. Purposive interpretation is derived from the mischief rule and is said to be an integrated approach which replaces the three rules mentioned above. An important aspect of purposive interpretation is the permissibility of referring to extrinsic material (meaning outside of the statutory provisions) such as parliamentary debates. Previously, this was not allowed. Whilst reference to extrinsic material can assist in discovering parliamentary intention, it also makes the exercise of interpretation a lengthier and more complicated one.

致荒谬，则避免字面含义）和弊端规则（找出法规旨在解决的弊端并推进补救措施）。

现代的做法则是采用目的性解释，即在该条的目的范围内解释法定条款，换句话说，根据议会的意图来解释。目的性解释源自弊端规则，据说是一种综合的方法，取代了上述三种规则。目的性解释的一个重要方面是允许参考外部材料（从法条之外找含义），如议会辩论。以前这是不允许的。虽然，参考外部材料可以帮助发现议会的意图，但它也使解释工作变得更加漫长和复杂。

Chapter 21
Regulatory Law

Rules help us live our lives when we lose the will to do it on our own.

——Yvonne Woon

We move now to law that is found, not in the cases or in the statutes, but in regulations. A preliminary point may usefully be made here. For countries adopting the Westminster model of government, there is a separation of powers in the three branches of the legislative, the executive and the judiciary. Laws are made by all the three branches and, broadly speaking, we have statutes from the legislative, case law from the judiciary and regulations from the executive.

It should be noted that the term "regulations" is confusing; for indeed, it is sometimes the label used for subsidiary legislation. In this chapter, we look at the financial advisers law for illustration.

As an example, in Singapore, the relevant legislation comprises, mainly, the Financial Advisers Act or FAA (primary legislation) and the Financial

第 21 章 监管规则与法律

当我们失去意志力的时候，规则引领我们过好生活。

——伊冯娜·沃恩

我们接下来要讨论的，不是案例或成文法，而是藏在监管规则里的法律。在此，先明确这样一个基本观念是有用的：对于采用西敏制政府模式的国家来说，政府被分为立法、行政和司法三个机关。法律由这三个机关共同制定，广义上讲，立法机关制定法案、司法机关产生判例法、行政机关制定监管规则。

需要注意的是，“监管规则”一词概念模糊容易混淆。原因是在实际运用中，“监管规则”有时也被用作附属法例的标签。在本章中，我们以金融顾问法为例来说明。

在新加坡，金融顾问法的相关立法主要包括作为基础性立法的《金融顾问法》（FAA）和作为辅助性立法的《金融顾

Advisers Regulations or FAR (subsidiary legislation) . In financial advisers law, product suitability is a key concern. Section 27 of the FAA says that a financial adviser should not make a recommendation on a financial product unless he has a reasonable basis for his recommendation. Regulation 18B of the FAR follows up by requiring a financial adviser to do a due diligence exercise to ascertain the suitability of a new product for its target segment. The FAA and the FAR are the normal or conventional law.

The law on product suitability is not confined to the normal or conventional law. In addition, the financial adviser has to be aware of and comply with regulatory law — the regulations put in place by the authority which oversees the type of business in question. In Singapore, the Monetary Authority of Singapore (MAS) sets out and frequently updates a raft of regulations in the form of Guidelines, Notices and other instruments.

The usual approach to regulating a business activity is first to "proscribe" (disallow) a business activity unless one is licensed. Next, provision is made for one to apply for a licence and the criteria are set out. If and when approval is given, the authority sets out conditions of the licence. The licensee will also be subject to the whole regulatory framework that is put in place.

Whilst the framework may be detailed and complicated, it is useful to know that regulation generally involves two aspects: prudential regulation and conduct of business (COB) regulation. Prudential regulation deals with the financial soundness and proper governance of the business organisation. COB regulation is concerned with the manner the organisation goes about trying to sell its products and services.

It should be noted that while breach of normal laws attracts legal sanctions,

问条例》(FAR)。金融顾问法非常重视产品的适当性。FAA第27条规定，金融顾问不应就某一金融产品向客户提供建议，除非有合理的建议依据。FAR的第18B条补充要求金融顾问做尽职调查以确定新产品对目标群体的适当性。FAA和FAR属于法律与行政法规。

产品适当性这方面的法律不局限于法律与行政法规。除上述法条外，金融顾问还必须了解并遵守监管规则，即由监督相关业务类型的机构制定的规范。在新加坡，新加坡金融管理局(MAS)以指南、通知和其他文书的形式制定并实时更新一系列法规。

监管商业活动的惯用做法，首先是“禁止”(即不允许)一项商业活动。除非持有许可证，否则不得进行。然后允许申请许可证，有关部门会阐明申请的要求，有时还会规定持证条件。持证经营者，还将受到一个完善的监管框架的约束。

具体监管框架可能是具体而复杂的。我们需要了解的监管规则通常涉及两个方面：审慎监管和商业行为监管。审慎监管涉及商业机构的财务稳健性和管理是否恰当。商业行为监管涉及产品和服务的销售方式。

应当注意，违反法律与行政法规会受到法律制裁，如刑法上的罚款或监禁，以及侵权和合同法上的赔偿责任；而违反监管规则会受到监管制裁。制裁方式包括谴责、产品禁令(禁止该金融顾问销售某些产品)，在极端情况下，还会吊销执照。

回过头来说产品适当性，《新加坡金管局公平交易指南》列举了公平交易的几项预期目标，其中，第2项为“金融机构提供适合目标客户群的产品和服务”。具体而言，该指南的第

such as a fine or imprisonment for criminal law, and liability for compensation for tort and contract, the contravention of regulatory law attracts regulatory sanctions. They include reprimand, product ban (prohibiting a financial adviser from selling certain products) and, in the extreme of cases, revocation of the licence.

Coming back to product suitability, the MAS Guideline on Fair Dealing sets out several outcomes of fair dealing, one of which is Outcome 2: "Financial institutions offer products and services that are suitable for their target customer segments". More specifically, paragraph 2.2.1 of the Guideline requires the financial adviser to conduct due diligence for every product it intends to market, and to identify segments for which it is suitable, and segments for which it is not suitable. (It will be observed that this overlaps substantially with Regulation 18B of FAR.)

As for Notices, MAS Notice FAA-N16 requires financial advisers to conduct a "know your client" (KYC) exercise to understand the client's needs in order to recommend a suitable product. For complex products, the Notice requires enhanced due diligence, including assessing the client's financial knowledge.

And there are yet other MAS regulations which directly or indirectly relate to the subject of product suitability.

Clearly, where a business activity is subject to regulatory constraints, the composite legal and regulatory framework can be a labyrinth of principles and conditions where objectives and concepts are woven into different pieces of law and regulation. The picture can be very complex and expert advice may be indispensable. The challenge is for that advice to be comprehensive and yet easy to understand.

2.2.1 节要求金融顾问围绕每一种打算推广的产品做尽职调查，并细分适合该产品的客户群以及不适合该产品的客户群。（我们可以观察到这部分指南与 FAR 第 18B 条法规大致吻合。）

至于通知，新加坡金管局 FAA–N16 通知要求金融顾问通过进行客户身份审查（KYC）来了解客户的需求，以推荐适合的产品。如果想要推荐复杂金融产品，就要进行更严格的尽职调查，包括评估客户在投资理财方面的知识。

金管局还颁布了其他一系列直接或间接与产品适当性有关的监管规则，这里不再一一赘述。

我们已经能感受到，当一项商业活动受到监管限制的时候，其中的法律法规的框架可能是一座由原则和条件构成的迷宫，不同的监管目的和概念被编织在各条法律和监管规则里。全局可能非常复杂，要准确解读很可能需要专家意见。而对专家来说，提供周详又易懂的意见则是一大挑战。

PART IV

Complexity in the Law

The complexity of things — the things within things — just seems to be endless. I mean nothing is easy，nothing is simple

——Alice Munro

第四部分

法律中的复杂性

事物的复杂性——一环套一环——似乎是无止境的。我的意思是没有什么是容易的，没有什么是简单的。

——爱丽丝·门罗

The world is a very complicated place. The continuing evolution of civilisation adds to the breadth and depth of the diversity and the tensions. The challenge is for the law to comprehend and accommodate change as the intricate landscape gets ever more difficult. It should not surprise that there is much complexity and controversy in the whole body of law and in many of its constituent parts (see Fig. 3) . In this part of the book, we seek to understand these myriad difficulties.

As regards case law, the task of ascertaining what the law is on a particular point or issue can, for a variety of reasons, be challenging, even exasperating (Chapter 22) . We have seen earlier that law is made by parliament and also made by judges. The difficulty is in discerning which issues or topics fall within the province of parliament and which are left to the courts (Chapter 23) .

The law seeks to be fair to the parties in a particular scenario or dispute, but the interests and perspectives of the different parties are often competing and conflicting; as the number of parties increase, the pressure mounts (Chapter 24) . A particular instance of this is the three-party situation where A gets B to perform a task for him and B, in the process, injures C. That B should be liable to C is obvious enough, but whether A should be liable to C, in the event that B is unable to pay, is a matter of great controversy (Chapter 25) .

Law caters to the environment and is sensitive to it. So, when the environment changes, law has to as well. But change does not often take place

世界非常复杂。文明的持续演变增加了多样性和紧张局势的广度和深度。法律所面临的挑战是如何理解和适应变化，因为错综复杂的局面会变得更加困难。在整个法律体系及其许多构成部分中存在着许多复杂性和争议，这并不奇怪（见图 3）。在本书的这一部分，我们将试图理解这些数不胜数的困难。

关于判例法，出于各种原因，确定某一点或某一议题的法律属性可能具有挑战性，甚至到了令人恼火的程度（第 22 章）。我们前面已经看到，法律可以由议会制定，也可由法官制定。困难在于如何辨别哪些问题属于议会的管辖范围，哪些问题是留给法院的（第 23 章）。

法律力求对特定情况下或特定争端中的各方公平，但各方的利益和观点往往相互竞争和冲突；随着当事人数量的增加，压力也在增加（第 24 章）。这方面有一个特殊的例子：A 让 B 为他完成一项任务，而 B 在此过程中伤害了 C。B 很明显应该对 C 负责，但在 B 无力支付的情况下，A 是否应该对 C 负责，这是一个极具争议的问题（第 25 章）。

法律迎合了环境，并且对环境很敏感。因此，当环境发生变化时，法律也必须随之变化。但变化往往并不及时也不够有序。每当法律发生变化时，受影响的各方和观察者都会努力去理解这种变化及其影响（第 26 章）。

第 3 章中提到，法律有几十个领域。一个事实场景可能会

in a timely or orderly fashion. Each time the law changes, the affected parties and the observer alike may struggle to understand the change and its implications (Chapter 26) .

It was mentioned in Chapter 3 that there are dozens of areas of law. A factual scenario may trigger legal principles from multiple areas of law, sometimes as many as four or five areas. Where there are multiple or overlapping areas of law, there is the question of whether the application of different principles and concepts to the situation should lead to the same outcome or to different outcomes, and this is an exceedingly difficult question (Chapter 27) .

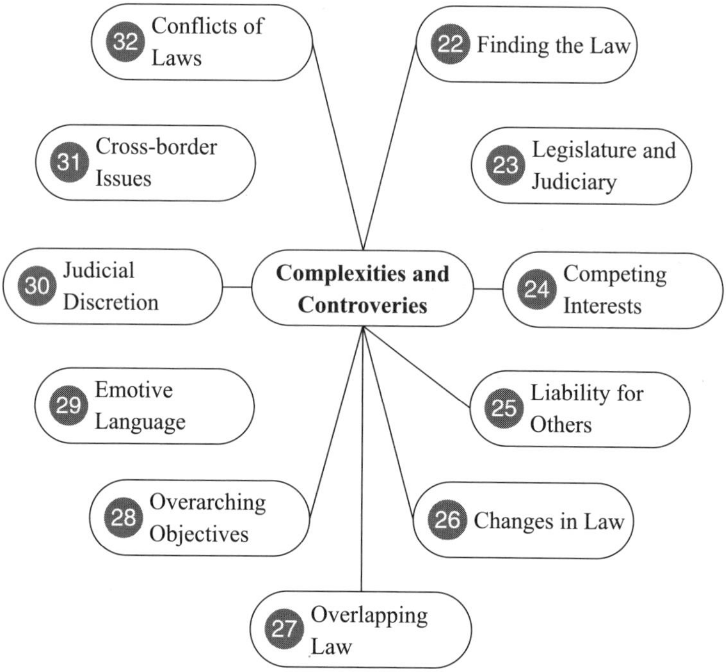

Fig. 3: Complexities and Controversies
(numbers indicate the chapters in which the topic is covered)

触及多个领域的法律原则，有时甚至多达四五个领域。如果出现多个或重叠的法律领域，就会出现对同一情况适用不同的原则和概念是否应导致相同的结果或不同的结果的问题，而这个问题极难解决（第 27 章）。

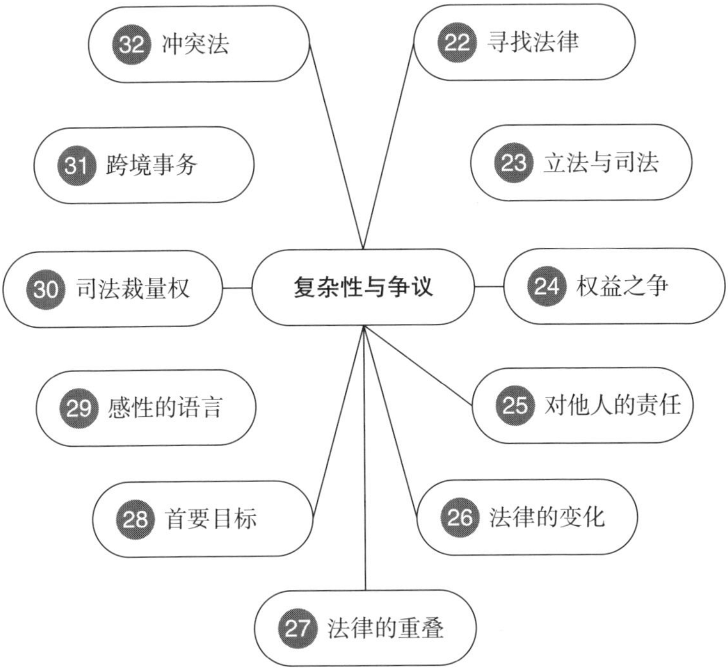

图 3：复杂性与争议
（数字代表讨论相关课题的章节号）

虽然在每个法律领域都可能有一个主要的目标或目的，但有时也会有额外的或非核心的目标。这里的困难在于能否预测何时会对这些非核心目标产生诉求，从而导致不同的法律结果（第 28 章）。理解某一特定法律观点或领域的另一个障碍是法官采用感性的语言，或者逻辑学家所说的“说服者的话”，这

While there may be, in each area of law, a primary goal or aim, sometimes there are additional or peripheral objectives as well. The difficulty here is the ability to predict when these peripheral objectives may be resorted to and thus lead to a different legal outcome (Chapter 28). Another obstacle to understanding a particular point or area of law is where the judge adopts emotive language, or what logicians call "persuader words", which may lead the observer to accept a legal proposition without really understanding it (Chapter 29).

Further, in the judge's toolbox, there is often this tool called "discretion". Where the legal framework in a particular area or issue of law includes judicial discretion, the legal position may become quite unpredictable (Chapter 30).

In this increasingly globalised and IT-enabled world, interactions across borders, whether on a governmental, business or personal level, is commonplace. This leads to cross-border legal implications, including the need to have some knowledge of the laws and legal systems of other countries (Chapter 31). It is also important for the global citizen to have some understanding of what is known as a conflict of laws (Chapter 32).

可能导致观察者在没有真正理解的情况下接受一个法律主张（第 29 章）。

此外，在法官的工具箱中，经常提到一种叫作“自由裁量权”的工具。当某一特定领域的法律框架包括司法自由裁量权时，法律的立场可能会变得相当难以预测（第 30 章）。

在这个日益全球化和信息技术化的世界中，无论是政府、企业还是个人层面的跨境互动都很常见。这产生了跨境法律问题，包括需要对其他国家的法律和法律体系有一定的了解（第 31 章）。对于全球化的公民来说，对所谓的冲突法有一定的了解也很重要（第 32 章）。

Chapter 22
Finding the Law From Cases

Finding is reserved for those that search.

——Jim Rohn

In the common law world, much of the law is to be found in the cases — the reported judgments of the courts. In Chapter 19, we looked at a passage from the case of *Donoghue v. Stevenson* and saw how the judge articulated and crafted a principle of law. The challenge of discerning or discovering the law from cases can be a difficult thing, and this is so for a variety of reasons, including lengthy judgments, obscure language and those discussed below.

The common law world subscribes to the doctrine of precedent (or *stare decisis*) — that when deciding on a particular issue, a judge should follow preceding decisions; like cases should be decided in a like manner. But which parts of a judgment are binding? It is the *ratio decidendi* — the reason for the decision — that is binding. In contrast to *ratio decidendi*, there are statements of law made by a judge but which may not be necessary for his decision. Such statements are

第 22 章 案例中寻法

只有寻找才会有发现。

——吉姆·罗恩

在普通法的世界里，许多法律原则都在案例中，被记载在法院的判决记录里。在第 19 章，我们以 *Donoghue v. Stevenson* 案的一段引文为例，探讨了法官是如何阐述和制定法律原则的。冗长的判决书、晦涩的语言，还有下面即将讨论的其他因素，使从案例中找出并辨别法律原则变成一项艰巨的任务。

普通法世界"遵循先例原则"（又被称为"因循先例原则"），它要求法官在作出裁决时遵循先前对该争议点已有的裁决，让相似的案件得以用类似的方式裁决。你也许会问，一份判决中的哪些部分有约束力呢？答案是"判决依据"——也就是一项判决的理由。与之相对的是法官在判决中提到的，但并非得出判决结论所必需的观点，被称为"附带意见"。举一个欺诈案的例子，法官在认定被告有欺诈行为后，可能还会探讨假如被

known as *obiter* dicta (or *dictum*, if singular) . For example, in a fraud case, the judge may, after finding the defendant guilty of fraud, venture to explore the legal position if the defendant had been negligent instead. The judge's statement of law on this latter aspect would be *obiter*. *Ratios* are binding whereas *dicta* are only persuasive.

The ascertainment of the *ratio* or *ratios* of a case may not be straightforward. For one thing, there are different levels of generality. For example, is the *Donoghue* principle confined to a manufacturer's liability to the ultimate consumer, or can it be applied more generally to a citizen's duty to his fellow man?

Another difficulty is where several judges in a panel agree to the outcome but each gives a different reason for the agreed outcome. In such a situation, what principle or principles may be deduced from the case? This uncertainty continues until clarified by later decisions.

A further difficulty is where the decision is a majority decision, such as where two out of the panel of three judges decide in favour of the plaintiff. Whilst the majority view determines the outcome, the persuasiveness of the case may be weakened. This is especially so if the dissenting judge is a well-respected one, sparking the possibility of the law being changed in the future. Also, a slim majority, such as a 3–2 decision (incidentally, *Donoghue* was a 3–2 decision) suggests that the matter is highly controversial. This is even more so if, on appeal, the decision goes the other way, and again on a slim majority.

Some of the difficulties mentioned in the paragraphs before may be ameliorated if the case report contains good "headnotes" (a headnote is a short summary appearing at the front of the report), which are now a feature in modern

告的行为是出于过失，法律后果又会怎样。法官后面的这些议论就是“附带意见”。判决依据具有法律约束力，而附带意见只具有说服性意义。

确定一个案件的判决依据和附带意见有时并非直截了当。首先，判例的普遍适用性程度不同。例如，Donoghue 原则是仅限于制造厂商对最终消费者的责任，还是可以更普遍地适用于公民对其同伴的责任？

其次，当合议庭的几位法官同意判决结果，但各持不同理论时，另一个问题就出现了。在这种情况下，我们该从此案中推导出什么样的原则？是不是可以得出多条原则呢？这种不确定性将一直持续到被后来的判决澄清为止。

最后，当判决并非合议庭的一致意见而只是多数意见时，解读会异常艰难。例如，由三个法官组成的合议庭，两位的判决有利于原告，剩下的一位的判决不利于原告。虽然多数人的意见决定了最终结果，但作为判例，对之后类似案件判定的说服力会被削弱。如果持反对意见的法官恰好德高望重，那就更是如此，这份反对意见很可能预示着法律的未来走向。在此之外，一份仅有微弱优势的多数判决——比如 3 比 2 的决定（顺便一提，*Donoghue v. Stevenson* 案就是一个 3 比 2 判决的案例），可能表明对这个问题还有很大争议和辩证空间。假如上诉时判决又是另外的走向，而且又是以微弱优势险胜决出，情况就更不明了了。

不过，案例报告开头有归纳准确的判例摘要的话，以上提到的问题可以得到缓解。判例摘要是现代案例报告的一大特色。优秀的案例报告会总结甚至解读案件的判决依据和附带意

case reports. A good case report assembles and even crafts the *ratios* of the case, identifies the *dicta* and points to the relevant paragraphs of the judgment, substantially aiding the reader in searching for the law.

Another challenge in ascertaining the legal position is where the authorities (precedent cases) are in conflict, with authorities to support alternative opposing positions. Where there are conflicting authorities, one would need to scrutinise the decisions and discern what is likely to be the correct legal position.

It should be noted, further, that there is a hierarchy of courts, and that there is vertical *stare decisis* but not horizontal *stare decisis*. In other words, courts of a certain level are bound by decisions of courts of higher levels but are not bound by courts of the same level. For example, in the UK, where the Supreme Court sits at the apex and just below it is the Court of Appeal, the Court of Appeal is bound by previous Supreme Court decisions but not by previous Court of Appeal decisions.

So, for the reasons stated in this chapter (and others), the search for the precise legal principle or position on a particular issue may not be an easy one.

见，还会标出判决书的相关段落，对我们的法律检索有极大的帮助。

当判决与先例相矛盾，即有支持其他观点甚至相反观点的先例时，确定法律观点就难上加难了。如果有相互冲突的法律依据，我们就需要仔细审视这些判决，自行分辨可能的法律观点。

在这里还需要指出，法院是有等级之分的。只有纵向因循先例，没有横向因循先例。换句话说，法院只受更高一级法院的裁决的约束，不受同一级别法院的约束。例如，在英国，最高法院是最高等级的权威，下面一级是上诉法院，上诉法院受到最高法院的判决先例约束，而不受其自身的先例判决约束。

从本章所述的原因（以及其他还没来得及详述的原因）可以看出，要确定一个特定争议的法律原则或法律观点道路崎岖，需“上下”而求索。

Chapter 23
Legislature-Judiciary Interplay

Power must never be trusted without a check.

——John Adams

In common law countries, law is made by parliament, and law is also made by the judiciary (in civil law countries, judges, notionally at least, do not make law; they just interpret law) . Law is found in both legislation and the decisions of judges; statute and case law run alongside each other in providing the legal framework of rules and principles. Somewhat like the double helix in a DNA molecule.

The interplay between legislature and the judiciary is intricate and may puzzle the observer. What exactly is the relationship between the two institutions of lawmakers? The questions would include the following:

- Who is supreme — parliament or the judiciary?
- Are there matters which are within the exclusive domain of each

第 23 章
立法与司法的相互作用

对权力的信任不可代替监督。

——约翰·亚当斯

在普通法国家，法律不仅由议会制定，还由司法部门裁定（而在大陆法国家，法官只能解读而不能制定法律，至少理论上是这样）。在普通法系里，成文法和判例法都写着法律，成文法和判例法双管齐下编织成了有条理有原则的法律框架。有点像 DNA 分子里的双螺旋。

立法和司法的互动很微妙，让人难以捉摸。这两个机构之间到底是怎样的一种关系呢？具体的疑问有以下几个：

- 议会和法院哪一个权力至高无上？
- 哪些议题分别属于其中一个的专属管辖范围？
- 这两个机构在履行制定法律的职能时，会有合作或竞争关系吗？

institution? And

- Do the two compete or collaborate in making law?

As a preliminary point, it should be mentioned that common law countries typically subscribe to the Westminster model of governance where there is a separation of powers amongst the three branches of the legislature, the executive and the judiciary. Our focus, in this chapter, is on the legislature and the judiciary.

The responsibility of parliament is to pass legislation. Likewise, it is the judiciary's responsibility to develop the common law through cases. However, each, in carrying out its role, may interact with and affect the other in the other's performance of its role. While parliament makes law in the form of legislation, the interpretation of that law is done by the judiciary. The duty of courts and judges is to ascertain the meaning of the statute and the intention of parliament. Where the relevant statutory provision is clear, there is no room for the judge to make law; he just applies it.

But, in situations of ambiguity or where there are gaps in the law, the judge can — through interpretation or gap-filling — in effect, make law. For example, does the statutory requirement that commercial premises should have fire extinguishers apply where an entrepreneur works from his home? A judge deciding such a case may use rules of interpretation to arrive at his conclusion that the entrepreneur needs to comply with the requirement.

Further, in some countries, such as the US, Canada, Australia and Singapore (surprisingly, the UK does not have a written constitution), the judiciary is explicitly or implicitly given the task of safeguarding the constitution.

前面我们已经提到过，普通法国家采用西敏制政府模式，包括立法、司法和行政三个机构。我们这一章的聚焦集中在立法和司法。

议会的主要责任是通过法案；法院则负责用判例来健全普通法。不过，各尽其责的时候，两个部门不免会接触和互相影响。议会颁布法案时，解读法案的责任在法院。法庭和法官的职责是确认法案条例的含义和议会的意图。在裁决一个案子的时候，如果相关成文法意思清楚不容歧义，法官就没有空间“创造”法律了，只能应用已有的成文法。

不过，在成文法意思模糊或在有法律空白的情况下，法官能够通过合理解读或填补空白的方式来“创造”法律。例如，成文法规定商业场所必须配置灭火器，这一法律对居家办公的创业者是否适用？裁定这样一宗案件的法官可以运用合适的解读规则来得出他认为公平公正的结论，比如创业者也需要遵守这一消防安全的规定。

再者，在一些普通法国家，如美国、加拿大、澳大利亚和新加坡（令人惊讶的是，英国没有成文宪法），司法机关被明确或隐含地赋予维护宪法的职能。在这些国家，如果议会通过的新法案与宪法相左，法院则有权力和义务宣告该法案无效。这个概念被称为宪法的至高无上性。

总之，法院可以告诉我们法案里的法律的含义，以及某一部法案是否违宪。

反过来，司法的权力也受议会的影响。

法院有权力通过裁决案件来健全法律，议会则有权力确认、更正，甚至废除具体的普通法。确认通常是以默许的方式，

In these countries, if parliament passes a piece of legislation that contravenes the constitution, the judiciary has the power and responsibility to declare that statute invalid. It is said that there is constitutional supremacy.

In short, the judiciary tells us what the statute means, and whether the statute is unconstitutional.

Conversely, the power of the judiciary is also affected by parliament.

While the judiciary has the power to develop the law through its decisions, parliament has the power to affirm it, vary it or even to abolish it. Affirmation usually takes the form of acquiescence, meaning parliament does nothing and simply lets the judicial development continue. Affirmation can also take the form of encapsulating it in a statute. The Unfair Contract Terms Act 1977 essentially endorsed the judicial position that an exclusion clause is valid only if it is fair and reasonable.

Alternatively, if parliament disagrees, wholly or partly, with the new development, it can pass legislation to set out the desired legal position. For example, the Frustrated Contracts Act departed from the common law position that the losses lie where they fall and instead set out a new legal position that all payment obligations are nullified and the court will decide what, in the circumstances, is fair allocation of loss.

From this perspective, it would appear that, generally, parliament has substantial supervisory power over the judiciary's law-making ability. It should be pointed out, however, that the legislation so passed is again subject to the court's interpretation. Perhaps, from this perspective, one could say that parliament has qualified supremacy.

A further question needs to be answered — are there scenarios where the courts would or should avoid making law, leaving the task to parliament? There are

也就是说，议会任由该法律发展而不采取任何行动。确认有时也以更明确的方式，将这部分的普通法包含在新法案里。《不公平合同条款法》（1997年颁布）就基本上认可了普通法里免责条款只有在公平和合理的情况下才有效的立场。

如果议会不同意司法部门建立起来的某个或某部分法律的发展方向，议会可以通过颁布法案来阐明更理想的法律观点。比如，《合同落空法案》就偏离了普通法里“损失落在谁家头上就算谁家”的立场，另行规定了一条新的原则，即所有的支付义务因无法预见事件而失效，再由法院决定具体案例中的损失分配。

从这一视角分析就能看出，总体来说，议会对法院制定法律的工作有实质性的监督权。然而这里需要指出，被议会通过的法案又由法院解读。或许换个角度，我们可以说议会享有有限的最高权力。

另一个需要被解答的问题是：在什么情况下法院会选择或者应该避免制定法律，把这项任务留给议会呢？有三个相关的答案。

首先，根据传统，法院立法带来的法律变化通常会循序渐进、由浅入深（其中主要的原因是法官倾向于聚焦在手头案件的具体事实所引起的法律问题上）。司法引起的法律变动通常不会激进或者毫无征兆。

其次，当法庭不能清晰、全面地制定法律解决某个问题时，这项任务最好留给议会。不过，议会是否一定比一个由学识渊博、经验丰富的法官组成的合议庭更具备制定法律的能力，这个问题值得探讨。毕竟判决书都是公开发表的，并且可以受到

three related answers.

First, conventionally, legal change through judicial lawmaking tends to be incremental and moderate (especially since judges tend to confine themselves to legal issues raised by the facts before them). Judicial legal change tends not to be abrupt or radical.

Secondly, it is said that where the law cannot be clearly and comprehensively made by the judiciary, the matter is best left to parliament. It is arguable whether parliament is necessarily more equipped than a panel of very experienced and distinguished judges. After all, judgments are published and are subject to appraisal and criticism by other judges, academics, lawyers and others in the marketplace of ideas.

Finally, and perhaps most importantly, where the change is heavily policy-laden, it is thought that parliament is the more appropriate lawmaker. Parliament, having been elected by the people, appears to have greater legitimacy to make important changes in law, such as tackling money laundering, dealing with illegal immigration, overhauling workplace safety and health, and the controlling of fake news.

Further, where policy is concerned, it would be preferable for the matter to be discussed and debated in the well of parliament. Letting judges decide policy matters runs the risk of the judiciary proceeding based on personal views and subscriptions rather than on widely-accepted public policy.

Parliament and the judiciary make law. The interaction is an interesting one as there is independence as well as interdependence. The intricate balance appears to provide an optimal way for developing the legal framework.

其他法官、法学学者、律师还有其他思想市场上的参与者的评核和批评。

最后一点或许是最重要的一点，如果变动涉及大量的政策，通常认为议会是更合适的制定人。由人民选举产生的议会被认为更有决定法律上的重大变化的正当性，这些议题包括打击洗钱、安置非法移民、全面改革工作场所的卫生安全以及控制虚假新闻等。

需要补充的是，涉及政策上的问题，通常经过议会讨论、辩论后再做决定更合适。让法官做政策方面的决定可能让司法程序的判定受个人观点和信仰左右，而非出于公众政策的考量。

总结来说，议会和法院都制定法律，且二者之间的相互作用很耐人寻味——各自独立，又互相依存、相互影响。这一错综的关系和微妙的平衡给法律建设提供了一条理想途径。

Chapter 24
Competing Interests

Justice cannot be for one side alone but must be for both.

——Eleanor Roosevelt

A boundary separates two adjoining landowners. If you shift the boundary towards one of them, he gains and his neighbour loses. So it is with the allocation of legal rights in general. The law is involved in the balancing of interests and deciding where the equilibrium should be.

This competition of interests is seen in many legal realms. The law of nuisance, for instance, decides what a landowner is entitled to as he enjoys his land; at the same time, it is also deciding what his neighbour has to put up with as the latter enjoys his land. One person's enjoyment of music, for example, may impinge on his neighbour's right to peace and quiet. A certain "give and take" is involved and both considerateness and tolerance are relevant here. An example of striking a compromise is that renovations within a residential estate are restricted, such as by confining pounding and grinding work to certain hours of the working

第24章 此消彼长的法律权益

正义不只为一方伸张，在另一方身上也不应该缺席。

——埃莉诺·罗斯福

想象一条边界将两家相邻的土地所有者分开。如果将这条边界为其中一家扩大一点，这家有得，那家就会有失。一般来说，法律权利的分配也是如此。法律参与了平衡多方权益的过程，并决定达到平衡的位置。

这种利益之争在许多法律领域都随处可见。例如，管治滋扰的法律决定了土地所有者在享受其土地时有什么权利，同时也决定了他的邻居必须遵守什么规矩，做出什么让步。举个例子，一个人在家大声外放音乐可能会影响到邻居享有安宁的权利。这涉及一定的“取舍”，与双方的体贴和宽容也密不可分。达成妥协的一个实例，是限制住宅区内装修的共识，例如，限制敲打和研磨工作，约定在工作日的特定时段

week.

This challenge of competing interests takes on an added dimension when one of the parties is a public authority. Take the problem of falling branches and trees and the harm thereby caused. In deciding the level of care and diligence the park authorities should take, it is important to remember that they serve the public interest and that resources may be limited. If an inordinately high standard is placed on them, it is conceivable that they may limit the facilities they provide, such as to have fewer trees or severely restrict opening hours in times of inclement weather. Thus, it seems reasonable to give some allowance to public bodies.

Take another area — defamation. The maker of a statement, which is critical of another person, asserts his freedom of expression. The person being criticised protests that his reputation is being attacked. So, a balance has to be struck between the maker's freedom to express and the subject's interest to preserve his reputation.

And the right of yet other parties may be relevant too. In the case of defamation, the hearer or reader of the statement may assert the right to know and to form his own opinion on the matter. Thus, in deciding whether a statement is defamatory, the interests of at least three parties have to be considered, which makes the matter even more challenging.

Taking an example from the commercial realm, where several persons come together for a business venture, there can be debates as to how decision-making should proceed. Naturally, the common basis is that majority prevails. So, if three venturers wish to make a business decision, apart from situations of unanimity, the decision usually proceeds based on the wishes of the majority.

However, in some situations, it may be unfair to disregard the interest

才能进行。

当争议一方是公共机构时，这种利益冲突带来的问题就增加了一个层面。以掉落的树枝和树木造成的人身伤害问题为例。在决定公园当局应采取哪种程度的谨慎态度和防护措施时，重要的是不能忘记公共机构是为公众利益服务的，且资源通常有限。如果对公园当局的职责标准定得过高，可以预见到他们能提供的设施就会减少，例如园内树植会减少，或恶劣天气时段里园区的开放时间会大幅度受限。这样看来，法律对公共机构给予一定的宽容合情合理。

再谈另一个领域——诽谤法。发言的人批判另一个人，算是主张他的言论自由。被抨击的人则以自己名誉受损为由抗议。也就是说，法律必须在发言人的表达自由和被提及者维护个人名誉的权益之间取得平衡。

非当事方的权利有时也会被牵扯进来。在诽谤的案件里，所谓诽谤言论的听众或读者可以主张知情权和对此事形成自己的看法的权利。也就是说，在决定某一言论是否具有诽谤性质时，至少要考虑三方的利益，这是一个极大的挑战。

以商业领域为例，几个人合作谋划商业投机，时常会在共同决策时产生争论。大部分时候共识是少数服从多数。也就是说，假如有三个创业者希望做一个商业决定，除了一致通过的情况外，通常会按照多数人的意愿进行决策。

然而，在某些情况下，无视少数人的利益可能是有失公平的。公司法承认这一法律观点，并确认了“压迫少数股东”的概念。如果少数股东认为多数股东对其压迫，可以提起法律诉讼来得到救济。不过，对少数股东的压迫作为一个概念听起来

of the minority. Company law acknowledges this and recognises a concept of oppression of the minority. Where a minority shareholder feels that the majority is oppressing him, he can bring legal action to remedy this. Suffice it to say that the oppression of the minority sounds good as a concept but is challenging in its application to practical dilemmas.

Another interesting illustration in company law is where, in the liquidation of a company, many creditors (and types of creditors) compete in claiming from the limited assets of the company. In the first place, a distinction is made between secured creditors (those who have taken security over the debtor's assets, such as a mortgage) and unsecured creditors. Secured creditors claim first, followed by unsecured creditors.

As amongst unsecured creditors, the general rule is that they rank equally and claim proportionately (the legal term is *pari passu*). However, there is usually a statutorily prescribed order of priority for unsecured claims, namely:

- the costs of winding-up (including the liquidator's fees);
- the claims of employees (for salaries, provident fund contributions and work injury compensation); and
- the claims of the tax authorities.

So, the costs of winding up get paid first, followed by the claims of employees and then the claims of the taxman. All other unsecured creditors, such as the suppliers or the customers, get paid after these claims have been met.

There are, of course, good reasons for the preference and priority accorded. Without the involvement of the liquidator and associated expenses, the

绝妙，但是在应用于实际困境时却极其不易。

公司法中另一个有意思的例子，是在公司清算时，许多不同类别的债权人竞相从公司有限的资产中索赔。首先，有担保的债权人，即那些有公司的资产等作担保的债权人和无担保的债权人之间的权益是有区别的。有担保的债权人首先索赔，之后才轮到无担保的债权人。

至于无担保债权人之间，一般的规则是地位平等，按债权比例从剩余资产中索赔（法律称“同等权益”）。然而，法定以下无担保债权优先：

- 清算费用（包括清算人的费用）；
- 雇员请求权（工资、公积金供款和工伤赔偿）；和
- 税务机关请求权。

也就是说，清算费用应首先得到支付，其次是雇员的债权，然后是税务人员的债权依次得到满足。所有其他无担保债权人（如供应商或客户等）在这些债权得到满足后才能得到赔偿。

当然，这些优先权背后是有充分缘由的。没有清算人的参与和相关开销，清算过程就无法顺利进行。至于员工，社会普遍认为公司的员工处于弱势地位，需要有一定限度的保护（比如，最多优先偿还六个月的工资）。税务机关的权利更值得商榷；普遍认为是因为未缴税款是对公众的债务，所以应给予一定的优先权。

根据以上的例子我们可以认识到，制定法律是为了划定边

liquidation process cannot proceed. As for employees, it is perceived that they are in a vulnerable position and need some limited protection (for example, up to six months' wages). The claim of the tax authority is more debatable; the justification appears to be that unpaid taxes is a debt to the public and hence, should be given some priority.

Making law is about drawing boundaries and balancing competing interests. And someone has to be an arbiter. The task of achieving equilibrium can be a difficult one.

界，以平衡各方相互竞争的不同权益。总有人要充当仲裁者。实现平衡的任务时常让人难以定夺，很容易此消彼长。

Chapter 25
Liability for Acts of Others

A man can't ride your back unless it is bent.

——Dr Martin Luther King, Jr

The law imposes obligations and liabilities on each of us. If our act breaches a legal duty, we face legal consequences. The question is: What if the act is not ours but that of someone else with whom we have some relationship? When does the law make a person liable for wrong or harm committed by another person?

This seemingly simple question actually raises difficult and complicated scenarios and issues of law. As for scenarios, there are many possible contexts, such as:

- the liability of a service provider for wrongdoing by his appointed agent, such as pocketing money belonging to the client;
- the liability of an employer for a careless act of his employee, such as a delivery driver who speeds and injures a passer-by in an accident; and

第 25 章
为他人的行为承担责任

卑躬屈膝的人才会被人骑在背上。

——小马丁·路德·金博士

法律规定了每个人的义务和责任。一旦一个人的行为违背了法律责任，这个人将面临法律后果。问题是，如果该行为不是我们实施的，而是与我们有某种关系的其他人实施的，又该怎么办？什么时候法律会让一个人对另一个人犯下的错误或造成的伤害负责？

这个看似简单的问题实际上能引出困难而复杂的事实情景和法律问题。先看事实情景，有许多可能的情况，例如：

- 服务提供者是否应当为其指定的代理人的错误买单，例如偷窃客户钱财的行为；
- 雇主是否应当对其雇员的粗心大意负责，如送货司机超速、撞伤行人；以及

- in a casual or social context, where a person asks a friend for a favour to perform some task, such as bring the dog out for a walk, and the dog bites the friend in the course of the walk.

The question traverses many areas of law, including the three core areas of crime, tort and contract. Where A instructs B to do an act, the result of which C is harmed, can A be convicted of a criminal offence? Likewise, in tort, can C (apart from suing B) sue A for the tort committed by B? And, in contract, can A's liability be affected by the action of B, such as, that B had, prior to the entering into the contract, made a false statement about the product to C? The reader might hope or expect that the legal framework across the three areas has a high degree of uniformity and consistency. Regrettably, this is not the case. The law on this looks more like patchwork than a neatly designed mosaic.

Further, since the scenario involves three parties instead of just two, the challenge of competing interests (see Chapter 24) becomes more acute and the task of establishing the desired equilibrium is made more difficult.

Broadly speaking, in seeking to lay down the law, the lawmaker addresses many considerations and utilises many concepts, including:

- authorisation (and prohibition);
- participation;
- knowledge of act;
- integration;
- benefit from act;
- hazardous activity; and

- 在日常社交的背景下，一个人请友人代劳做某件事，比如出门遛狗，而这位友人在遛狗时不幸被狗咬伤。

这个问题可以说贯穿了法律的许多领域，包括刑法、侵权法和合同法这三大核心领域。倘若 B 受 A 的指示的行为给 C 造成了伤害，那么，A 是否可以被判定为刑事犯罪？同理，在侵权行为中，C 是否可以（除了起诉 B 之外）就 B 的侵权行为起诉 A？在有合同关系的情况下，A 的责任是否受 B 的某个行为的影响，比如说，在签订合同之前，B 向 C 做了关于产品的虚假陈述这样的情况？读者可能希望或者期待这三个领域的法律框架能有高度的一致性。然而，遗憾的是其实不然。这方面的法律，比起设计整齐的马赛克，看起来更像是一张拼凑缝合在一起的花布。

此外，由于这种情况涉及三方而不仅仅是两方，利益竞争带来的挑战（见第 24 章）变得更加突出，建立一个理想的平衡的任务也格外艰巨。

广义上讲，在寻求制定法律时，立法者要考虑许多因素，用到许多概念，其中包括：

- 授权（和禁止）；
- 参与；
- 对（他人）行为的知情度；
- 整合；
- 从（他人）行为中是否受益；
- 危险活动；以及

- vulnerability of victim.

Space and practicality permit only a quick elaboration of the above.

Authorisation, as the word suggests, is the argument that A had given B the authority to do the act in question and, hence, should bear liability. The concept of authority figures prominently in the law of agency.

Authorisation, however, has to take into account prohibition. Should A be liable if he had prohibited B from certain types of conduct? The instinctive answer appears to be negative. And one approach is that a prohibited act is unauthorised and so A is not liable. Another approach, arguably a more holistic one, is to ask if A had exercised sufficient due diligence. This issue is a very controversial and difficult one.

Participation is concerned with A's involvement in B's act. Criminal law talks about abetting, or being an accessory to, a crime. In the context of corporate crime, the law asks if the individual director (or officer) who did the wrongful act is the "directing mind and will" of the company; if he is, then the company is liable for the offence. In the tort of nuisance, in deciding if a landlord is liable for a nuisance committed by his tenant, the law asks if the landlord had "participated" in the nuisance, for example, by helping the tenant organise the activity which caused the nuisance.

Knowledge is also a relevant aspect. In certain circumstances, if A knows about B's intending act, the law may attribute liability to him. But knowledge, as we have seen in Chapter 12, involves a whole spectrum, and the lawmaker has to decide, in the given scenario, what is the appropriate level of fault.

Integration is the perspective that B is part of the set-up of A and so B's act

- 受害者的脆弱程度。

由于篇幅和实际情况的限制，我只能对上述内容进行相对简单的阐述。

授权——正如字面的意思，是指因为 A 授予了 B 进行该相关行为的权力，所以应该承担责任的观点。授权的概念在代理法中占有突出的地位。

然而，有授权也就会有禁止。假如 A 表示了禁止 B 作出某些类型的行为，A 是否仍应对这类行为承担责任？我们本能的答案应该是否定的。被禁止的行为未经授权，所以 A 不承担责任，这是一种思路。另一种思路——或许是更全面的一个解决问题的思路——是探讨 A 有没有充分地谨慎尽职。回答这个问题并非易事，相关争议很多。

参与是指 A 对 B 的行为的参与度。从刑法上来讲，就是教唆，或成为犯罪行为中的帮凶。在公司犯罪的具体事例中，法律会问做了不法行为的董事（或高管）是不是公司里“指导思想和意志”的关键人物；如果是，那么公司就要对其犯罪负责。在扰民的侵权行为中，在决定房东是否对租户实施的扰民行为负责时，法律会询问房东是否“参与”了该扰民行为，比如，帮忙组织该扰民活动等。

知情也是一个相关的方面。在某些情况下，倘若 A 知晓 B 意图实施的行为，法律便可以追究责任。但是，正如我们在第 12 章中所提到的，知情或认知涉及一系列的不同程度，而立法者必须在特定的情况下决定适当的过错门槛。

整合，是指 B 是 A 组织架构中的一部分，因此 B 的行为

is essentially A's act. So, sometimes, there are debates as to whether B is part of A's set-up or not. An employee is likely to be part of the employer's set-up. In contrast, a contractor (or, independent contractor) is not. A is "vicariously" liable if B is an employee but not if B is a contractor. This distinction, and its soundness, has been put under strain by the trend of outsourcing of important functions of an organisation.

Another relevant consideration is whether A benefitted from B's act. If he did, then the law is inclined to make him liable as well. He who takes the benefit also should bear the burden.

For example, in the scenario where B, in selling A's product to C, acts contrary to A's prohibition and misrepresents an essential feature, is A legally affected by B's misrepresentation? And can A hide behind a contract clause which says that C is not relying on any statement made by B? The short answer to this complicated question is that the judge will look at the reality of the situation (that B had, in fact, made a false statement) and the extent to which A had taken steps to ensure that C was not misled, such as checking with C before he signs the contract.

Another consideration is where a particular conduct or activity involves especial danger. In such a situation, the law is likely to make A liable even if he engages B to perform it for him. In legal terms, it is said that A is under a non-delegable duty.

Finally, there are situations where C is in a vulnerable or dependent position and, on account of that vulnerability, the law imposes liability on A even though the action is carried out by B. An example is where a school is held liable for the carelessness of an external swimming instructor where swimming is part of the

本质上属于A的行为的观点。所以，有时会有一些就B是否隶属A的讨论。雇员可能属于雇主机构的一部分；而承包商（或独立承包商）则不是。如果B是雇员，A要承担“替代”责任，但如果B是承包商，A则不承担责任。不过，面对现在越来越多公司外包重要职能的趋势，这种区别对待及其合理性受到了不少的非议。

另一个相关的考量是A是否从B的行为中受益。如果是，那么法律也倾向于让其承担责任。利益既得者应当承担起相应的责任。

举个例子，B在向C销售A的产品时违反了A的禁止性规定，对产品的重要特征进行了虚假描述，那么A在法律上是否受到B的虚假陈述的影响？A能不能躲在合同条款后面，主张C没有依赖B的任何陈述？对这一复杂问题的简短回答是，法官会考察现实情况（即在事实上B确实做出了虚假陈述），以及A在多大程度上采取了措施确保C不被误导，例如在C签署合同前与C核实。

另一个考虑因素是某一特定行为或活动涉及特殊的危险。在这种情况下，法律可能会让A承担责任，即使他雇用B代他执行。用法律术语来说，就是A有不能转移的责任。

最后，在有些情况下，C处于一个易受伤害或依赖他人的处境，而由于这种脆弱性，法律要求A担责，即使相关行为是由B执行的。举一个例子，当游泳属于学校课程的一部分时，学校要对外聘的游泳教练的疏忽承担法律责任（见*Woodland v. STA*案）。

总之，通过采用本章提到的概念的不同组合和相互作用，

school curriculum (see *Woodland v. STA*) .

So, by adopting varying combinations and interactions of the concepts mentioned in this chapter, the law comes up with legal principles, such as accessory liability in criminal law, actual authority and apparent authority in agency law, and vicarious liability and non-delegable duty in tort law.

As we go beyond the broad generalisations and delve deeper into each of the specific branches of law, things get a lot more complicated and controversial.

法律得出了一些法律原则，如刑法中的从属责任，代理法中的实际授权和表见授权，以及侵权法中的替代责任和不可转移的责任。

当我们不再通过广义概括浅尝辄止，而是深入每一个具体的法律分支时，便会不可避免地发现不同维度的争议与难题。

Chapter 26
Changes in Law

Change is the only constant.

——Heraclitus

Change takes place constantly in this world. Change can be cyclical or linear. It can be done in an orderly or in a chaotic manner. At times, the change is minor; at other times, it is transformative or revolutionary.

Likewise, legal change occurs all the time. In each country, annually, there are dozens of statutory changes, whether in the form of new statutes or amendments of existing statutes. And there are scores of cases, some of which alter the existing law.

Why does law change incessantly? There are two main reasons. The first is that law exists within, and serves, its context (Chapter 3). If there is a change in the context, resulting in a change in the accepted policy — be it economic, social or political — law has to change as well, in order to implement the new policy or to catch up with it.

For example, in recent years, countries around the globe have introduced

第 26 章
法律中的变化

唯一不变的是变化本身。

——赫拉克利特

在这个世界上，变化不断发生。变化可以是周期性的，也可以是线性的；它可以一种有序的方式进行，也可以一种混乱的方式进行。有时，变化是细微的；有时，它又是变革性的乃至革命性的。

同样地，法律中的变化也一直在发生。在每个国家，每年都有几十项法律变化——无论是新法规的颁布，还是现有法规的修正案。同时也会有许许多多案例涌现，其中一些调整了现有的法律。

为什么法律会不停地变化？有两大主要原因。第一个原因是，法律存在于其适用的社会环境之中并为其服务（第 3 章）。如果大环境发生变化，导致公认的政策发生变化，无论是经济的、社会的还是政治的，法律也必须随之变化，以实施新的政

laws to deal with fake news, a development facilitated by the evolving social media world and the advancement in digital manipulation. New developments and challenges call for new laws.

As for the updating of existing laws, tax laws are a prime example. Each year, as parliaments decide the budget for the forthcoming fiscal year, the changes in tax — whether in the form of new categories of taxes, new rates of tax or new incentives in the form of exemptions or deductions — have to be effected by amending the existing tax statutes.

The second reason for legal change is to evolve or improve the legal framework. Invariably, law is a work in progress. This is particularly true of law that is crafted by judges. As canvassed in Chapter 19, the subject of duty of care in the tort of negligence is a classic illustration of this evolution. Over a period of some six decades, the legal framework for ascertaining the existence of a duty of care moved from a single-stage test of foreseeability, to a two-stage test of foreseeability and policy and, finally, to a three-stage test of foreseeability, proximity and policy.

The improvement of the law may also involve rectifying an error or an injustice (actual or perceived). For example, as regards a doctor's duty to disclose materials risks of a proposed treatment, the position in the UK was, for many years, that the Bolam test (or rule) applied — that a doctor is not negligent so long as what he did accorded with a substantial and respectable body of opinion in the field. Hence, if a significant number of doctors (even if it were a small minority) would not have warned the patient of the dangers, the doctor in question is not negligent for not informing. In 2015, the UK Supreme Court decided to remedy this injustice and held that a doctor is under a duty to disclose to his patient all the material risks of the proposed treatment and even of reasonable alternative treatments.

策或至少反映时事。

例如，近年来，全球各国都出台了针对假新闻的法律，这一发展是由日新月异的社交媒体世界和数字操纵技术的进步促成的。新的发展和挑战需要新的法律。

至于现有法律的更新，税法是一个最好的例子。每年，当议会决定下一个财政年度的预算时，税收方面的变化都必须通过修改现有的税收法规来实现，无论是增加新的税种、更新税率，还是推行新的免税或抵扣等激励措施。

法律变化的第二个原因是为了法律框架的演变或完善。法律无疑是一项持续进行中的工程，在普通法系里由法官制定的法律更是如此。正如第 19 章所述，过失侵权中的注意义务是这种演变的一个典型例子。在大约 60 年的时间里，确定注意义务存在的法律框架从单一阶段的可预见性测试，到两阶段的“可预见性”和“政策”测试，最后到目前的三阶段的“可预见性”“接近性”“政策”测试。

法律的改进也可能涉及纠正错误，改变实际的或人们认为的不公正。例如，关于医生披露所建议的治疗方法的重大风险的责任，多年来，英国的立场是适用 Bolam 标准（或规则），即只要医生的所作所为符合该领域里一定数量的、值得尊重的同行的意见，就不存在过失。也就是说，假如相当一部分（即使是少数）的医生不会警告病人某些危险的存在，那么被告医生不告知病人这些危险就没有过失。2015 年，英国最高法院决定纠正这一不公正现象，认为医生有义务向病人披露推荐疗法，甚至是其他合理的替代疗法的所有重大风险。

然而，要理解法律变化和它们带来的影响并非轻而易举的

But it may not be easy to understand the legal changes and their implications. In the case of change through case law, the judgment or judgments have to be carefully scrutinised. For lawyers and even for non– lawyers (especially as regards law outside their field of competence or expertise), the task may be a difficult one (as we have seen in Chapter 22) . To this end, the commentaries of lawyers and academics may be very helpful.

Where the change is a statutory one, there may be the added complication that the change is implemented through several channels, and the full picture emerges only when we piece all the parts together.

For example, some years ago, the financial regulators in Singapore decided to implement a balanced scorecard framework (BSF) to affect the remuneration of financial advisers. The basic idea is that when rewarding the bank's sales officer, regard should be given to the amount of sales achieved as well as to whether the officer did his due diligence and gave the client good and proper advice. An unprofessional or irresponsible adviser would have his remuneration appropriately reduced.

However, four instruments were used to effect this change: an amendment to the Financial Advisers Act, the introduction of a new piece of subsidiary legislation, the Financial Advisers (Remuneration) Regulations, the issuance of a new MAS Notice on BSF and the issuance of a new MAS Guideline on BSF. So, unless the reader is legally trained and is familiar with the subject, it would be a great challenge to understand the new law and its implications. Again, the availability of commentaries from lawyers or academics may be helpful here.

Change is unavoidable and it is often necessary. Sometimes, the changes are complicated and perplexing, and may confuse rather than clarify. For those affected by any legal change, steps have to be taken to understand and to respond to the change.

事。在判例法推动法律变化的情况下，这些判决须经过仔细审查。对于律师而言，尤其是对非法律专业人士而言，完成这项任务时常如雾里看花，正如我们在第 22 章中所看到的。为此，律师和学者的评论文章和学术讨论通常能助我们一臂之力。

当变化反应在成文法上时，也可能会有额外的棘手问题，即变化将通过多头并进来实现，而我们只有把不同方面的情况全部拼凑在一起时，才能看出全貌。

举个例子，几年前，新加坡的金融监管机关决定实施“平衡计分卡框架”（BSF）来决定金融顾问的薪酬。该政策的基本理念是在奖励银行的销售人员时，应考虑到其所实现的销售量，以及该人员是否尽职尽责，为客户提供了良好、适当的建议。不专业或不负责任的顾问应被适当地减薪。

然而，实现这一变化的过程中涉及了四份法律法规：《金融顾问法》的修正案，引入的新的附属立法《金融顾问（薪酬）条例》，新发布的《新加坡金融管理局关于 BSF 的通知》，以及新发布的《新加坡金融管理局 BSF 指南》。所以说，除非读者受过法律专业培训并熟悉这一领域，否则要理解这方面的新法律及其影响需要大费周折。不过，参考律师或学者提供的评论文章在这时同样可能会有帮助。

变化是不可避免的，且往往是必要的。有时，变化复杂且令人困惑，甚至会混淆而不是澄清问题。因此，可能受某项法律变化影响的群体，需要付出努力才能理解和应对这种变化。

Chapter 27
When Legal Concepts Overlap

The more complex the network is, the more complex its pattern of interconnectedness.

——Fritjof Capra

It is common that in a given scenario or dispute, multiple issues or areas of law may be applicable. This can occur within an area of law, such as contract law, for example, where a customer who is dissatisfied with a financial product wants to sue the bank for misrepresentation or for a breach of a term of contract.

It could also occur across areas of law. In the above scenario, it is possible that customer may also wish to sue the bank under the tort of negligence. Further, the authorities may want to prosecute the bank for a criminal offence in relation to the misrepresentation.

Before proceeding further, it must be cautioned that the subject of multiple overlapping laws is a very complex area and much remains unclear. A preliminary point should be made here. It may seem that one would expect different paths of

第 27 章
法律概念的重叠

越复杂的网状结构，其间相互联系的模式也越复杂。

——福瑞特季夫·卡普拉

通常，在一个特定的场景或争端中，会涉及多个法律问题，或适用多个领域的法律。这有可能发生在某一个法律领域里，比如合同法里一个对金融产品不满意的客户想起诉银行的虚假陈述或违反合同条款的情况。

同一事件也可能同时涉及好几个法律领域。就第 26 章所举的例子，客户可能也考虑就过失侵权行为起诉银行。此外，相关当局也可能考虑追究银行的虚假陈述行为的刑事责任。

在进一步开展讨论之前，我们必须注意的是，重叠法律是一项非常复杂的课题，学术上有很多疑点尚不明朗。这里需要先指出一点——人们期待的，是不同的分析路径会导致相同的结果。毕竟，法律的终点是正义，不是吗？其实法律的全貌要

analysis to lead to the same result. After all, law is about justice, isn't it? The full picture is much more complicated than that.

The application of the different issues or areas may lead to the same outcome or to different outcomes. Sometimes they should lead to the same outcome; sometimes they should not. The difficulty for the judge (as well as the onlooker) is to understand and discern when they should and when they should not lead to the same outcome.

When two different legal principles or concepts are potentially applicable, there are several possibilities:

(a) the two principles are essentially the same in substance, and are different ways of saying the same thing;

(b) the two principles are concentric circles — one principle is larger than the other and encompasses it; and

(c) the two principles intersect and overlap, with each having a part which does not apply to the other.

In possibility (a), one would expect the answer to be the same. This scenario is rare. A possible example is found in contract law, in the concept of substantial performance and the concept of a warranty. From the performance angle, the law says that where the performing party has substantially performed the contract, he is entitled to payment of contract price less the part unperformed or imperfectly performed.

From the perspective of breach of contract and the award of damages, the law says that for a breach of a term which is a warranty (in contrast to a condition), the innocent party cannot terminate the contract but may claim compensation.

复杂得多。

不同法律问题或领域的适用实则可能导致相同的结果，也可能导致不同的结果。有时候它们应该导致相同的结果；有时候又不应该。法官（以及局外人）面对的难题在于理解和辨别什么时候不同法律领域应该导致相同的结果。

当两条不同法律原则或概念可能同时适用时，有以下几种可能性：

（a）这两条原则在实质上是相同的，是表达同一道理的不同方式；

（b）这两条原则的范围像同心圆——其中一条原则比另一条原则范围广，包含了那条应用更具体的原则；以及

（c）这两条原则相交、重叠，且各有不适用于另一条原则的部分。

在（a）可能性中，我们会期待两条原则给同一法律问题带来一致的答案。这种情况其实是罕见的。一个可能的例子是在合同法里，在实质性履行的概念和保证条款的概念中。从履约的角度看，法律规定，如果履约方实质上履行了合同，他有权获得除去未履约或未完全履约部分的合同价款。

从违约和损害赔偿的角度来看，法律规定，对于违反保证（与违反条件相对），无过错方不能终止合同，但可以要求赔偿。

当我们对比以上两条法律原则的应用情况，我们可以看到，实质性履行的理论和保证条款概念实际上是硬币的两面。因此，当人们适用实质性履行和违反保证的损害赔偿时，结果是一样的，因为这两个概念的实质是同一道理的正反面，一个是从履行的角度看，另一个是从违约的角度看。事实上，合同

As we juxtapose the two, it may be observed that the doctrine of substantial performance is in fact the flip side of the concept of a warranty. So, as one applies substantial performance and damages for breach of warranty, the outcome is the same as the substance of the two concepts are obverse sides of the same, one looking from the perspective of performance and one from the perspective of breach. Indeed, a contract may be discharged by performance and may also be discharged by breach.

We come to situation (b) . In Chapter 16, we considered the *Hedley Byrne* concept of "special relationship" for deciding duty of care for negligently-made statements. On a broader level, to decide a duty of care, the law requires three things (or concepts) — foreseeability, proximity and policy. The *Hedley Byrne* special relationship is but one way by which proximity may be satisfied (other proximities include the concept of voluntary assumption of responsibility) . So, proximity is the outer circle while special relationship is a smaller circle within the bigger circle.

In the third situation (c), the two (or more) applicable concepts overlap but each, in its own way, has a part of its ambit that the other does not cover. If, on the facts, an element in the overlapping part is not satisfied, then the claims fail on both approaches. For example, in a tort claim, if there is no causation, the claim will not succeed whether the claim is in the tort of negligence or in the tort of inducing a breach of contract.

But where, on the facts, the non-overlapping area is relevant, the outcomes differ depending on which tort is being scrutinised. For example, where a guest is injured by a wild animal kept by the host in his premises, the tort of negligence is committed if the host failed to take reasonable care, such as muzzling or chaining

可以因履行而终止，也可以因违约而终止。

我们来看看（b）可能性。在第16章中，我们考虑了Hedley Byrne案中的“特殊关系”以判断有关过失言论的注意义务。在更广泛的层面上，要决定注意义务，法律需要三项要素（或概念）——可预见性、接近性和政策。Hedley Byrne案中的“特殊关系”概念只是满足接近性的一种方式（其他接近性包括自愿承担责任等概念）。因此，接近性是外圈，而特殊关系是大圈内的小圈。

在（c）可能性中，两个（或更多）适用的概念重叠，但每个概念各自有一部分要素是另一个概念所不涵盖的。如果一项案件的事实不满足两者重叠部分的要素，那么，无论依据哪项法律概念，索赔都不会成功。例如，在侵权索赔中，如果损失和侵权行为没有因果关系，无论是主张过失侵权还是主张诱导违约，索赔都不会成功。

但是，如果案件事实涉及的是两者的非重叠区域，那么结果就会因从哪种侵权行为的角度分析而不同。例如，假如客人被主人在其处所饲养的野生动物伤害，如果主人没有采取合理的行动照顾客人的安危，如给动物戴上口罩或链子，就属于过失侵权。但这位饲主也会负有野生动物侵权的责任。这项责任是绝对的，也就是说，即使该饲主已经采取了合理的预防措施，例如用铁链拴锁，但动物意外挣脱了，饲主仍然要为后一种侵权行为负责，即使他可能不需要承担对客人的过失侵权的责任。

在有重合的法律原则产生冲突时，其中一条原则可能占上风的另外一种原因是，法庭认为该原则或领域的总体目标比另

the animal. But there is also the tort of liability for wild animals and here the liability is strict or absolute. Even if the host had taken reasonable care, such as by chaining, and the animal unexpectedly broke free, the host is still liable for the latter tort even though he may not be liable under the tort of negligence.

In a clash of overlapping principles, another reason why one may prevail is that the court considers that the overarching aim or goal of one principle or area is more important than that of the other. This is interestingly illustrated in the scenario where a contracting party seeks a return of his monies under an illegal contract, such as where a person places a bet with an unlicensed bookie. By conventional contract law principles, such an action would fail on the policy of courts refusing to render assistance when parties engage in illegal transactions.

Here, the policy goal of courts refusing to render assistance to parties engaged in illegal transactions is prioritised over the aim of enforcing promises in contract law.

As an alternative, a person may seek a return of his monies (such as where the bookie did not place the bet) under the law of unjust enrichment.

According to this area of law, where a person is unjustly enriched at another's expense, the court may allow restitution of monies, in order to redress the unjust enrichment. But when the plaintiff seeks such a remedy, a conservative court is likely to reject such an attempt on the ground that to do so would "stultify" (or obstruct) the policy in contract law.

As said earlier, this whole subject remains complex and uncertain.

一条的更重要。这一点在以下情况中很有趣地体现出来：合同一方要求归还其在一项非法合同下支付的款项（如一个人在没有执照的博彩公司下注）。根据传统的合同法原则，这种诉讼会因法院不帮助当事人从事非法交易的政策而败诉。

此处，法院拒绝向从事非法交易的当事人提供帮助的政策目标被置于合同法中执行双方约定的目标之上。

另一种选择是，允许一个人根据不当得利的法律要求得利者返还钱财（例如在上述赌徒没有成功下注的情况下可能适用）。

根据不当得利法，如果一个人以他人的利益为代价获得了不正当的利益，法庭可以允许归还金钱以达到纠正不正当得利的目的。不过，当原告寻求这种救济时，保守的法院兴许还是会拒绝这种主张，理由是如此一来会“窒息”（或阻碍）合同法的政策。

所以，如同我们上面已经提到的，本章讨论的课题目前仍然复杂而不确定。

Chapter 28
Overarching and Ancillary Objectives

> Objectives can be compared to a compass bearing by which a ship navigates.
>
> ——Peter Drucker

As mentioned in Chapter 2, there are dozens of areas of law, of which crime, tort and contract form the foundational three. Within each area of law, what are of utmost importance are the overarching aims, goals or objectives of that area (see Chapter 3).

These objectives lead to the key concepts of law, and then to the elements and the detailed rules. Whenever doubts or controversies arise regarding a legal rule or proposed legal rule, the overarching objectives are referred to for guidance.

For example, tort law seeks to compensate an innocent party who has been harmed by the wrongful act of another party (the tortfeasor). In deciding who should pay and how much, the central idea of tort law is corrective justice. What

第 28 章

总体目标与附属目标

目标如同大海航行中船舶的罗盘。

——彼得·杜拉克

如第 2 章提到的，法律有几十个领域，其中刑法、侵权法和合同法是最基础的三大领域。在每个法律领域中，最重要的是该领域的总体目标和宗旨（见第 3 章）。

这些目标直接导致了法律的关键概念的产生，然后是要素和详细规则。每当我们对某项法律规则或拟议的法律规则产生怀疑或争议时，就应参考该部法律的总体目标指引的方向。

举个侵权法的例子，侵权法寻求对受到侵权人不法行为伤害的无辜方进行赔偿。在决定哪方应该支付赔偿和赔偿多少时，侵权法的中心思想是矫正正义。这意味着，法律应该决定由侵权行为人向受害者赔偿，而且赔偿金额应使受害者还原到仿佛没有发生侵权行为时的状态，但不是更多。

this means is that it is the tortfeasor who should pay the victim, and he should compensate the amount necessary to put the victim in the position he would be in if the tort was not committed, but not more.

In contrast, as mentioned in Chapter 3, tort law sometimes, in order to advance a remedy to a claimant perceived to be deserving, mentions distributive justice. For example, distributive justice may motivate a court to make a defendant pay, or pay more, because he has "deep pockets" or because the victim is poor.

So, although corrective justice is said to be central to tort law, courts do, from time to time, refer to distributive justice and make decisions in accordance with it. And the outcome may be contrary to what the application of corrective justice would dictate. Despite nice statements such as, that "... tort law is a mosaic in which principles of corrective justice and distributive justice are interwoven" (*MacFarlane v. Tayside*, per Lord Steyn), one is really uncertain when and how distributive justice will be applied.

There is yet another objective of tort law — deterrence. As mentioned in Chapter 3, the court may impose liability on the defendant, or impose a higher than usual sum of compensation, not so much because of victim compensation but rather to deter would-be tortfeasors. A simple objection to such action by the court is that deterrence — a form of punishment — belongs to criminal law. Like distributive justice, deterrence is, from time to time, mentioned as a relevant consideration but it is difficult to predict when it will surface and how much weight to give to each objective.

The problem caused by ancillary or peripheral objectives is also seen in contract law. When awarding damages for a breach of contract, the law's aim

相反，如第 3 章所述，有时为了向应得救助的索赔人提供法律救助措施，侵权法也会考虑分配正义。例如，根据分配正义，法庭可以因为被告有“雄厚资金”，受害者贫困潦倒，而让被告向受害人支付赔偿，或支付更高的赔偿。

因此，尽管矫正正义被认为是侵权法的核心，但法庭其实不时地提到分配正义且根据分配正义做决定，而得到或许与应用矫正正义相左的判决。尽管有人说“……侵权法是一片马赛克，其中纠正性正义和分配性正义的原则交织在一起”（*MacFarlane v. Tayside* 案，按 Steyn 大法官的话），以及诸如此类动听的话，但人们实在不确定法庭在何时，以及会如何应用分配正义原则。

侵权法还有一个目标——震慑。如第 3 章提到的，法庭可能会要求被告承担赔偿责任，或判处高于常理的赔偿金额，这与其说是为了赔偿受害者，不如说是为了震慑潜在的犯下同样侵权行为的人。反对法庭这种行为的一个简单观点是，震慑作为一种惩罚形式应属于刑法管辖。与分配正义一样，震慑也时常作为一个相关的考量被提及，但人们很难预判它何时会出现，以及法庭将会赋予每个目标多少比重。

在合同法中也可以看到辅助性或边缘性目标带来的问题。在对违约行为进行赔偿时，法律的目的是对无辜的一方进行补偿，并使其处于假设合同得到正常履行会出现的状况。这种理念的一个应用是，如果合同以违约金条款的形式规定了违约方要支付的赔偿金（例如，在完成合同方面每延迟一天需支付 1000 美元），该条款只有在它是对损失的“真实预估”时才有效。相反，如果金额过高甚至类似勒索，且该条款旨在“恐吓”

is to compensate the innocent party and to put him in a position he would have been in if the contract had been properly performed. An application of this thinking is that if the contract provides for the compensation to be paid, in the form of a liquidated damages, or LD, clause (e.g, $1,000 for each day of delay in completing the contract), the clause is valid only if it was a "genuine pre-estimate" of loss. In contrast, if the amount was exorbitant or extortionate and the clause was aimed at "terrorising" the contract party, it would be invalid.

However, in recent times, English courts have tempered with this principle by recognising that one party may have a "legitimate interest" to "encourage" the other party to observe the contractual obligation (see *Parking Eye v. Beavis*) . In so doing, they have introduced an ancillary objective to the law on LD clauses, namely giving regard to a contracting party's interest to ensure that the contract is performed, albeit through the threat of a penalty.

The *Parking Eye* case concerned a parking scheme whereby motorists could park for free up to two hours but were charged a hefty £85 if they exceeded the two-hour limit. The defendant, who parked beyond the two-hour period, was unsuccessful in challenging the LD clause. The court held that so long as the clause did not impose a detriment on the contract- breaker "out of all proportion to any legitimate interest" of the innocent party to have the contract performed, it was valid. Hence, the defendant had to pay the £85.

The change in law is controversial in two respects. First, there appears to be a shift in philosophical thinking. Until *Parking Eye*, it was established law that for an LD clause to be valid, it must have been a genuine pre-estimate of loss; no threat of penalisation was permitted. Now, the court has introduced an element of penalisation, which goes against the pre-existing philosophy.

合同相对方，那么，它在法律上将是无效的。

不过，近来英国法院对这一原则进行了调整，承认合同一方可能有“合法利益”来“鼓励”另一方遵守合同义务（见 *Parking Eye v. Beavis* 案）。这样一来，他们为违约金条款的法律引入了一个辅助目标，即考虑到合同当事人的利益，以确保合同的履行，即使是威胁对违约进行惩罚。

Parking Eye 案涉及一项停车场的规定，根据该规定，驾驶者可以免费停车两小时，但如果超过两小时，则要收取 85 英镑的高额费用。被告停车超过了两小时的时间，最终未能成功挑战那条违约金条款。法庭认为，只要该条款带给违约者的损失没有“与无过错方要求履行合同的合法利益完全不成比例”，它就是有效的。因此，被告必须支付原告停车场 85 英镑。

这一法律变化面临两方面的争议。其一，该法律背后的哲学思想似乎发生了转变。根据 Parking Eye 案之前既定的法律规定，有效的违约金条款必须是对损失的真正预估；不允许有惩罚的威胁。现在，法院引入了惩罚的因素，这与之前存在的理念相悖。

其二，法律现在承认确保合同相对方不违约是一种合法利益。但缔约一方希望另一方履行合同而非违反合同，难道不是双方制定合同时几乎无一例外的情况吗？因此，在 Parking Eye 案之后，加入金额比以前更极端、更不成比例的违约金条款可能成为常见的做法。这样看来，什么样的违约金条款是可接受的，这个问题已经变得难以揣摩。

正如本章开头所讲，每个法律领域都有其目标，既有总体

Secondly, the law now recognises a legitimate interest to ensure that there is no breach. But is it not almost invariably the case that a contracting party wants the other party to perform the contract and not breach it? So, post-*Parking Eye*, it may become common practice to include LD clauses which monetary sums are less moderate and proportionate than previously witnessed. So, the issue of what is an acceptable LD clause has become much more uncertain.

As mentioned at the start of this chapter, each area of law has its objectives, overarching as well as ancillary. Often, it is unpredictable when the ancillary objectives will surface and how the court will balance the competing objectives.

This uncertainty adds to the complexity of the law.

目标，也有辅助性目标。通常情况下，我们无法预测辅助性目标在何等情况下相关以及法庭将如何平衡这些相互竞争的法律目标。

这种不确定性进一步增加了法律的复杂性。

Chapter 29
Emotive Words, Obscure Language

> We are searching for things in nature that are hidden behind the veil of appearance.
>
> ——Franz Marc

As we have seen in Chapter 14, words convey thoughts and ideas. In judgments, they are used to explain and illuminate — or are supposed to — so that the reader understands the factual situation of the dispute, the issues and the reasons for the outcome.

However, at times, the words mislead or obscure. They become obstacles to the reader's understanding of the decision and of the law. This happens in two ways.

First, emotive words are sometimes used. An emotive word, instead of being neutral, contains the speaker's (or writer's) approval or disapproval of the person or event being reported or discussed and colours, sometimes unfairly, the reader's impression or perception of the factual scenario.

第 29 章
感性的语言，晦涩的表达

我们寻求着自然界中隐藏在表面那层面纱背后的东西。

——弗兰茨·马尔克

正如我们在第 14 章中所看到的，文字传达我们的思想和观念。在判决书中，文字被用来解释和说明（或者说应该被用来解释和说明），以便读者了解该争议的事实情况、法律问题和判决理由。

然而，有时这些词语会误导读者或令人一头雾水。它们反而成了读者理解判决和法律的障碍。这种情况以两种形式发生。

首先，有时判决书会使用情感性词语。一个情感性的词做不到传达理性和中立的意思，而是包含了说话人（或作者）对被报道或讨论的人或事件的认可或否定，有时候会给读者对事实情况的印象或看法带来不公平的影响。

A journalist reporting an event can refer to terrorists or freedom–fighters, rebels or pro–democracy activists, and the reader will automatically and subconsciously (unless he consciously struggles to keep an objective view) adopt the bias so purveyed by the words used.

Likewise, as the judge narrates the facts of a case, the reader is influenced by his choice of words. The defendant can be described as having "arranged" for something to happen, which is quite neutral language, or has having "schemed", "conspired" or "manipulated" . A person who enters a disused property without permission can be described somewhat positively as a "sporting enthusiast" or negatively as a "thrill seeker" . And, a defendant who had omitted to perform a duty can be said to have done so "unwittingly" or "carelessly" . So, to get a clear and true picture of the scenario, the reader has to be alert to the use of emotive language and persuader words.

Obscure words or language can also be an obstacle to understanding. For example, a particular area of law may be very controversial and in need of change, perhaps radical change. The judge, however, may be reluctant to upset what he perceives to be a familiar and established legal distinction or framework of law, even though he is aware of its defects or imperfections.

Let us illustrate this with the context of a person's liability for another person's actions (see Chapter 25) . Here, there are two legal concepts (there is a third — agency — but, for simplicity sake, we look at two) that have evolved independently: vicarious liability and non–delegable duty.

In vicarious liability (VL), the liability of an employer for torts of his employee, the legal analysis is that the employee is personally liable for his tort, and that liability is primary. The employer, in contrast, is secondarily liable.

记者在报道某一事件时，可以提到恐怖分子或自由斗士、反叛者或民主积极分子，而读者通常会自动和下意识地被所使用的词语带来的偏见潜移默化（除非该读者能有意识地努力保持客观的观点）。

同样，当法官叙述案件事实时，读者也会受到他所选词语的影响。被告可以被描述为“安排”了某些事情的发生——这是很中性的语言——也可以被描述为“策划”“密谋”“操纵”了事件。一个人未经许可进入废弃的他人领地，可以被打上积极的标签比如“运动爱好者”，也可以被描述为“寻求刺激的那类人”。一个疏忽履行职责的被告可以说是“不知不觉”或“疏忽大意”地未尽职责。因此，为了清楚和真实地了解情况，读者必须警惕情绪化的语言和劝导性的词语。

晦涩艰深的词语或语言也能成为我们理解的障碍。例如，一个特定的法律领域可能极具争议，需要改变，甚至是彻底的变革。然而，法官即使在意识到该法律的缺陷的情况下，可能也不愿大刀阔斧地打乱他熟悉的、既定的法规类别或法律框架。

让我们以一个人对另一个人的行为的责任为例来说明这一点（见第 25 章），其中有两个独立发展的法律概念：替代责任和不可转移的责任（其实还有第三个代理的概念，但为简单易懂起见，我们只分析两个）。

在替代责任，即雇主对其雇员的侵权行为的责任中，法律分析是，雇员对其侵权行为负有个人责任，而且该责任是主要的。相比之下，雇主则负次要责任。

从可转移责任的角度来看，法律所采取的立场是，通常可

From the perspective of delegable duty, the position taken by the law is that, in general, a duty of care can be delegated. For example, A needs something to be done and he gets B to do it. The law says as long as A had chosen B carefully, he is not liable even if B commits a tort against C. A is not liable to C. However, the law creates limited exceptions where A is liable to C. In these situations, there is a non–delegable duty (NDD) . Judges take pains to emphasise that NDD should remain exceptional because A is being made liable for another person's act and not his own act. They also stress that, in NDD, the duty is primary and not secondary.

The problem arises in a case when C raises VL and NDD as alternative grounds to make A liable for B's tort. The VL argument may fail because the court is of the view that B was not, strictly speaking, A's employee or because B's act was done outside rather than within his course of employment. As C raises the NDD argument, the court, if it is reluctant to extend the application of NDD to cover the case at hand, will emphasise the differences between VL and NDD, that the two doctrines are "separate and distinct" (see, for example, *MCST Plan No. 3322 v. Tiong Aik*, where the main contractor of a development project was held not liable for defective work by the subcontractors) and should remain so.

But the reader may be perplexed. Because if one takes a step or two back, the scenario that the two concepts deal with is essentially the same — the question of A's liability for harm done to C by A's representative B, as B goes about achieving A's purpose. B's act is not simply the act of another person; it is an act done for A and, in a sense, is his act as well. And whether you term A's liability secondary or primary, the objective and effect are the same whether one term or the other is used. So, are they really totally different or is it more a matter of

以委托他人尽到注意义务。例如，A 需要做一些事情，他能让 B 来做。法律规定，只要 A 谨慎地选择了 B，即使 B 对 C 实施了侵权行为，A 也不承担任何责任。法官们不厌其烦地强调，不可转移责任应该是例外，因为它要求 A 对另一个人的行为而不是他自己的行为负责。他们还强调，不可转移责任是主要责任而非次要责任。

当 C 提出替代责任和不可转移责任作为两个不同主张，要求 A 为 B 的侵权行为负责时，麻烦就出现了。替代责任的论点可能会失败，因为法院认为 B 严格来说不是 A 的雇员，或者因为 B 的行为是在其工作范围之外而不是在其工作过程中完成的。当 C 提出不可转移责任的论点时，如果法院不愿意将不可转移责任的适用范围扩大到涵盖该案，就会强调替代责任和不可转移责任两个概念之间的区别，即这两个学说是"独立和不同的"（例如，在 *MCST Plan No. 3322 v. Tiong Aik* 案中，一个发展项目的主要承包商被认定不对分包商的缺陷工作负责），并且应该保持这种状态。

但读者可能会感到疑惑。因为退一步来看，这两个概念所处理的情况基本上是一样的——当 B 去实现 A 的目的时，A 的代表（B）对 C 造成的伤害的责任问题。B 的行为不仅仅是另一个人的行为；它是为了 A 所做的行为，在某种意义上，也属于 A 的行为。无论你说 A 的责任是次要的还是主要的，无论使用一个术语还是另一个术语，其目标和效果都是一样的。那么，这两个概念真的完全不同吗，还是说这只是一个语义学问题，是技术和形式上的区别？

我倾向于是后者。但是，为了得出这样的结论、看到真实

semantics, of technical and formalistic distinctions?

I am inclined to think that they are the latter. But in order to reach such a conclusion and see the true picture, I would need to surmount the obstacles created by the emphatic and extreme language used by the judges and engage in objective and deep analysis of the whole matter.

So, at times, when law is confusing and incomprehensible, the problem is that emotive and/or obscure language has been used. It is then necessary to look beyond the appearance into the reality, beyond the form to the substance. Only when the veil is lifted can one see the true picture and appreciate the incongruence, conflict and tension involved. Only then can one start to work out the solution to the complexities and controversies at hand.

的情况，我需要克服法官所使用的强调和极端语言带来的障碍，对整个问题进行客观和深入的分析。

因此，当法律令人困惑和无法理解时，有时候问题出在情绪化和 / 或晦涩的语言的使用。那么，我们就有必要超越表象洞察现实，透过形式看本质。只有揭开面前那层面纱，人们才能对真实的情况明察秋毫，得以理解其中的不协调、冲突和张力。只有在那时，人们才能开始找出解决手头复杂问题和争议的办法。

Chapter 30
Judicial Discretion

Discretion is a synonym for intelligence.

——Eloisa James

What is meant by "discretion"? As is common in the world of words, there is more than one meaning or usage. The first is about having the freedom or power to do as one chooses or pleases. The second is about being wise, responsible or circumspect when making a decision. Clearly, the two meanings are quite far apart. Both figure prominently in definitions of the word.

Discretion is present in the law or in the administration of the law. In this book, we have seen the importance of principles, rules and concepts in crafting the law. On a given issue, the lawmaker attempts to set out the boundaries clearly.

If the elements of a particular principle of law are satisfied, then the principle applies to the situation at hand and legal implications attach. However, the meaning of a principle or its elements may be open to different interpretations and, in a sense, the judge's freedom to choose the interpretation he favours is a

第 30 章
司法裁量权

酌情处理是智慧的同义词。

——艾洛伊莎·詹姆斯

什么是“自由裁量权”？正如英语词汇海洋中常见的那样，这个词有不止一种含义或用法。第一个意思是指一个人做愿意或选择的事的自由或权力。第二个意思是指在做决定时要明智、负责或谨慎。很明显，这两种含义相差甚远，而两种都在这个词的定义中占有突出地位。

裁量权存在于法律或法律的实施中。在本书中，我们已经看到了原则、规则和概念在制定法律中的重要性。在一个特定的问题上，立法者试图清楚地列出界限。

如果某项法律原则的要素得到满足，那么该原则以及相应的法律后果就适用于当前的情况。然而，对一项原则或其要素的含义可能会有不同的解释，从某种意义上说，法官自由选择他更认可的解释是一种自由裁量权。

form of discretion.

However, in this chapter, we are more interested in situations where the law specifically gives a judge discretion — leeway to decide what to do in the case before him.

Let us take an example from contract law. A remedy for misrepresentation is rescission, meaning the innocent party may cancel the contract and need not fulfill his part of the bargain. If a plaintiff satisfies the elements of misrepresentation, he is entitled to rescission. However, in common law countries, there is usually a statutory provision such as:

… the court… may declare the contract subsisting and award damages in lieu of rescission, if of opinion that it would be equitable to do so….

So, what this provision says is that if the judge thinks it is fair to do so, he may decide that the contract continues and award monetary compensation instead. Of course, the plaintiff may have preferred to be able to rescind the contract and return the product that he is unsatisfied with.

Let us take another example, this time from company law — the winding up of companies. The typical statutory provision lays down situations in which a company may be wound up, such as that the company is not doing any business, is unable to pay its debts or is conducting its affairs in a way that oppresses minority shareholders. Apart from listing out specific grounds, the provision also provides a general ground:

"the court is of opinion that it is just and equitable that the company be

然而，在本章中，我们更感兴趣的是法律明确赋予法官自由裁量权的情形，换句话说，在他手中的案件里决定做什么的余地。

让我们举一个合同法的例子。对虚假陈述的法律补救措施是撤销合同，这意味着无辜的一方可以撤销合同，不再需要履行他应该交易的部分。如果原告满足了虚假陈述的要素，他就有权撤销合同。然而，在普通法国家，通常有这样一条成文法条款：

法院……认为公平的情况下，可宣布合同继续存在，并判予损害赔偿以代替合同的撤销……

这条法律规定的意思是，法官可以决定合同继续存在，并以金钱赔偿替代对合同的撤销，如果法官认为这样做公平的话。当然，原告可能更希望能够撤销合同并退回他不满意的产品。

让我们再举一个例子，这次是公司法中的例子——公司的清算。典型的法定条款规定了公司可能被清盘的情况，如公司没有任何业务，无力支付债务，或以压迫小股东的方式处理其事务。除了列出具体的理由外，该条款还规定了一个一般性的理由：

“法院认为对公司进行清算是公正和公平的。”

在迄今为止提到的每一个例子中，法律都赋予了法官自由

wound up".

In each of the examples mentioned so far, the law gives the judge discretion, in the first, to award damages instead of allowing rescission and, in the second, to wind up a company. The inquisitive observer may wonder: Why does the law give judges discretion? Is such a practice good or bad?

There are at least two possible answers to the first question. First, the reality of the diversity of this world and the limits of mortal intelligence (see Chapter 41) suggest that it is often impossible to foresee every conceivable circumstance to which a principle may or may not apply. It is difficult for the law to be spelt out comprehensively and exhaustively. Secondly, sometimes, one knows instinctively or intuitively what the fair outcome should be even though it may be difficult to articulate the exact reasoning (read Malcom Gladwell's fascinating book, *Blink: The Power of Thinking Without Thinking*).

Generally, courts do not have discretion unless discretion is provided for in the law. However, in the matters of procedure, courts are said to have discretion (the term used is "inherent jurisdiction") to make orders to ensure fairness and efficiency and to prevent an abuse of process.

Is discretion good or bad? Some view it as a good thing; some view it as bad. Advocates of judicial discretion point out that it gives flexibility to a judge and enables him to award individualised justice. They say that a judge who exercises his discretion does so judicially and not arbitrarily. Opponents, however, argue that the exercise of discretion results in uncertainty and unpredictability. Further, outcome of the decision may flow from the judge's personal attitudes and biases. One judge expressed it rather cynically: "The

裁量权，在第一个例子中，法官可以判决赔偿而不是允许撤销合同；在第二个例子中，法官可以将公司清盘。好奇的观察者可能会问：为什么法律赋予法官自由裁量权？这种做法是好是坏？

对于第一个问题，至少有两个可能的答案。首先，这个世界现实的多样性和人类智慧的局限性（见第 41 章）表明，法律往往不可能预见到一个原则可能或不可能适用的每一种可想象的情况。法律也很难被全面和详尽地阐述出来。其次，人们有时可本能地或直觉地知道公平的结果应该是什么，尽管可能难以阐明确切的推理（详情推荐阅读 Malcom Gladwell 的精彩著作《眨眼：不假思索的力量》）。

一般来说，除非法律明确规定，否则法庭没有自由裁量权。然而，在程序问题上，法庭被认为有很大的自由裁量权（术语是“固有管辖权”）来颁布法庭命令以确保程序的公平和效率，防止滥用程序。

自由裁量权到底是好是坏？有些人认为这是一件好事；有些人认为这是一件坏事。倡导司法自由裁量权的人指出，司法自由裁量权给法官带来了灵活变通的空间，让法官能够实现为案件量身定制的正义。这些人认为，行使自由裁量权的法官是依法行事，而不是任意行事。然而，反对者认为，行使自由裁量权会导致不确定性和不可预测性。此外，最终决定的结果可能源于法官的个人态度和偏见。一位法官就颇为嘲讽地表达了这一点——“据说法官的自由裁量权是暴君的法则：它总是未知的……在最好的情况下，它经常是任性的”（Lord Camden, LCJ）。可以肯定的是，自由裁量权的行使必然涉及法官的主

discretion of a judge is said to be the law of tyrants: it is always unknown; ... In the best, it is oftentimes caprice."（Lord Camden, LCJ）. To be sure, the exercise of discretion necessarily involves subjectivity on the part of the judge, as we may deduce from the various expressions used in the legal provision, such as "deems", "thinks", "considers", "of the opinion" and "of the view". The danger is that a judge might be influenced by his personal beliefs or philosophical subscriptions.

But one should also note that the subjectivity is not unbridled, for the provision proceeds to use qualifiers such as "fit", "just", "equitable", and "appropriate". Often, there is also reference to "in all the circumstances" and "on the facts of the case".

It appears then that judicial discretion is to be exercised wisely and not whimsically. The judge is constrained by justice, even if that be a general and amorphous term. So, sometimes, in the interest of meting out justice in a particular case, predictability may have to be sidelined. Perhaps rightly so.

观性，这一点我们可以从法律条款中使用的各种表达方式，如“认定”“认为”“考虑”“持以下观点”“持以下见解”中推断出来。其中的危险在于，法官可能会受到其个人信仰或哲学观念的影响。

但人们也应该注意到，主观性并非肆无忌惮、信马由缰，因为这些允许自由裁量权的法律条文使用了诸如“适合”“公正”“公平”“适当”等限定词，通常还提到“综合各种情事”和“根据案件的事实”。

这样看来，司法自由裁量权的行使应该是理智的，而不能异想天开。法官受到正义的制约，即使那只是一个笼统的、无形的束缚。因此，有时为了在特定案件中伸张正义，可预测性不得不被搁置——而这样做或许是正确的。

Chapter 31
Cross-border Complications

When in Rome, do as the Romans do.

——St Ambrose

As mentioned in Chapter 2, there is a whole compendium of areas of law, and each country has hundreds of statutes and thousands of court decisions. It is a real challenge for one to acquire a good grasp of the laws just in his or her country.

As one goes beyond the borders of one's country, the diversity and complexity of laws increase exponentially. There are basically three additional sets of laws to be aware of if one ventures abroad, namely:

- the laws of the host country;
- the specific foreign investment law of the host country; and
- private international law.

Regarding the first set of laws, it is obvious that when in Rome, one must

第 31 章
跨境难题

入国问禁，入乡随俗。

——圣安博

正如在第 2 章中提到的，法律的不同领域有一个完整的汇编，且每个国家都有数以百计的法规和成千上万的法庭判决，仅仅掌握好自己国家的法律就已经是个不小的挑战。

当一个人走出自己国家的边界，法律的多样性和复杂性就会成倍增加。对于一个探索跨境发展的人，基本上还有三套法律需要注意：

- 东道国的法律；
- 东道国的特定外国投资法；以及
- 国际私法。

关于第一套法律，很明显，如果一个人在罗马，就必须像

do as the Romans do. There are two aspects of the laws of the host country to be concerned with — the substantive laws and the legal system.

The substantive law deals with the actual rules and principles governing acceptable conduct in society and in business. Each country has some rules and principles that are different from others. For example, some countries, such as Thailand and the Philippines, have usury laws, that is, laws that set a maximum rate of interest chargeable. Another example is that in some countries, such as Indonesia, the matrimonial home may not be used to secure a person's commercial debt. So, in seeking to do as the Romans do, one has to abide by the laws of the host country.

One should bear in mind, however, the issue of extraterritoriality. In general, a country's laws apply to its citizens as regards their conduct in their home country. One would not expect these laws to apply to their conduct abroad. Exceptionally, however, some country's laws can be extraterritorial, meaning they can extend to the conduct of their citizens abroad. For example, many countries make their bribery laws extraterritorial, with the result that their citizens may be prosecuted for a bribery offence committed in another country. Other areas of extraterritorialism include terrorism, sexual offences against children and taxation. So, when one is abroad, there is a need to bear in mind the extraterritorial laws of one's home country.

It should be mentioned that, for certain select issues and areas of law, some degree of uniformity of law is achieved when countries sign treaties with each other or participate in a convention. For example, the UN Convention for the International Sale of Goods (or CISG) was signed in Vienna in 1980 with the objective of introducing some uniformity in law so as to facilitate transborder

罗马人一样行事。东道国的法律有两个方面需要关注——实体法和法律体系。

实体法涉及管理社会和商业中可接受行为的实际规则和原则。每个国家都有一些与其他国家不同的规则和原则。例如，一些国家像泰国和菲律宾有高利贷法，即规定了可收取利息的最高比率的法律。另一个例子是，在一些国家如印度尼西亚，婚姻住所不得用于担保一个人的商业债务。因此，在寻求"像罗马人那样做"的过程中，人们必须遵守东道国的法律。

然而，人们应该注意长臂管辖权的问题。一般来说，一个国家的法律适用于其公民在本国的行为。人们不会料想这些法律会适用于他们在国外的行为。然而，在特殊情况下，一些国家的法律可以具有长臂管辖权，即它们可以延伸到其公民在国外的行为。例如，许多国家规定其反贿赂法具有长臂管辖权，结果是该国公民可能因在另一个国家犯下的贿赂罪而被起诉。治外法权的其他领域包括恐怖主义、针对儿童的性犯罪和税收。因此，当一个人在国外时，仍有必要牢记自己国家法律的长臂管辖权。

值得一提的是，对于某些特定的法律问题和法律领域，当各国相互签署条约或参与一项公约时，可以实现某种程度的法律统一。例如，《联合国国际货物销售公约》（CISG）于1980年在维也纳签署，目的是引入一些统一的法律，以促进跨国界商业。截至2019年12月，已有93个国家批准了该公约，换句话说，这些国家在自己的议会中批准了该公约，并出台了实施该公约的立法。

法律制度涉及如何制定和执行法律。我们将在本章的后半

commerce. As at December 2019, 93 states have ratified the Convention, that is, approved it in the participating country's own parliament and introduced legislation to effect the Convention.

The legal system deals with how laws are made and enforced. We consider the subject of the world's legal systems in the second half of this chapter.

The second set of laws — foreign investment law (FIL) — refers to law directly addressing investment flows into a country. The typical FIL deals with more than a dozen matters, such as:

- areas of business which are open to foreign investors;
- type of permitted business vehicle (s);
- extent of foreign ownership and management;
- repatriation of profits;
- exchange control;
- tax incentives; and
- expropriation of assets.

Thus, the intending investor needs to scrutinise the FIL in order to operate legitimately and optimally in the host country.

The third set of laws concerns the problem and challenge of resolving a cross-border dispute where the laws of different countries dictate conflicting results. This subject is covered in Chapter 32. For the rest of this chapter, we take a quick look at the world's legal systems.

Essentially, there are five types or categories of legal systems around the world, namely:

部分考虑世界上的法律体系。

第二套法律，外国投资法（FIL），是指直接应对投资流入一个国家的法律。典型的外国投资法涉及十几项事务，比如：

- 对外国投资者开放的商业领域；
- 允许的商业实体的类型；
- 外国所有权和管理权的范围；
- 利润返还；
- 外汇管制；
- 税收优惠；以及
- 资产的征用。

因此，有意向的投资者需要仔细研究 FIL，以便在东道国合法和最佳地经营。

第三套法律涉及在不同国家的法律规定了相互冲突的结果的情况下，如何解决跨境争端。这个问题将在第 32 章中阐述。在本章的其余部分，我们会快速浏览一下世界上的法律体系。

基本上，全世界有五种类型或类别的法律体系，即：

- 大陆法系；
- 普通法系；
- 宗教法系；
- 社会主义法系；以及
- 混合法系。

- the civil law system;
- the common law system;
- the religious system;
- the socialist system; and
- the mixed system.

Naturally, each system has its own strengths and weaknesses.

The civil law system is the most commonly adopted system and is in use in Continental Europe and in many other countries around the globe. In this system, the law is contained, quite comprehensively, in codes or statutes. These codes are the primary sources of law. It would be common for a civil law country to have three major codes — the criminal code, the civil code and the commercial code to cover the three major areas of law (see Chapter 2) — which are supplemented by other codes to deal with other areas of law.

In the civil law system, case law or judicial decisions are of minor importance; there is no doctrine of binding precedent (unlike in the common law system). Interestingly, the opinions of respected academics are of greater importance than past judicial decisions.

The common law system is adopted by the UK and other member countries in the Commonwealth of British Nations. Essentially, this Commonwealth comprises current and former colonies of Britain. To this list, we should add the USA, the eastern parts of which were former British colonies.

An integral feature of the common law system is the role of judges. Judges make law. A judicial decision sets a precedent, within a hierarchy, for future courts deciding on the same issue. In a common law country there are

自然地，每个体系都有其自身的优势和劣势。

大陆法系是最普遍采用的体系，欧洲大陆和全球许多国家都采用大陆法。在这个体系中，法律被全面地包含在法典或成文法中。这些法典是法律的主要渊源。一个大陆法系国家通常会有三部主要的法典——刑法、民法和商法，以涵盖三个主要的法律领域（见第 2 章），并由其他法典补充，以处理其他法律领域的问题。

在大陆法系中，判例法或司法判决的重要性不大，不存在具有约束力的先例理论（与普通法系不同）。有趣的是，一些德高望重的学者的意见比过去的司法判决更为重要。

普通法系存在于英国及其他英联邦国家，英联邦本质上由英国现在的和从前的殖民地组成，在英联邦之外，我们还要加上美国，美国东部曾经是英国的殖民地。

普通法系的一个不可或缺的特点是法官的作用。法官制定法律。一项司法裁决在一个等级体系内为未来的法庭在同一问题上的裁决设定了一个先例。在普通法国家，即便有数以百计的成文法，法官在解释这些法律方面依然发挥着重要作用，他们的裁决可能为解释这些法律设定先例。

另一个值得注意的方面是抗辩制和纠问制诉讼程序之间的区别。前者是对立双方的律师互相竞争的一个过程，法官在寻求确定事实（和法律）时充当裁判员。相比之下，纠问式是一种官方调查，法官在查明真相方面发挥着非常积极的作用。普通法国家采用抗辩制，而大陆法国家，如法国和意大利，则采用纠问制。

接下来，还有宗教法系。在这种法系中，宗教法（及其信

statutes — usually hundreds of them — but even here, judges play an important role in interpreting these statutes and their decisions may set precedents in the interpretation of the provisions.

Another aspect worth noting is the difference between the adversarial system and the inquisitorial system of court proceedings. The former is a competitive process between opposing counsel, with the judge acting as a referee as the facts (and law) are sought to be determined. In contrast, an inquisition is an official inquiry where the judge plays a very active role in ascertaining the truth. Common law countries adopt the adversarial system while civil law countries, like France and Italy, subscribe to the inquisitorial approach.

Next, we have the religious system. In this system, the religious law (with its variations of belief) becomes or is the national law. The Islamic system is the most prominent religious system and there are some 50 Islamic countries, the most notable of which are Saudi Arabia, Pakistan, Afghanistan and Iran.

The fourth is the socialist legal system, a key feature in the socialist system is the Marxist–Leninist ideology.

Finally, there is the mixed or pluralist system, where the legal system of a particular country is a mixture of two (or more) of the four legal systems above. Most notable of the countries with a mixed system is China, which is basically a mix of the civil legal system and the socialist system. Some scholars go so far as to say that most countries do not have a pure system; instead, almost all have mixed legal systems.

In addition to the four mentioned above, analysts often mention customary law as yet another system. For example, even in colonised countries, as the colonial law was applied, it was often modified and adapted to local conditions

仰的变化）成为国家法律。伊斯兰体系是最突出的宗教法系，有大约 50 个伊斯兰国家采用，其中最引人注目的是沙特阿拉伯、巴基斯坦、阿富汗和伊朗。

第四种是社会主义法律体系，社会主义制度的一个关键特征是马克思列宁主义意识形态。

最后，还有一种混合或多元体系，即某一国家的法律体系是上述四种法律体系中两种（或更多）的混合。在混合制度的国家中，最值得一提的是中国，它基本上是大陆法律制度和社会主义制度的混合体。一些学者甚至认为，大多数国家都没有一个纯粹的制度；其实几乎所有国家都是采用混合的法律制度。

除了上面提到的五种，分析家们经常提到习俗法是另一种体系。例如，即使在殖民地国家，殖民者的法律在应用过程中，往往被修改并适应当地的条件，在一定程度上成为习俗法。

假如我们不担心过于简化事实的风险，那么可以说，现代世界的大部分地区都采用了大陆法系或普通法系。在这个方面，一个方便的标志是看一个国家的殖民历史，基本上就是看它是英国的殖民地还是欧洲大陆强国的殖民地，如法国、西班牙或德国。此外，宗教法系（更具体地说是伊斯兰法）适用于穆斯林国家。最后，一些国家有两种或两种以上的法律体系的混合。

为了完整起见，还应该提到一些实行联邦政府制度的国家。如第 1 章所述，在一些国家，如美国、加拿大和澳大利亚，联邦和州在制定和执行法律方面分享权力。因此，各州的法律可能会有偏差或变化，尽管从广义上讲，总体原则和政策是相

and accommodated, to some degree, the customary laws.

At the risk of simplification, we can say that much of the modern world adopts either the civil law system or the common law system. Here, a convenient guide is to look at the colonial past of the country, essentially whether it was a colony of Britain or a colony of a Continental European power, such as France, Spain or Germany. In addition, the religious system (more specifically Islamic law) is applied in the Muslim countries. Finally, some countries have a mixture of two of more legal systems.

For the sake of completeness, some mention should be made of countries with a federal system of government. As noted in Chapter 1, in some countries, such as the USA, Canada and Australia, there is a sharing of power, between the federation and the state, in the making and the enforcement of the law. Consequently, there may be deviations or variations of the law from one state to another, even though broadly speaking, the overarching principles and policies are the same. The European Community is like a federation of states.

Clearly, the subject of cross-border legal implications is a complex one. Broadly speaking, there are a few takeaways. First, the laws of the foreign country on specific issues may differ significantly from those of your country. Secondly, there is a need to have a basic understanding of the foreign country's legal system. Thirdly, there is a need to scrutinise the host country's foreign investment law.

同的。欧洲共同体就像一个国家的联盟。

显然，跨境法律影响的问题非常复杂。大体上来讲，对我们有几个方面的启示。第一，外国关于具体问题的法律可能与我们本国的法律有很大不同。第二，对外国的法律体系有一个基本的了解很重要。第三，仔细研究东道国的外国投资法十分必要。

Chapter 32
Conflict of Laws

Globalisation makes us painfully aware of the limitations of our instruments to meet its challenges.

——Anna Lindh

In Chapter 31, we looked at cross-border legal complications. In this chapter, we consider a specific subject, within these complications, called private international law (which stands in contrast to public international law, which is about the law between nations). It is also known as conflict of laws. As the latter name suggests, where the two (or more) transacting persons or entities are from different countries, there is a problem if the two (or more) laws may apply but they are in conflict. For example, a transaction between the two persons, A and B (each from a different country), may be legal in A's country but illegal in B's country. Which law prevails?

As you may suspect, private international law is a very complex subject. In this chapter, only a brief overview is given. It should be noted that different

第 32 章 冲突法

全球化让我们痛苦地意识到我们试图应对其挑战的工具的局限性。

——安娜·林德

在第 31 章中，我们考察了跨境法律的复杂性。在本章，我们将考虑在这些复杂问题中的一个具体法律部门——国际私法（与国际公法相对，后者是关于国与国间的法律），也被称为冲突法。正如后一个名称所表明的，当两个（或多个）交易方来自不同国家时，就会有两部（或多部）法律可能适用，但要是它们之间相冲突，就会造成一种困境。例如，A 和 B 分别来自不同的国家，他们之间的交易，在 A 的国家可能是合法的，但在 B 的国家却是非法的。这种情况下，哪国的法律优先？

正如你可能猜到的那样，国际私法是一个非常繁复的法律部门。在本章中，我只做一个简单的概述。应该注意的是，不

countries may have their own view or version of private international law. Broadly speaking, the private international law of countries in the common law world is largely similar, and the same may be said of those in civil law countries.

The key legal issues, here, of private international law are:

- jurisdiction;
- applicable law; and
- enforcement of judgments.

Let us discuss the issues by considering a simple scenario where A, a Singaporean, and B, a Chinese (from the People's Republic of China) decide to enter into a joint venture to start a business in Indonesia. In the event there is a dispute between A and B, the preliminary issue is: Where can the lawsuit be brought? The choices are Singapore, China and another country. But when will a court hear a case? When will it have jurisdiction?

The common grounds on which courts exercise jurisdiction are:

- the transaction took place in that country;
- the defendant is resident there; and
- the parties "submitted" or voluntarily agreed to be subject to the jurisdiction of the court.

For practical purposes, submission is the most important basis of jurisdiction. Submission takes two forms: actual submission (by appearing in court at the start of the lawsuit) and agreement to submit via a jurisdiction clause.

同的国家可能对国际私法有自己的看法或版本。广义上讲，各个英美法系国家的国际私法基本相似，不同大陆法系国家的国际私法也可以说是如此。

国际私法的关键法律问题有：

- 管辖权；
- 准据法；以及
- 判决的执行。

让我们通过一个简单的场景来讨论这些问题：新加坡人 A 和中国人 B 决定成立一家合资企业，在印度尼西亚创业。如果 A 和 B 之间发生了纠纷，初步的问题是：各方可以在哪里提起诉讼？选择分别是新加坡、中国或其他国家。但法庭在什么情况下会受理一宗案件？换句话说，一个法庭什么时候会有管辖权？

法庭行使管辖权的常见理由是：

- 交易发生在该国；
- 被告是该国居民；以及
- 当事人“服从”或自愿同意接受该法庭的管辖。

从实际操作来讲，服从是管辖权的最重要基础。服从有两种形式：实际服从（在诉讼开始时表示出庭）和通过双方合同约定的管辖条款表示服从。

在有外国元素的合同中，通常会发现一类条款，即当事人

In contracts with foreign elements, it is common to find a clause whereby the parties agree to submit to the jurisdiction of particular courts. So, in our joint venture example from before, it could be that there is a clause saying: "The parties hereby submit to the non-exclusive jurisdiction of the courts of the People's Republic of China and of Singapore respectively."

In such a case, both the Chinese and Singapore courts have power to hear the case. There can also be an "exclusive" choice of one country's court instead. Of course, that is a matter of negotiating power.

Even where a court has jurisdiction, there is a further matter — it is possible that the court may decline to exercise jurisdiction. The court may be of the view that there is another court which is more appropriate to hear the case. In the common law world, the objection is a Latin phrase *forum non conveniens*, literally, inconvenient forum. The label "*conveniens*" is misleading as the concern is to find the appropriate or natural forum for the lawsuit. Convenience is but one of the many aspects in determining appropriateness.

An example of inappropriateness, in relation to *forum non conveniens*, is the fact that there is a pending lawsuit between the parties over the same subject matter in another jurisdiction (the legal term is *lis alibi pendens*). Another factor for a court declining jurisdiction is that there is a foreign jurisdiction clause, namely that the parties had in their contract expressly chosen to submit to the courts of another country. The argument has even greater force where the clause involves an exclusive choice.

The second area of conflict is, which law or laws apply to the transaction. Generally, in many countries, the parties are allowed to choose the law to apply to their transactions. For example, there may be a clause stating: "This contract

同意服从特定某国法院的管辖权。因此，在我们之前的合资企业例子中，可能会有一个条款表明："双方在此接受中华人民共和国和新加坡法院的非专属管辖权。"

在这种情况下，中国和新加坡的法院都有权审理此案。合同方也可以选择约定一个国家的法院有"专属"管辖权。当然，这是一个谈判能力的问题。

即使一个法院有管辖权，还有另一个问题——法院有可能拒绝行使管辖权。法院可能认为，有另一个法院更适合审理该案件。在普通法世界中，有一个拉丁短语 *forum non conveniens* 来表达法院拒绝管辖的理由，字面意思是"不方便的法院"。"方便"这个标签有误导性，因为我们关注的是，为诉讼找到合适或合乎案件常理的法院。方便性只是确定适当性的众多方面之一。

比如，以"不方便法院"为名，实际是不适合管辖的一个例子是，当事人之间在另一个司法管辖区就同一争议有一个未决的诉讼（法律术语是 *Lis alibi pendens*）。法院拒绝管辖权的另一个因素是有外国管辖权条款，即当事人在其合同中明确选择服从另一个国家的法院。在该条款涉及排他性选择的情况下，这一拒绝理由就更有说服力。

冲突的第二个方面是，哪种或哪几种法律适用于交易。一般来说，在很多国家，当事人被允许选择适用于其交易的法律。例如，可能有一条条款规定"本合同应受印度尼西亚共和国法律的管辖"。同样，选择哪个国家的法律作为准据法是一个议价能力的问题。这听起来很奇怪，但合同当事人可以选择他们愿意接受管辖的那个法院所在国的法律之外的法律。

shall be governed by the laws of the Republic of Indonesia". Again, it is a matter of bargaining power which country's laws would be chosen. This may sound odd, but contracting parties can choose a law other that of the court (s) which they have chosen to submit to.

In the absence of an express choice, the court may imply a choice. For example, the language in which the contract is expressed may lead a court to read in such an implied choice. Alternatively, the court may impute a choice and find a certain country has the "most real and substantial connection" with the parties and the dispute. Through the process of ascertaining a choice, the court would arrive at the "proper law" of the contract.

There is a further complication. Apart from the proper law, it is possible that other laws apply (together with the proper law). For example, a contracting party's capacity to contract is determined by the *lex domicili* (law of the country of domicile or permanent home) and the validity of a contract is affected by the *lex loci contractus* (law of the place where the transaction was entered into). In short, the proper law as well as other applicable laws will govern the transaction.

The third area of conflict is, assuming the plaintiff obtains a judgment from a foreign country against the defendant, whether he will be able to enforce it in another country. In our joint venture example, if A obtains a judgment in Singapore against B, will A be able to enforce the judgment in China where, let us assume, B's primary assets are? Or does he have to commence a fresh lawsuit in China?

For countries in the British Commonwealth, enforcement is relatively easy as many of these countries have arrangements for the reciprocal enforcement of each other's judgments — a judgment from one Commonwealth country can be

在没有明确选择的情况下，法院可以认定一个合同双方的默示选择。例如，合同所表达的语言可能会导致法院读出这样一个隐含的选择。或者，法院可以通过发现某个国家与当事人及争端有“最真实和最重要的联系”来推定这样一种选择。通过确认这种选择的过程，法院将得出合同适用的“适当法律”。

还有一个更复杂的问题。除了适当法律之外，还有其他法律（与适当法律一起）可能适用。例如，签约方的签约能力是由住所地法（住所或永久居所所在国的法律）决定的，而合同的有效性则受合同地法（交易发生地的法律）影响。简而言之，适当法律以及其他适用的法律都将管辖相关交易。

第三个冲突法的领域是，假设原告从外国获得了针对被告的判决，能否在另一个国家执行该判决。在我们先前合资企业的例子中，假若 A 在新加坡获得了针对 B 的判决，A 的问题是能够在中国（我们假设 B 的主要资产在中国）执行该判决吗？还是说 A 必须在中国开启新的诉讼程序？

对于英联邦国家之间，执行是相对容易的，因为这些国家都有相互执行对方判决的约定，也就是说，一个英联邦国家的判决可以在另一个国家“登记”并执行。2005 年《海牙法院选择协议公约》提供了一个更普遍的制度（该公约涉及管辖权以及判决的执行）。然而，目前已经签署和批准该公约的国家数量不多。

面对没有互惠执行安排的情况，执行外国判决是一个难题。一个替代办法是双方通过合同同意仲裁并寻求执行仲裁裁决。世界上绝大多数国家（包括中国）都签署并批准了 1958

"registered" and enforced in another country. A more general regime is provided by the 2005 Hague Convention on Choice of Court Agreements (which deals with jurisdiction as well as enforcement of judgments) . However, the number of countries which have signed and ratified the Convention remains small.

Where there are no reciprocal enforcement arrangements, the enforcement of a foreign judgment is a difficult matter. An alternative would be to agree to arbitration and to seek to enforce an arbitral award. The great majority of countries in the world (including China) are signatories to and have ratified the 1958 New York Convention, which facilitates the enforcement of arbitral awards. Hence, practically, the arbitration option is an important one where reciprocal enforcement of foreign judgments is not available.

The discussion so far has focused on private international law as it affects commerce. It should be noted that similar difficult issues can also arise in relation to matters of marriage and parenthood. In a cross-border situation, there are questions such as when a foreign marriage or divorce is recognised and which country's law decides the rightful custody of a child from that union.

Clearly, the issues in private international law are complex. In cross- border dealings, ideally, to assure oneself on these issues, it is necessary to obtain foreign legal opinions from all the relevant jurisdictions. Of course, that may be costly and time consuming.

年的《纽约公约》，该公约为仲裁裁决的跨国执行提供了便利。所以说，在无法对等执行外国判决的情况下，仲裁是一个重要的选项。

到目前为止，我们讨论的重点是国际私法，因为它影响到商业金融。但是值得指出的是，类似的困难也可能出现在婚姻和亲子关系的问题上。在跨国界的情况下，存在诸如外国婚姻或离婚何时被承认，以及哪个国家的法律决定该婚姻中孩子的合法监护权等问题。

显然，国际私法中的问题很复杂。在进行跨境交易时，理想情况下，一方有必要从所有相关的司法管辖区获得外国法律意见，以保证其在这些问题上的周全。当然，这多半会需要大量的时间并产生昂贵的费用。

PART V
Error and Unfairness

The greatest mistake is to imagine that we never err.

——Thomas Carlyle

第五部分

错误与不公

想象我们从不犯错才是最大的错误。

——托马斯·卡莱尔

Laypersons generally have two complaints against the law. The first is that law is too complicated and complex and cannot be understood.

We have considered these matters in the preceding part.

The second is that law is either wrong or unfair. The two are often but not always related. The assertion that the law is wrong could suggest that either the current law is wrong or the judge's perception of the law is wrong. Naturally, the above errors would lead to unfairness or injustice. But there are other contributors to unfairness, or the perception of unfairness (see Fig. 4). They include:

- the challenge of polarity — the ability to discern if the situation at hand is binary or ranged (Chapter 33);
- inclusiveness — the difficulty of precise circumferencing, and avoiding under-inclusion and over-inclusion (Chapter 34);
- presumptions — how the law sometimes uses presumptions in respect of the elements of a legal principle (Chapter 35);
- the challenge of causality — the difficulty of determining the actual cause of a particular injury (Chapter 36) and, where there are several causes, the correct apportionment of liability amongst the causes (Chapter 37);
- grey areas — unfairness simply because the situation is really borderline or grey, and the law or the judge is faced with two options, both of which are not entirely satisfactory (Chapter 38);
- justice or law — that, for a particular dispute before a court, there is a

非专业人士对法律通常在两方面有所抱怨。一是认为法律过于复杂，无法理解。

我们在前面的部分已经考虑了这些问题。

二是认为法律要么是错误的，要么是不公平的。这两者经常但并不总是相关的。说法律错误，可能指要么现行法律错误，要么法官对法律的认知错误。自然地，上述错误会导致不公平或不公正。但是其他因素也会导致不公平或令人产生不公平的感觉（见图 4）。它们包括：

- 两极化问题——辨别面对的情况是二元化的还是区间化的能力（第 33 章）；
- 囊括性——精确圈定范围时面临的困难，以及避免囊括不足和过度囊括性（第 34 章）；
- 推定——法律时而采用的对法律要素的推定方式（第 35 章）；
- 因果关系的难题——确定某一特定伤害的实际原因时遇到的困难（第 36 章），以及在有多个原因时，如何在各个原因之间正确分配责任（第 37 章）；
- 灰色地带——不公平仅仅是因为情况确实处于边缘或灰色地带，法律或法官面临两种选择，而无论哪种选择都不完全令人满意（第 38 章）；
- 正义还是法律——法院审理特定纠纷时，存在一个法官

fundamental question of whether the judge's role is to administer justice or to administer the law. A judge who focuses on the former would be inclined to interpret, bend or change the law whereas a more conservative judge would apply the law, even if the outcome is not so just (Chapter 39); and

- hindsight reasoning — as with other disciplines and areas of life, the law sometimes fall prey to hindsight reasoning (Chapter 40).

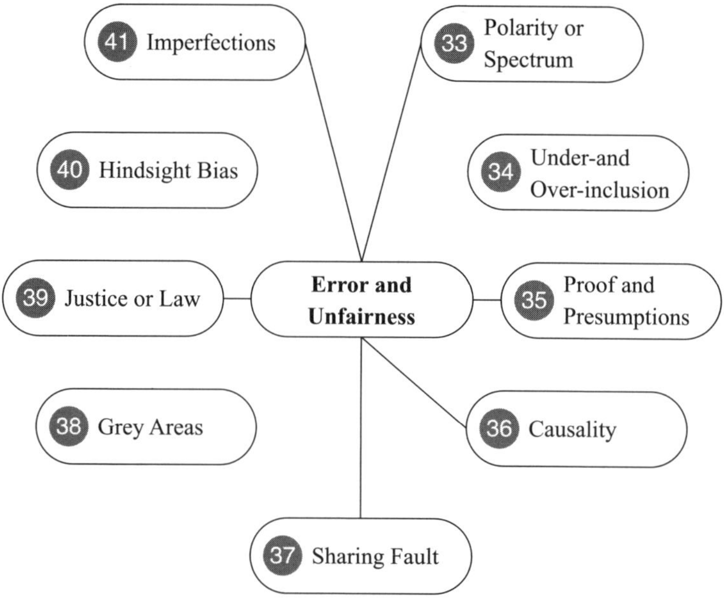

Fig. 4: Error and Unfairness
(numbers indicate the chapters in which the topic is covered)

Finally, as one seeks to understand why laws are often imperfect and sometimes unjust, it needs to be acknowledged that in the imperfect world, lawmakers are imperfect and sometimes do make mistakes (Chapter 41).

的角色究竟是实现正义还是执行法律的基本问题，注重前者的法官会倾向于解释、扭曲或改变法律，而更保守的法官则会严格适用法律，即便结果不那么公正（第39章）；以及

- 事后推理——与其他学科和生活领域一样，法律有时会成为事后推理的牺牲品（第40章）。

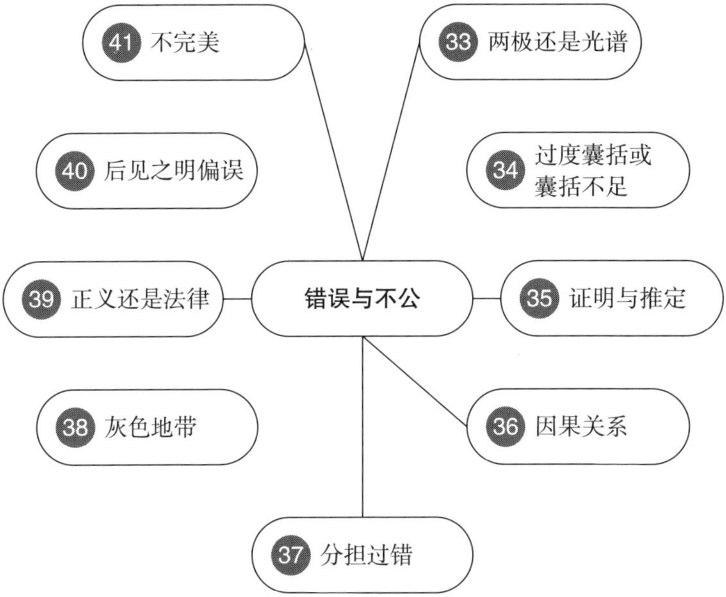

图4：错误和不公平
（数字代表讨论相关课题的章节号）

最后，当人们试图理解为什么法律常常是不完美的，并有时是不公正的时候，需要承认在一个不完美的世界里，立法者也注定是不完美的，有时确实会犯错误（第41章）。

Chapter 33
Polarity or Spectrum

Instead of two opposed polarities, there is a continuous spectrum.

——Ian Stewart

In seeking to understand the myriad things in this complex universe, we try to simplify. A good way to simplify is to categorise or classify.

For example, the world of nature can be placed into three broad categories: animals, plants and minerals. Each of these may be described as a kingdom. The animal kingdom can be classified into birds, fish, mammals, reptiles and insects. And each of these can, in turn, be further subcategorised.

In fact, the compendious varieties pose great challenges for the observer; grouping can be a complicated matter. Biological classification, for example, has no less than seven levels of hierarchy: kingdoms, phylum, classes, orders, families, genus and species. That's mind-boggling.

One approach in categorisation is polarisation. Something is either this or that, such as hot or cold, light or darkness, and, in this social media world, like

第33章
两极还是光谱

我们有一个连贯的光谱，而不是对立的两极。

——伊恩·斯图尔特

在寻求理解这个复杂的宇宙中的无数事物时，我们总是试图进行简化。分类或归类是简化的一个好方法。

例如，自然界可以被分为三大类：动物、植物和矿物。其中每一类都可以被描述为一个王国。动物王国可分为鸟类、鱼类、哺乳动物、爬行动物和昆虫。而其中每一种又可以进一步细分。

事实上，繁多的品种给观察者带来了巨大的挑战；分组可能是一个复杂的问题。例如，生物分类有不少于七个层次：界、门、纲、目、科、属和种。这有点令人头晕目眩。

分类的一个方法是二分化。一些东西要么是这样，要么是那样，像热或冷，光或暗，以及在这个社交媒体世界里，喜欢或不喜欢（大拇指向上或向下）。这两个类别被视为或描绘成

or dislike (thumbs up or thumbs down). The two categories are seen or portrayed as poles or opposites. Sometimes the difference is not so stark; the two are seen as distinct or discrete categories.

To be sure, polarity has its place. It is useful to know if a substance is a metal or a non-metal. A metal is a good conductor of heat and of electricity, whereas a non-metal is a bad conductor of both. So, if your purpose requires the conduction of heat or electricity, use a metallic appliance. To avoid getting burnt or electrocuted, use an appliance made of non-metal. Binary categorisation can be useful, such as whether a chemical is acidic or alkaline, whether a reaction is biological or chemical, or, in job compatibility, whether a person is an introvert or an extrovert.

But binary categorisation is unsuitable where the situation at hand or the subject being examined is not naturally amenable to polar division. In many scenarios, there is a middle category in between the poles. An object may be grey rather than black or white, a drink may be lukewarm rather than hot or cold, and someone may be neutral or ambivalent rather than having an inclination one way or the other. Even in the metals example, above, scientists have introduced an intermediate category called metalloids (which are weak conductors of heat and electricity).

Another problem is where the item being scrutinised has attributes belonging to both categories. For example, birds fly while fish swim, but what do we do with fish that can fly? (One might ask further: What is the meaning of "fly"? Do such fish glide rather than fly?) As a matter of fact, there are 64 species of flying fish under the family of *exocoetidae*. (Furthermore, some birds can swim!)

In such situations, a forced binary categorisation would result in an incorrect

两极或对立。有时，区别并不那么明显；两者就被视为不同的或不相关的类别。

可以肯定的是，二分化有它的作用。知道一种物质是金属还是非金属是很有用的。金属是热和电的良好导体，而非金属是两者的不良导体。因此，如果你的目的是需要传导热或电，请使用金属器具。为了避免被烧伤或触电，则使用非金属制成的电器。二元分类法可能是有用的，例如，一种化学品是酸性还是碱性，一种反应是生物反应还是化学反应，或者在工作兼容性方面，一个人是内向还是外向。

但是，当手头的情况或所研究的主题不能自然地进行两极划分时，二元分类法就不适合了。在许多情况下，在两极之间存在着一个中间类别。一个物体可能是灰色的，而不是黑色或白色的；一种饮料可能是温的，而不是热的或冷的；一个人可能是中性的或矛盾的，而不是有一种倾向性的。即使在上面的金属例子中，科学家们也引入了一个中间类别，称为类金属（它们是热和电的弱导体）。

另一个问题是，被考察的物品有属于两个类别的属性。例如，鸟会飞而鱼会游，但我们该如何处理会飞的鱼呢？（人们甚至可能会进一步发问："飞"的含义是什么？这种鱼是滑翔而不是飞行吗？）事实上，外海鱼科下有 64 种飞鱼。（而且，有些鸟类也会游泳！）

在这种情况下，强行的二元分类会导致对当前问题的不正确描述或理解。这将是一个错误的二分法。不正确地选择二元分类而不是范围分类会导致困惑和不公正。（但两极可能比区间更容易处理。）

portrayal or understanding of the matter at hand. A false dichotomy. Incorrectly choosing a binary rather than a ranged categorisation results in perplexity and injustice. (But polarity may be easier to deal with than spectrum.)

For example, as regards a crime or a tort, the law may require the mental element of knowledge, such as: Did the accused know that the parcel he was carrying contained prohibited drugs? As we have seen in Chapter 12, there is a spectrum of fault. In such a case, rather than taking a binary approach of knowledge and no knowledge, the law has to identify carefully the ranges of culpable knowledge and to calibrate the penal consequences to the seriousness of the wrongful act.

To take another example, in the law of contract, a fundamental tenet is the freedom of contract. Basically, the general position is that a clause in a contract is binding since the parties had freely agreed to it. If a binary approach is taken, only two possibilities are entertained — that a party freely agreed, in which case the clause in question binds him, or he did not freely agree, in which case he is not bound by it.

But, in the real world, there is only a small percentage of transactions where both parties freely agree to all the clauses, in the sense that they knew and understood all the clauses and their implications, and had enough bargaining power to protect themselves, along with the option of walking away if necessary. In the great majority of cases, the freedom is partial, minimal or even illusory. For instance, telecos which dominate the industry may offer almost the same standard terms and conditions to which consumers have no power to refuse. So, in such situations, it is facile to resolve the issue on a simplistic argument of freedom of contract.

例如，关于犯罪或侵权行为，法律可能要求具备知情的心理要素，如：被告是否知道他携带的包裹里有违禁药物？正如我们在第 12 章中所看到的，有一个过错程度的轴。在这种情况下，法律不是采取知道和不知道的二元方法，而是要仔细确定应受处罚的知情程度的范围，并根据不法行为的严重程度来调整刑事后果。

再举个例子，在合同法中，其中一条基本原则是合同自由。基本上，一般的立场是，合同中的条款是有约束力的，因为各方都是自由同意的。如果采取二选一的方法，只有两种可能性——一方当事人自由同意，在这种情况下，有关条款对他有约束力；或者他没有自由同意，在这种情况下，他不受其约束。

但是，在现实世界中，只有一小部分交易是双方自由同意所有条款的，即他们知道并理解所有条款及其影响，并有足够的议价能力来保护自己，以及在必要时选择离开。在绝大多数情况下，这种自由是部分的、最小的甚至是虚幻不存在的。例如，主导行业的电信公司可能提供几乎相同的标准条款和条件，消费者没有权利拒绝。因此，在这种情况下，用简单的合同自由论来解决这个问题便过于轻率了。

幸运的是，法律经常对这一点有所认识。例如，在免责条款方面，法律将可执行性置于对公平和合理性的考虑。在非竞争条款（贸易限制条款）和违约金条款方面也有类似的态度。

不幸的是，有时法律并不那么干预主义，而是满足于在合同自由的口号下不作为。例如，在租赁协议中，常见的是承租条件和违约事件条款，其综合起来的效果是使房东有权在可能不公正的情况下驱逐其租户。

Fortunately, the law often recognises this. For example, in the area of exemption clauses, the law subjects the enforceability to considerations of fairness and reasonableness. A similar attitude is seen with regard to non-compete clauses (restraint of trade clauses) and liquidated damages clauses.

Unfortunately, sometimes the law is less interventionist and is content to take refuge under the mantra of freedom of contract. For example, in tenancy agreements, it is common to find covenants and event of default clauses, the combined effect of which entitles the landlord to evict his tenant in circumstances which may be unjust.

For instance, a "covenant" (or undertaking) in the tenancy agreement may prohibit a tenant bringing pets onto the premises while an "event of default" clause may give the landlord the right to terminate the tenancy for any breach of the covenant. As such, a tenant may be evicted simply for the reason that he allowed a stray cat to stay on his premises. In many countries, the courts would countenance the landlord's action, and the declared justification is freedom of contract.

The problem is also seen in the law relating to an occupier's liability to visitors of his premises. A common categorisation is to divide the entrants into lawful entrants and unlawful entrants, with lawful entrants having substantial protection against harm and unlawful entrants having little or no protection. But it is simplistic to use such binary classification. Unlawful entrants, that is those who enter without permission, cover a whole range of persons, with greatly differing culpability and/or deservedness. The long list, in descending order of innocence, includes:

例如，租赁协议中的“承租条件”（或承诺）可能禁止租户将宠物带入房内，而“违约事件”条款可能赋予房东在违反契约的情况下终止租赁的权利。因此，一个租户可能仅仅因为允许一只流浪猫留在他的房子里而被驱逐。在许多国家，法院会支持房东的行为，并宣布这是出于合同自由。

这个问题也出现在与土地占有者对其访客的责任有关的法律中。一个常见的分类是将进入者分为合法进入者和非法进入者，合法进入者受到很大的保护，不受伤害，而非法进入者则很少受保护或完全不受保护。但是，使用这种二元分类法是很简单的。非法进入者，也就是那些未经许可进入的人，涵盖了一系列的人，他们的可归责性或应受惩罚的程度大不相同。在这个长长的名单中，按可归责性从低到高排列，包括：

- 好心人；
- 取回物品的邻居；
- 走捷径的人；
- 聚会活动的闯入者；
- 窃贼；以及
- 刺客。

以同样的方式对待所有上述人员可能会导致对一些人保护不足而对另一些人保护过度，就像统计学中存在第一类错误（拒绝本应接受的结果）和第二类错误（接受本应拒绝的结果）。这个问题将在下一章详述。

对合法进入者和非法进入者的二元分类，使法律无法公平

- a good Samaritan;
- a neighbour retrieving an item;
- a short-cut taker;
- an event gatecrasher;
- a burglar; and
- an assassin.

To treat all the above persons the same way is likely to result in under-protecting some while overprotecting others, much like how in statistics there are Type 1 errors (rejecting what should have been accepted) and Type 2 errors (accepting what should have been rejected). This subject is elaborated upon in the next chapter.

A binary classification of lawful and unlawful entrants would not lead to a fair and nuanced treatment of rights and liabilities of visitors who are injured whilst on the occupier's premises.

Hence, it is important for the law, as it seeks to categorise persons and situations in order to lay down legal principles and provide for rights and liabilities, to be sensitive to the scenario. In some situations, a binary categorisation is appropriate; in others a spectrum of categories, along with its differentiated legal consequences, is needful. And in the spectrum scenario, there is the further challenge of deciding how many categories there should be and how the law can, especially from a practical perspective, tailor itself to so many categories. It is not surprising that the law tends towards simplicity.

In summary, where the law falters in not correctly recognising whether a binary or ranged approach should be adopted, error and injustice will occur.

和细微地处理在土地占有者处所内受伤的访客的权利和责任。

因此，当法律试图对人和情况进行分类以制定法律原则并规定权利和责任时，我们必须对这种情况保持敏感和警惕。在某些情况下，二元分类是合适的；而在其他情况下，则需要有一系列的分类，以及不同的法律后果。然而，在光谱式渐变的情况下，还有一个挑战，即决定应该有多少个类别，以及法律如何适应这么多类别（特别是从实践的角度）。如此一来，法律趋向于简单化也就不足为奇了。

总之，如果法律没有正确认识到应该采用二元法还是光谱法，就会出现错误和不公正。

Chapter 34
Under-inclusion, Over-inclusion

To look for precision in each class of thing so far as its nature admits.

——Aristotle

As the law goes about its task of regulating conduct in society and in business, it imposes legal liability and accords rights. In so proscribing and prescribing, there is always the challenge of precise and appropriate circumferencing. Quite simply — who are the persons who should be affected by the law in question?

If the boundaries are drawn too narrowly, there may be under- inclusion. There will be persons who should be covered by the law but are not. Conversely, if the boundaries are drawn too broadly, they may be over–inclusion; there will be persons who should not be affected but they are. Again, the challenge of dealing with Type 1 errors and Type 2 errors.

To illustrate, let us look at an area of company law — the control of abuse

第 34 章
过度囊括与囊括不足

其性质所允许的范围内，对每一类事物都力求精确。

——亚里士多德

当法律执行其规范社会和商业行为的任务时，它规定了法律责任并赋予了权利。这样的禁止和规范总是存在着如何精确和适当地确定范围这一挑战。简单来说，谁应该受相关法律的影响?

如果界限划得太窄，可能会出现囊括不足的情况。有些人本应受到法律的保护却没有。相反，如果界限划得太宽，则可能会出现过度囊括的情况；有些人本不应该受影响却受到了影响。这又是处理第一类错误和第二类错误的挑战。

为了说明这一点，让我们看一下公司法的一处规定——对公司董事滥用权力的控制。更具体地说，我们将考虑向公司董事贷款的问题。这方面的总体理念或政策是，一般来说，禁止

of power by directors of a company. More specifically, we shall consider the issue of loans to the directors of a company. The overall philosophy or policy on this is that, in general, a company is prohibited from giving a loan (or provide some other credit facility, such as giving a guarantee in support of a loan) to its director. The thinking is that if the director is creditworthy, he should be able to get a loan from elsewhere; if he is not creditworthy, neither should the company lend to him.

So, it is common that a country's company law makes provision to prohibit loans to directors (and other "related party" corporate transactions) . Such a provision goes further to extend to loans to persons close to the director and typically says that "reference to a director includes reference to his spouse, son, adopted son, step-son, daughter, adopted daughter and step-daughter" (Section 162 (8), Singapore Companies Act) .

As one reads this, several thoughts surface. First, the provision covers the spouse and the children. What about other close family members such as parents and siblings? Should not a loan to the director's parent or sibling also be prohibited? Is not the provision under-inclusive? And what about the close friends of a director?

Let us leave these questions in abeyance for a moment as we consider further the control of director abuse. Well aware that the director may attempt to sidestep the legislation by arranging for the loan (or other facility) to be made to a company instead of an individual, company law goes further and prohibits loans to director-related companies (see, for example, Section 163 of the Singapore Companies Act) .

Such a provision might say that Company A may not give a loan (or other

公司向其董事提供贷款（或提供一些其他信贷服务，如为贷款提供担保）。理由是，如果董事有足够信用，他应该能够从其他渠道获得贷款；如果他没有足够信用，公司也不应该向他贷款。

因此，一个国家的公司法通常禁止公司向董事贷款（以及其他与“关联方”进行的交易）。这种规定进一步扩大到向与董事关系密切的人提供贷款，并且通常说“提到董事，包括他的配偶、儿子、养子、继子、女儿、养女和继女”[新加坡《公司法》第162（8）条]。

当人们读到这一点时，有几个想法会浮现出来。首先，该条款涵盖了配偶和子女。那么，其他近亲属，如父母和兄弟姐妹呢？难道不应该禁止向董事的父母或兄弟姐妹贷款吗？这条规定是不是包容性不足？那么董事的亲密朋友呢？

让我们暂时搁置这些问题，因为我们要进一步考虑控制董事滥用职权的问题。意识到董事可能试图通过安排向公司而不是个人提供贷款（或其他融资）来规避法律的限制，公司法更进一步禁止向与董事有关的公司提供贷款（如新加坡《公司法》第163条）。

这样的规定可能是，如果A公司的一名或多名董事在B公司拥有20%或更多的投票权，则A公司不得向B公司提供贷款（或其他融资），除非A公司的股东被告知并批准该贷款。然而，该条款也涵盖了“视为董事利益”这一概念。如果公司或其董事按照某人的意愿行事，该人将被视为在公司中拥有股权利益。因此，例如，如果X公司拥有B公司的股份，而X公司或其董事按照A公司董事P的意愿行事，那么X公司在

facility) to Company B if a director or directors of Company A are interested in 20% or more of the voting power of Company B, unless the shareholders of Company A are informed and they approve of the loan. However, the provision also covers the "deemed interests" of the directors. A person is treated as interested in the shares of a company if the company or its directors act in accordance with the wishes of that person. So, for example, if Company X has shares in Company B, and Company X or its directors act in accordance with P, a director in Company A, then Company X's interest in Company B are deemed to be the interests of P.

So, in practice, the ascertainment of whether a loan by Company A to Company B requires prior approval involves a complicated exercise of considering the total cumulative share interests, both direct and deemed, of all the directors of Company A.

Two observations may be made here. It is conceivable that since a company has many directors and these directors may have direct interests and also deemed interests, the prohibitory scheme may, in certain situations, be over-inclusive. Secondly, it may be observed that such an exercise of ascertaining if the threshold is triggered can be a very time consuming and complicated one. Both these comments are fair ones.

The challenge is to find a simpler solution which is also effective. The difficulty is inevitable where the factual network of connections of the corporate background is a complicated one and perfect classification is often illusive.

The challenge of drawing the precise ambit of a legal framework can be a difficult one. Often, the lawmaker ends up making a choice which will result in either over-inclusion or under-inclusion.

B 公司的利益就被视为 P 的利益。

因此，在实践中，确定 A 公司对 B 公司的贷款是否需要事先批准涉及一项复杂的工作，即考虑 A 公司所有董事直接拥有的和被视为拥有的股权总额。

在此，我们可以看到两点。第一，可以想象，由于一家公司有许多董事，这些董事可能有直接利益和被视为拥有的利益，在某些情况下，这条法律禁止规定可能会囊括过度。第二，我们可以看到，确定是否触发禁止条件可能是一项非常耗时和复杂的工作。这两点恐怕都并非言过其实。

我们面临的挑战是如何找到一个更简单且有效的解决方案。当公司内部人士的关系网络错综复杂的时候，这种困难不可避免，完美的分类往往不切实际。

划定一个法律框架的准确范围其实是极其困难的事。通常情况下，立法者最终不得不做一个选择，于是就会导致囊括不足或过度囊括的结果。

Chapter 35

Proof and Presumptions

When truth and reason cannot be heard then must presumption rule.

——Barbra Tuchman

It seems intuitive that a person who makes an assertion has to prove it. The law requires that whoever wishes to make a legal claim against another must prove his case. So, a prosecutor has to prove that the accused committed an offence, and a plaintiff has to show that the defendant infringed his legal rights.

As we have seen in the introduction to Part III, legal principles are comprised of elements. So, when a person makes an allegation against another (such as that a salesman had made a misrepresentation about a product), he has to substantiate his claim against that other and adduce evidence as regards each of the elements.

On occasion, the law utilises presumptions. Perceiving that a party to a claim requires or deserves some assistance, the law may provide that a particular element is to be presumed. This effectively shifts the burden to the defendant,

第 35 章
证明和推定

当真理和理智无法被听到时，就必须由推定说了算。

——巴巴拉·塔奇曼

所谓谁主张谁举证，这似乎是合乎直觉的事。法律规定，无论谁想对他人提出法律请求，都必须证明自己的案件。因此，检察官必须证明被告犯了罪，而原告则必须证明被告侵犯了他的合法权利。

正如我们在第三部分的介绍中所看到的，法律原则是由要件组成的。因此，当一个人对另一个人提出指控时（比如说一个销售员对产品做了虚假陈述），他必须证实他对另一个人的指控，并就每个要件举出证据。

有时，法律会利用推定。考虑到索赔的一方需要或应该得到一些帮助，法律可以规定对某一特定要素进行推定。这实际上是将责任转移到被告身上，被告必须举证反驳该要素。当然，

who has to disprove the element. Of course, this may seem unfair. Thankfully, the law seldom resorts to presumptions but when it does so, the dynamics are radically altered. Let us look at some examples from crime, tort and contract.

In criminal law, the challenge of controlling drug trafficking is a difficult one. The elements of the offence typically include possession, knowledge (that the article is a prohibited substance) and the intention to traffic (or sell) drugs. For example, at an airport terminal, a security officer detects, through the scanning device, a packet of drugs in a passenger's luggage. The passenger expresses surprise at its presence, and protests that he had no idea how the packet got there, and certainly no knowledge that the contents were prohibited drugs. Or, an accused who is in possession and with knowledge argues that the substance was for his own consumption (and so he is not guilty of trafficking). And the prosecutor may encounter serious obstacles if he has to prove these elements.

In some jurisdictions, these obstacles are surmounted by employing presumptions of possession, of knowledge and of trafficking. So, a person who is found or caught with a receptacle which contains proscribed drugs in excess of a certain quantity may face one or more of presumptions of possession, knowledge and trafficking. If so, he has the uphill task of disproving the allegation that he was trafficking drugs. So, be very careful before agreeing to help someone carry a bag or some other item at airports and similar places of vulnerability.

Under contract law, a binding contract requires the elements of agreement (offer and acceptance), consideration (giving value for a promise) and intention (to create legal relations). As regards intention, the law lays down two contrasting presumptions.

In social and domestic contexts, the law presumes that, in their dealings,

这或许看起来不公平。值得庆幸的是，法律很少采用推定的方式，但当它这样做时，举证的动态就会发生根本性的变化。让我们看一下犯罪、侵权和合同中的一些例子。

在刑法中，控制毒品贩运困难重重。该罪行的要件通常包括拥有、知晓（该物品是违禁物质）和贩运（或出售）毒品的意图。例如，在机场航站楼，一名安检人员通过扫描设备发现一名乘客的行李中有一包毒品。该乘客对毒品的存在表示惊讶，提出抗议称不知道这包毒品是怎么来的，当然也不知道里面的东西是违禁毒品。或者，一个拥有毒品并知情的被告争辩说，该违禁物质是供他自己吸食的（因此他没有犯贩运罪）。而检察官如果要证明这些要素，可能会遇到严重障碍。

在一些法域，这些障碍是通过采用占有、知情和贩运的推定来克服的。因此，一个人如果被发现或被抓到携带装有超过一定数量的违禁药物的容器，可能会面临法律对占有、知情和贩运这几项要件中一个或多个作出推定。倘若如此，他要反驳关于贩运毒品的指控将十分困难。因此，在机场和类似的容易发生问题的地方，同意帮助他人搬运包裹等物品之前，一定要非常小心谨慎。

根据合同法，一个有约束力的合同需要有合意（要约和承诺）、对价（为允诺提供价值）和意图（建立法律关系）等要件。关于意图，法律规定了两种截然不同的推定。

在社交和家庭背景下，法律推定，在这样的交易中，当事人并不打算建立法律关系。所承担的义务只是道德上的义务，不应受到起诉。因此，儿子如果想从他父亲那里索取允诺的对优秀学业成绩的奖励，就必须向法院证明这对父子有意在他们

the parties did not intend to create legal relations. The obligations undertaken are only moral ones and are not to be sued upon. So, a son who wishes to claim a promised reward from his father for excellent academic results has to show to the court that the father and son had intended to create legal obligations between them.

Conversely, in commercial contexts, the law presumes that dealings and transactions are meant to be legally binding. If commercial parties wish not to create legal obligations, it is best that they give clear indications, such as by including a clause which reads: "This agreement is binding in honour only and is not intended to create legal relations" .

Finally, an example from tort law. A plaintiff who wishes to sue a defendant for negligence has to show the existence of a duty of care, a breach of that duty, causation and unremote damage. There is an interesting legal concept which goes by the Latin expression *res ipsa loquitur* — literally, the thing (or circumstance) speaks for itself. This includes situations where a passenger lift plunges or a plaintiff 's stationary car is rear-ended by the defendant's car.

Essentially, when the defendant is in control of the offending object and/or the circumstances, and the accident or harm-causing event would not ordinarily have occurred if there had been no negligence, the law puts the burden on the defendant to explain what happened. If he is unable to do so satisfactorily, he is liable. In effect, where *res ipsa loquitur* applies, the law is presuming a breach and also presuming that the breach caused the damage or injury.

The use of presumptions radically changes the dynamics of proof in legal allegations. In crafting law, the resort to presumptions should be done carefully.

之间建立相关的法律义务。

相反，在商业背景下，法律推定交易的目的是要具有法律约束力。如果商业当事人希望不产生法律义务，他们最好给出明确的指示，例如包括一个条款，内容为“本协议仅是君子协定，无意建立法律关系”。

最后，举一个侵权法的例子。原告如果想起诉被告过失侵权，必须证明存在注意义务、违反该义务、因果关系和有关联的损害。有一个有趣的法律概念，其拉丁语表达为 *res ipsa loquitur*——字面意思是事物（或情况）不言自明。这包括乘客电梯坠落或原告的静止的汽车被被告的汽车追尾的情况。

本质上，如果被告控制着造成损害的物体、环境，并且如果没有过失，事故或造成伤害的事件通常不会发生，法律将规定被告有责任解释发生了什么。如果他不能令人满意地做到这一点，就要承担责任。实际上，在适用“不言自明”规则的情况下，法律推定存在违反义务的行为，并推定这种行为导致了损害或伤害。

推定的使用从根本上改变了法律指控中的举证机制，因此，在制定法律时，应谨慎使用推定。

Chapter 36
The Challenge of Causality

> The law of causality is a relic of a bygone age, surviving, like the monarchy, only because it is erroneously supposed to do no harm.
>
> ——Bertrand Russell

The basic legal concept of causation is simple enough — a certain action leads to a certain result. For example, A spilt water on the floor and B slipped on the wet floor injuring himself. It appears that A's act of spilling a drink has caused B to fall and get injured. If we add to this scenario the fact that A's act was culpable, such as it was intentional or negligent, A should be held responsible and be made to compensate B.

The layman would expect that, in each claim, causation must be proven, and convincingly. Further, he would expect that the defendant should be made to pay only to the extent of his responsibility. The issue of legal causation may appear straightforward.

However, in reality, there are many situations where the matter is

第 36 章
因果关系问题

有关因果关系的法律是一个已经过去的时代的遗物，像君主制一样，得以幸存下来，只是因为人们错误地以为它不会带来伤害。

——伯特兰·罗素

因果关系的基本法律概念很简单——某一行为导致了某一结果。例如，A 将水洒在地板上，B 在潮湿的地板上滑倒受伤。至少从表面上来看，A 的洒水行为导致了 B 的摔倒和受伤。如果我们在这种情况下再加上 A 的行为是有过错的，比如是故意的或过失的，那么 A 就应该承担责任，对 B 进行赔偿。

外行人会认为，在每项索赔中，都必须证明因果关系，而且需要达到令人信服的程度。此外，外行人还会预料被告只在其责任范围内进行赔偿。法律上的因果关系问题可能看起来很直接明了。

然而，在现实中，这个问题在许多情况下又是具有挑战性

challenging and controversial. One is where there is difficulty of ascertaining what really happened, such as how a particular illness or medical condition results. Yet another is where there are several possible causes, as often occurs in real life, and it is difficult to ascertain which of the causes is instrumental or should properly be held responsible. Finally, the quantum or proportion which a defendant may be made to pay can be controversial, even unfair.

We begin with the general principle used to ascertain causation — the "but-for" test. If not for the defendant's conduct, would the injury (or damage) have occurred? If the answer is negative, then the defendant's conduct caused the injury. If the answer is positive, the defendant's conduct did not cause the injury.

A good illustration is found in the landmark case of *Barnett v. Chelsea & Kensington HA*. Barnett went to the hospital, complaining of vomiting. The duty officer did not attend to him but instead told the nurse to send him home. He died five hours later, of arsenic poisoning. The English court held that although the doctor was negligent in not attending to the patient, his negligence did not cause the patient's death since arsenic poisoning could not be diagnosed and treated within five hours. Hence, as a matter of law, there was no causation.

However, the but-for test can be too broad; almost anything can be a cause. Perhaps the doctor in the *Barnett* case did not attend to the patient because his superior called him into a meeting; in which his superior's decision could be a cause. And, in the water spillage example, it could be argued that A would not have spilled the drink if C had not given it to him in the first; in that case, C could also be a cause.

Also, as a matter of chronology, there may be causation using the but- for test. For example, using an illustration from *Rubenstein v. HSBC*, a mountaineer

和争议性的。一种情况是难以确定真正发生了什么，例如某种疾病或医疗状况是如何产生的。然而，另一种情况有几个可能的原因，就像现实生活中经常发生的那样，很难确定哪个原因产生了作用，因而应该适当地承担责任。最后，被告被要求赔偿的数量或比例可能产生争议，甚至出现不公平的结果。

我们从用于确定因果关系的一般原则开始——“若非”测试。若非被告的行为，伤害（或损害）是否已经发生？如果答案是否定的，那么被告的行为就造成了伤害。如果答案是肯定的，那么被告的行为并没有造成伤害。

Barnett v. Chelsea & Kensington HA 这一里程碑式的案件就是一个很好的例子。Barnett 到医院去，抱怨说他有呕吐症状。值班人员没有照顾他，而是让护士把他送回家。五小时后，他因砷中毒而死亡。英国法院认为，虽然医生没有对病人进行护理是一种疏忽，但他的疏忽并没有导致病人的死亡，因为砷中毒不可能在五小时内得到诊断和治疗。因此，从法律上来讲，因果关系不存在。

然而，“若非”测试也许过于宽泛；几乎任何东西都可以是一个原因。也许在 Barnett 案中，医生没有去照看病人是因为他的上司叫他去开会；在这种情况下，他上司的决定可能是一个原因。而且，在上文水洒到地上的例子中，可以说，如果 C 没有把水给 A，水就不会洒出来；在这种情况下，C 也可能是一个原因。

另外，使用“若非”检验标准还可能把时间先后视为因果关系。例如，在 *Rubenstein v. HSBC* 案中，一个登山者对自己的膝盖状况有疑问，在登山前向医生咨询（在第 14 章中讨

who has doubts about the condition of his knee consults a doctor before going for his climb (discussed in Chapter 14) . The doctor is negligent in his checking and wrongly certifies that his knee is fine. The mountaineer goes for a climb and, as a result of an avalanche (and not the condition of his knee), gets injured. In this situation, it would not be logical or fair to hold the doctor liable.

The law narrows the possibilities by ascertaining what is a proximate cause or what is the cause that is closely connected to the incident. (Another analysis is to ask what the defendant's scope of duty was; in the mountaineer's knee case, the condition of the mountain slope was not within the doctor's scope of duty.)

As mentioned earlier, there could be difficulties of finding out what really happened and who, amongst several persons, should be held responsible. Here, where the judges are inclined to allow the claim, such as where it is important to compensate the innocent victim, the difficulty of causality is overcome by using one of several concepts or devices, namely the concept of contribution, the reversing of the burden of proof and, even, dispensing with the need for causation.

In a case called *Bonnington Casting v. Wardlaw*, the House of Lords was faced with the difficulty of deciding whether the plaintiff 's illness was caused by avoidable dust particles (in which case the defendant is liable) or unavoidable dust particles (in which case the defendant is not liable) . To solve (or sidestep?) the problem, the court held that the avoidable dust materially contributed to the injury or illness (MCI) . As compared to causation, contribution is a weaker connection between an act and a consequence. But the court accepted contribution in place of causation.

In a subsequent case *McGhee v. National Coal Board*, there was another

论)。医生在检查中出现了疏忽，错误地证明了他的膝盖没有问题。这个登山者去登山，由于雪崩(而不是他的膝盖状况)而受伤。在这种情况下，让医生承担责任是不符合逻辑和公平原则的。

法律通过确定什么是近因，或者什么是与事件密切相关的原因，缩小了可能被当作损害原因的行为的数量。(另一种分析是询问被告的职责范围是什么；在登山者的膝盖案中，山坡的状况不在医生的职责范围内。)

如前所述，要找出真正发生了什么，以及在几个人中谁应该负责，可能会有困难。在这里，如果法官倾向于判决赔偿，例如对无辜的受害者进行赔偿是很重要的，那么因果关系的困难会借助某些概念或手段来克服，即“贡献”的概念、举证责任的倒置，乃至免除因果关系要件。

在 *Bonnington Casting v. Wardlaw* 案中，英国上议院面临着决定原告的疾病是由可避免的灰尘颗粒(在这种情况下，被告有责任)还是不可避免的灰尘颗粒(在这种情况下，被告没有责任)引起的这一难题。为了解决(或回避？)这个问题，法院认为，可避免的灰尘颗粒对伤害或疾病有重大“贡献”(MCI)。与因果关系相比，“贡献”是一种行为和后果之间较弱的联系。但法院接受了“贡献”理论，以取代因果关系。

在随后的 *McGhee v. National Coal Board* 案中，又出现了另一个问题。医学专家不知道有关疾病——皮炎——是如何引起的；因此，他们甚至不能说被告的过失对产生伤害有“贡献”。但这难不倒法官们，他们认为，被告对致害风险有重大“贡献”(MCRI)，因果关系由此得到满足。

problem. The medical experts did not know how the illness in question — dermatitis — was caused; hence, they could not even say that the defendant's negligent source contributed to harm. Undaunted, the court held that causation was satisfied on the basis that the defendant's source materially contributed to the risk of injury (MCRI).

As we take a step back, it is clear to see that contribution is not really the same as causation. Further, the threshold used is "material", which judges interpreted to meaning "not minimal". Hence, MCI and MCRI are really quite controversial ways of satisfying causation.

Even more controversial is the decision of *Summers v. Tice*, where the plaintiff was injured by two bullets but it could not be ascertained whether the bullets came from hunter A or hunter B (or both). The court overcame the problem by reversing the burden of proof; in other words, each of the two hunters had to prove his bullet did not hit the plaintiff, which they could not (at the time, it was not known that each barrel creates a distinctive pattern on the bullet that passes through it). Such reversal goes against the general rule of procedure that the plaintiff bears the burden of proving his case, including causation.

Further, in the case of *Chester v. Afshar*, the House of Lords held the defendant doctor liable for not disclosing a material risk of the surgery even though it was accepted that the patient would have gone on with the surgery anyway. In effect, the court dispensed with the need to show causation.

The controversies are not restricted to the issue of whether there should be liability; they extend to the quantum of liability. Logically, if the defendant contributed to the injury, he should pay a proportionate amount. In particular, if he contributed to the risk, he should pay only to the extent of his contribution

退一步看，就可以清楚地看到，“贡献”与因果关系其实并不一样。此外，成为“贡献”的门槛是“重大性”，而法官将其解释为“并非微不足道”。因此，对损害的重大“贡献”和对致害风险的重大“贡献”确实是饱受争议的确定因果关系的方式。

更有争议的是 *Summers v. Tice* 案的判决，原告被两颗子弹打伤，但无法确定子弹是来自猎人 A 还是猎人 B（或两者兼具）。法院通过颠倒举证责任来解决这个问题；换句话说，两个猎人都必须证明他的子弹没有击中原告，而他们却无法证明（在当时，人们并不知道每个枪管都会在穿过它的子弹上形成独特的图案）。这样的逆转违背了程序的一般规则，即原告有责任证明他的案件，包括因果关系。

此外，在 *Chester v. Afshar* 案中，上议院认为被告医生没有披露手术的重大风险，即使大家都认为病人无论如何都会继续手术，也要承担责任。实际上，法院免除了显示因果关系的需要。

争议并不局限于是否应该承担责任的问题；它们还延伸到了责任的量级。从逻辑上讲，如果被告促成了伤害，他应该赔偿相应的金额。特别是，如果他对风险有“贡献”，他应该只在其“贡献”的范围内赔偿，而不是被要求作出全部赔偿。然而，在这一领域，法院有一种倾向，即注重为值得赔偿的原告提供最大限度的赔偿。

例如，如果一个雇员在为三个连续的雇主工作后，得了一种疾病，但不清楚是谁造成的，法院倾向于说，每个雇主都要对全部伤害承担连带责任。这意味着他们集体负有责任，而个

and not be called to make full compensation. However, in this area, there is a tendency of the court to focus on maximising compensation for a deserving plaintiff.

For example, if after working for three successive employers, an employee comes down with an illness for which it is unclear who caused what, the courts tend to say that each is liable jointly and severally for the full injury. This means that collectively they are liable, and individually they are liable as well. The employer who pays has a right to claim from the other two employers, assuming they still exist and have the financial ability to pay.

From the foregoing, it is clear that causation can be a very controversial matter.

人也有责任。支付赔偿的雇主有权向另外两个雇主追偿，前提是他们仍然存在并且有支付能力。

从上述情况可以看出，因果关系也可能是一个非常有争议的问题。

comparative negligence in some countries) is often raised as a partial defence in a negligence suit. To the extent that the plaintiff's negligence contributed to the accident or the injury, his claim will be reduced. As a simple example, the defendant-motorist may have been negligent in speeding, but the plaintiff-pedestrian may have failed to keep a lookout. The application of contributory negligence would result in an appropriate reduction in the plaintiff's claim.

Likewise, in contract law, where there is a breach of contract, the law requires the innocent party to take reasonable steps to mitigate or reduce his losses. For example, in a breach of contract for the supply of materials, the plaintiff is required to seek alternative supplies as he tries to mitigate the losses which may flow from the breach.

But courts sometimes fail to spread the blame between the defendant and the plaintiff. A notable example is *Deutsche Bank v. Chang*. Chang, a brilliant scientist, lost a vast amount of money because he was drawn into a highly speculative product by a bank's officer. In a nutshell, Chang was initially a conservative investor with little knowledge of the product in question but within a short space of time became a lot more knowledgeable and risk-taking. Chang sued in both tort and contract.

The Singapore High Court awarded him damages to the tune of US$49 million, on the ground that the bank breached its duty of care to him. On appeal, the Court of Appeal reversed the decision and denied the US$49 million claim, holding instead that the shortfall of US$1.8 million in the account had to be paid by Chang. A key reason for the decision was that the court thought Chang was aware of the risks of his investment.

Of course, the case involved other legal arguments and technicalities,

的例子，被告机动车司机可能有超速的过失，但原告行人可能没有保持警惕。适用与有过失将导致原告索赔的适当减少。

同样，在合同法中，如果存在违约行为，法律要求无过错方采取合理的措施来减少自身损失。例如，在违反材料供应合同的情况下，原告被要求寻找替代供应，以试图减少违约造成的潜在损失。

但法庭有时未能在被告和原告之间分摊责任。一个值得注意的例子是 *Deutsche Bank v. Chang* 案。Chang 是一位杰出的科学家，因为被一家银行的高管吸引到一个高度投机的产品中而损失了大量的资金。简而言之，Chang 最初是一个保守的投资者，对有关产品知之甚少，但在很短的时间内，他的知识和风险承受能力大大增强。Chang 同时提起了侵权和违约之诉。

新加坡高等法庭判给他 4900 万美元的赔偿金，理由是银行违反了对他的注意义务。在上诉中，上诉法庭推翻了这一裁决，并驳回了 4900 万美元的索赔，还判定账户中 180 万美元的缺口必须由 Chang 支付。该判决的一个关键原因是，法院认为 Chang 明确知晓自己投资的风险。

当然，该案还涉及其他法律争议和技术问题，不便在此讨论。主要关注点是二元化的判决结果是否公平和适当。细究该案就会发现，Chang 一开始是一个无辜的投资者，后来成为一个知情的参与者。如果是这样，那么（高风险投资的）过错就应该是原告与被告双方共同的，应该适用与有过失。但现实却非如此，两个法庭截然相反的二元化判决结果使读者产生极大困惑。

Skandinaviska v. APB 案提供了另一个例证。该案涉及 APB

which are not appropriate for discussion here. The big picture concern is whether a binary outcome is the fair and appropriate one. A careful scrutiny of the case suggests that Chang started out as an innocent investor and became a knowing participant. If so, then the fault (for the risky investment) should be shared and contributory negligence should have been applied. Instead, the reader is left perplexed by the contrasting binary outcomes in the two courts.

Skandinaviska v. APB provides another illustration. The case involved an elaborate fraud carried out over several years by Chia, a finance manager of APB (the defendant), to personally avail himself of credit facilities from several banks (the plaintiffs) granted purportedly to APB. The banks suffered losses to the tune of S$29.5 million and claimed against APB, basing their claim on several grounds. The claim failed on all the grounds.

Dealing with the claim based on vicarious liability (see Chapter 25), the Court of Appeal noted that vicarious liability was a convenient loss distribution device to compensate an innocent victim. It explained that the imposition of such liability is not justified if the victim bears more fault than the defendant. Applying to the case at hand, the court noted that the banks were more at fault than APB for not detecting the fraud and hence denied the banks' claim.

The observer may ask: Is not the fault in this case shared by both APB and the banks? The banks were negligent for not taking better due diligence measures to ascertain the veracity of the account-opening and the transactions; but APB was also negligent for allowing this state of affairs to go undetected for several years.

If the court had applied contributory negligence and reduced APB's claim, then the loss would have been equitably shared. Further, such an outcome would

（被告）的财务经理 Chia 多年来精心策划的欺诈行为，他个人利用几家银行（原告）给予 APB 信贷资金。这些银行遭受了 2950 万新元的损失，并基于几个理由向 APB 提出索赔。该索赔最终被驳回，原告在所有的诉由上都败诉了。

在处理基于替代责任的索赔时（见第 25 章），新加坡上诉法庭指出，替代责任是一种方便的损失分配手段，用于赔偿无辜的受害者。法庭解释说，如果受害者比被告有更多的过错，那么施加这种责任是没有道理的。对于该案，法院指出，银行在没有发现欺诈行为方面的过错比 APB 更大，因此拒绝了银行的索赔。

观察者可能会问：难道该案的过错不是由 APB 和银行共同承担吗？银行没有采取更好的尽职调查措施来确定开户和交易的真实性具有过失；但 APB 允许这种状态在几年内没有被发现也有过失。

如果法院适用与有过失并减少 APB 的索赔，那么损失将被公平地分摊。此外，这样的结果会激励像 APB 这样的雇主在内部尽职调查中更加严密谨慎。

在有两个或多个被告的情况下，也会出现分摊责任的任务和挑战。一个常见的例子是，雇员在为几任雇主工作后感染了疾病，例如，一名员工在一段较长时间内在三个不同的公司工作时接触了化学尘埃，从而患了癌症。

这里有两个挑战。第一个是关于因果关系——哪个雇主的过失导致对了雇员的健康损害？因果关系问题我们已在第 36 章讨论。第二个是损害赔偿的数量或比例。如果我们假设三个雇主都促成了伤害，并且（可以说是）在法律上造成了伤害，

spur employers such as APB to be more cautious in their internal due diligence.

The task and challenge of apportioning liability also arises where there are two or more defendants. A common example is where an employee contracts an illness after having worked for successive employers, such as an employee who contracts cancer after having been exposed to chemical dust working for three different employers over a long period of time.

There are two challenges here. The first relates to causation — which employer's negligence caused the employee's injury? The causality problem is discussed in Chapter 36. The second is the quantum or proportion of damages. If we assume that all three employers contributed to and (hence, can be said to have) caused the injury, arguably they should be liable proportionately. However, the typical judicial approach is to make all three employers jointly liable. The motivation for imposing liability is maximising the claim of innocent employee.

The legal effect is that each employer is liable for the whole amount of compensation, leaving them to claim contribution from each other. If, for example, of the three employers A, B and C, only A has the financial ability to pay, then it ends up shouldering the full burden. From A's perspective, the outcome is unfair and the liability is grossly disproportionate.

Careful scrutiny is required where fault is shared between the defendant and the plaintiff, or between co-defendants. A failure to make appropriate allocations of fault will lead to injustice.

那么他们应该按比例承担赔偿责任。然而，典型的司法进路是让三个雇主共同承担责任。施加责任的动机是使无辜雇员的索赔最大化。

这样做的法律效果是，每个雇主都要对雇员承担全额赔偿责任，再让他们互相求偿。例如，如果在A、B和C三个雇主中，只有A有经济能力支付，那么他最终将承担全部责任。从A的角度来看，这个结果是不公平的，责任与过错也严重不相称。

在被告和原告之间或共同被告之间分担过错的情况下，需要进行仔细的审视。不对过错进行适当分配的话，就会导致不公正。

Chapter 38
Grey Areas

I've always been interested in the grey and that's where the complexity is.

——Robert Redford

A grey area is one which is unclear or ill-defined, or which does not readily conform to categories. It may also be a situation where there is no correct answer or solution, and no one is sure how to deal with it.

Ideally, law should be clear and predictable. There should be a precise and good answer to every legal question or issue. We wish the law to be black and white.

The reality is that law, like life or the world, is full of grey areas. There are a variety of ways in which grey areas exist. For ease of discussion, I shall classify them into three:

- there is incomplete or incorrect legal categorisation;

第38章
灰色地带

我一直对灰色的东西感兴趣，那正是复杂所在。

——罗伯特·雷德福

灰色地带是指不明确或定义不清的地方，或者不符合类别的地方。它也可能是一种没有正确答案或解决方案的情况，没有人确定如何处理。

理想的情况下，法律应该是清晰和可预测的。每一个法律问题或议题都应该有一个精确、满意的答案。我们希望法律是黑白分明的。

现实情况却是法律和生活或世界一样，充满了灰色地带。灰色地带的存在有多种方式。为便于讨论，我将它们分为三种：

- 法律分类不完整或不正确；
- 在法律立场方面存在相互冲突的法律渊源；以及
- 对于当前的挑战，确实不存在唯一最优解。

- there is conflicting authority as to the legal position; and
- there is really no one answer to the challenge at hand.

The law categorises in order to understand, manage and regulate. But the categorisation may be imperfectly done (arguably, classifications will never be perfect). For example, the law may have used a binary or polar classification when a spectrum or ranged analysis was the appropriate one (see Chapter 33). Social media platforms force us to like or dislike, whereas perhaps we are actually ambivalent about the matter. (Interestingly, Facebook has moved from a binary choice to a choice of no less than six emojis!)

Contract law, in some instances, asks if the parties are of equal or unequal bargaining power. The reality is that it is only in a very small percentage of cases that contracting parties can truly be said to have equal bargaining power. The truth is that in the great majority of cases, there is inequality of bargaining power; the question is only as to the degree. But the law takes the simple (and simplistic) binary approach (see Chapter 33) and, as a result, does not, and is not able to, calibrate the legal implications to the extent of inequality.

The second grey area is caused by conflicting authority for a particular proposition of law, and this happens quite often in the law. So, for example, where there are two English Court of Appeal decisions each taking an opposing side of the issue, the law can only be clarified if the Supreme Court comes along and resolves the conflict. It would surprise laymen how often there are conflicting authorities on questions of law.

The unsettledness on a particular legal issue can also arise because the leading authority is a majority decision but the judgment also contains a powerful

法律分类的目的是理解、管理和规范。但分类可能做得并不完美（或许可以说，分类永远不会完美）。例如，法律可能使用了二元化或极端化的分类，而光谱式或区间式分析才是合适的分类（见第 33 章）。社会媒体平台迫使我们喜欢或不喜欢，而实际上我们的真实感受也许并非泾渭分明。（有趣的是，脸书已经从二元选择转为提供不少于六个表情符号的选择！）。

在某些情况下，合同法会问双方的议价能力是否平等，而现实情况是，只有在极少数情况下可以说合同双方真正具有同等的议价能力。其实，在绝大多数情况下，双方议价能力都存在不平等；问题只是程度不同而已。但是，法律采取的是简单的（和简单化的）二元区分法（见第 33 章），因此，法官不会也不可能根据不平等的程度来调整法律影响。

第二个灰色地带是由某一法律观点的法律渊源冲突造成的，这种情况在法律中经常发生。举例来说，如果有两份英国上诉法院的判例，各自对某个法律问题持相反意见，那么只有当最高法院的判决出现并解决冲突时，法律才能得到澄清。在法律问题上经常出现相互冲突的判例，这一点可能会让外行人感到惊讶。

在某一法律问题上的不确定性也可能是因为相关的权威判例是一个多数法官的决定，但判决书中存在一个强有力的反对意见。例如，关于医疗过失案件中的机会损失，在 *Gregg v. Scott* 案中，上议院的多数法官认为，只有当机会超过 50% 时，这种损失才可以得到赔偿。

然而，这样的观点是不符合逻辑的；法院误用了概率平衡的门槛（来确定事实），以此决定是否可以索赔机会损失，而

dissenting judgment. For example, on loss of chance in medical negligence cases, the majority of the House of Lords in *Gregg v. Scott* held that such a loss is recoverable only if the chance exceeds 50%.

However, such a view is not logical; the court had misapplied the threshold of balance of probability (which is used for establishing facts) to decide if a loss of chance may be claimed. It seems a matter of time before the opposing view of Lord Nicholls, the dissenting judge, will become accepted. Until then, one cannot say that the law is settled. It is also not predictable whether, on the next opportunity, the Supreme Court would decide that justice is more important than law (see Chapter 39) and bring about a change in the law (Chapter 26).

A variant of the conflicting legal position problem is where two or more areas of law are applicable to the issue at hand, and they do not lead to the same outcome (see Chapter 27). Overlapping legal concepts is a challenge courts often face, and it still remains unclear what the correct approach should be.

The third grey area is where there is really no good outcome or no good answer to the dilemma at hand. The court may really be asked to choose the lesser of two evils. As Lord Nicholls candidly acknowledged in *Fairchild v. Glenhaven Funeral Services*, "the unattractive consequence that one of the [potential] wrongdoers will be held liable for an injury he did not inflict" is outweighed by the "even less attractive alternative that the innocent [claimant] should receive no recompense". In the *Fairchild* case, faced with the difficulty of determining how the illness occurred, the court introduced a test of "material contribution to the risk of injury" which was a significant dilution of the conventional "but-for test" (discussed in Chapter 36).

Sometimes, the challenge at hand appears to be a Gordian knot. There is

持反对意见的法官 Nicholls 勋爵的见解被正式接受似乎是个时间问题。但是在此之前，我们不能说法律已经确定。同样无法预测的是，在下一次机会来临时，最高法院是否会认定正义比法律更重要（见第 39 章）而改变法律（第 26 章）。

法律立场冲突问题的一个变种是，两个或更多的法律领域适用于手头的问题，而它们会导致不同的结果（见第 27 章）。法律概念的重叠是法院经常面临的一个挑战，而正确的方法应该是什么，仍然不清楚。

第三个灰色地带是指对于眼前的困境，确实没有好的结果或好的答案。法院可能真的被要求两害相权取其轻。正如 Nicholls 勋爵在 *Fairchild v. Glenhaven Funeral Services* 案中坦率地承认，“其中一个［潜在］不法行为人将为他没有造成的伤害承担责任，这一不讨喜的后果”好过“无辜的［索赔人］得不到任何补偿的这一更坏的选择”。在 Fairchild 案中，面对确定疾病如何发生的困难，法院引入了“对伤害风险有重大贡献”的测试，这是对传统的“若非”测试标准（在第 36 章讨论）的大幅稀释。

有时，法律眼前的挑战似乎是一个死结。没有令人满意的答案；而问题似乎无法真正被解决。“错误出生”这类案件就是让人陷入两难。从本质上来讲，该案件是一个有出生缺陷的孩子起诉医生在母亲怀孕时因疏忽没有发现胎儿的异常，造成原告带着畸形生活，希望对其承受的痛苦和折磨提出索赔。

法官在裁决这类案件时，会遇到很大的困难。在实际层面上，这个案子不难理解——医生检查疏忽，怀孕继续，孩子出生，孩子受苦，孩子为这种痛苦要求赔偿（例如 *Harriton v.*

no satisfactory answer; the question appears unsolvable. Wrongful life cases are a great challenge. Essentially, the case is that an abnormal child sues the doctor for negligently failing to detect the abnormality in the foetus at the time of the mother's pregnancy. As a result, he lives with the abnormality and wishes to claim for his pain and suffering.

A judge who has to decide such a case encounters great difficulty. At the practical level, the case is simple enough — doctor is negligent in checking, pregnancy continues, child is born, child suffers and child claims damages for such suffering (see, for example, *Harriton v. Stephens*, where a disabled woman sued her mother's doctor for negligent advice which resulted in the pregnancy not being terminated). But, intuitively, the judge has serious reservation about allowing the claim.

The fundamental objection is a philosophical or moral one — many would feel that a human being does not have the right to say he should not be alive (which is somewhat similar to a person's insistence that he has a right to die, an issue for which different countries and cultures hold divergent views). One's philosophical subscription is a personal and subjective one, for which there appears to be no right answer.

So, in all the above ways (and more), grey areas abound in the law.

Stephens 案，一位残疾妇女起诉她母亲的医生，因为医生的疏忽，导致怀孕没有终止）。但是，凭直觉，法官会对允许这类索赔持严肃的保留态度。

最基本的反对意见是从哲学或道德角度出发的——许多人认为，一个人没有权利说他不应该活着（这有点类似于一个人坚持他有死亡的权利，不同的国家和文化对于这个问题有不同的看法）。一个人的哲学观是个性化的、主观的，对此似乎没有唯一正确的答案。

出于上述各种原因（或许还有其他更多原因），法律中充满了灰色地带。

Chapter 39
Justice or Law

Never give your reasons; for your judgment will probably be right, but your reasons will certainly be wrong.

——Lord Mansfield

Whenever a case is decided and a judgment is issued, the legal observer or analyst asks two questions, amongst others. The first is — is the outcome just? Is it fair that the plaintiff won, or lost, as the case may be? In a criminal proceeding, is it just that the accused was convicted (or acquitted)?

The second question relates to the law. Was the judge correct in his handling of the law? Did he perceive it correctly? Where he makes new law, did he craft it appropriately? Was his legal reasoning sound?

It may surprise the reader that there are these two separate questions. You may ask quizzically: "Isn't the law supposed to be just?" Fair response. Well, justice and law are not synonymous.

Justice is an abstract notion. Each of us, whether legally trained or not,

第 39 章
正义还是法律

永远不要说出你的理由；因为你的判断可能是正确的，但你的理由肯定是错误的。

——曼斯菲尔德勋爵

每当对一个案件作出决定并发布判决时，法律观察者或分析家都会提出至少两个问题。第一个问题是：结果是否公正？原告赢了还是输了，这公平吗？在刑事诉讼中，被告被定罪（或被宣告无罪）是否公正？

第二个问题与法律有关。法官对法律的处理是否正确？他的认识是否正确？如果他制定了新的法律，他是否适当地制定了该法律？他的法律推理是否经得起推敲？

读者可能会惊讶于有这样两个独立的问题。你可能会疑惑地问："法律不就应该代表正义吗？"这是一个合理的反应，但是，正义和法律并不是同义词。

公正是一个抽象的概念。我们每个人，无论是否受过法律

intrinsically has some thought, feeling or conviction about justice. If pressed to explain our view, we will take time, and in some situations encounter much difficulty, in trying to articulate the reason（s）for that view.

Law is a system or framework of rules and principles to guide behaviour. As law is crafted to regulate conduct, it seeks to be comprehensive but rarely is. It is impossible to foresee all the varied circumstances to which a legal principle should and should not apply. Law is always a work in progress. Besides, change takes place in society all the time, and law has to respond to change (see Chapter 26).

It should not surprise, then, that at times a particular principle may be imperfect or unjust, or that the application of an ostensibly just principle to a specific circumstance may produce an unjust result. In such a situation, the judge may find himself in a dilemma. In his judicial oath, he pledges to "administer justice according to law" or some other promise to like effect. So, is the judge's primary duty to administer law or to administer justice?

(A side point should be noted. In a dispute, one party wins and the other loses and it is understandable if the losing party feels the outcome is unfair. It is hoped, however, that even in this situation, the losing party perceives there is procedural fairness, in that he had his day in court and there was transparency in the decision-making. This may be a small consolation but is nevertheless important for a civilised society.)

A conservative judge would focus on the word "law". If the law is clear, even if the law is unjust, he would apply it to the case and accept the outcome. Likewise, where the application of an ostensibly just principle to the facts before him results in an unjust outcome, he will abide by it. Legal change, he reasons,

训练，本质上都对正义有一些想法、感觉或信念。但如果被要求解释我们的观点，我们会花费很多时间，甚至在某些情况下遭遇很多困难才有可能阐明我们所持观点背后的原因。

法律是一个指导行为的规则和原则的系统或者框架。由于法律是为了规范行为而制定的，它试图做到全面，但很少做得到。我们不可能预见一个法律原则应该和不应该适用的所有情况。法律始终是一项正在进行的事业。此外，社会一直在发生变化，而法律也必须对变化做出回应（见第 26 章）。

因此，有时一项特定的原则可能不完善或不公正，或者将表面上公正的原则适用于特定的情况时可能会产生不公正的结果，这些都并不令人震惊。在这种情况下，法官可能会发现自己处于两难境地。在他的司法宣誓词中，他承诺“依法维护正义”或其他一些类似的承诺。那么，法官的首要职责是执行法律还是推行正义？

（我们应该注意一个附带的问题。在纠纷中，一方赢了，另一方输了，如果输的一方觉得结果不公平，是可以理解的。然而，我们希望，即使在这种情况下，败诉方也会认为有程序上的公平，因为他在法庭上有过自己的机会，而且决策过程是透明的。这对个人来说可能仅仅是很小的安慰，但对一个文明的社会来说则至关重要。）

一个保守的法官会关注“法律”这个词。如果法律是明确的，即使法律是不公正的，他也会将其应用于案件并接受结果。同样，如果将表面上公正的原则适用于他面前的事实会导致不公正的结果，他也依然会遵守这项原则。他的理由是，法律变革最好留给议会去做（见第 23 章）。

is best left to parliament (see Chapter 23) .

In contrast, an activist judge, being more focused on the word "justice", may pay greater heed to his instinctive sense of what a just outcome demands for the case before him and then seek to rationalise or justify his decision. (Of course, rarely would judges admit to taking such an approach.)

He may try to stretch a particular principle so that it can accommodate the facts before him. For example, the principle of vicarious liability is about making employers liable for the wrongs committed by employees. In *Cox v. Ministry of Justice*, the plaintiff, a manager in a prison kitchen, was injured when a prisoner (who received nominal wages for doing some work whilst being a prisoner) carrying supplies accidentally dropped a sack of rice onto her back, injuring her. She sued the Minister of Justice for the prisoner's action on the principle of vicarious liability.

In the lower court, the judge held that the Ministry was not liable since there was no employer–employee relationship here. On appeal, the Court of Appeal (and, subsequently, the Supreme Court as well) held that the Ministry was vicariously liable since the prisoner was performing a task which was an integral part of the activities in the prison. In so doing, the doctrine of vicarious liability was extended to a situation where the wrongdoer was not strictly an employee but was in a situation said to be "akin to" an employee. (Interested readers are referred to *Armes v. Nottingham CC* for an even more radical extension of the doctrine.)

Where a judge is so minded, he may, within the bounds of *stare decisis* (the doctrine of precedent; see Chapter 22) change the law or create new law in order to achieve a result which he perceives to be fair. And there are many tools at his

相比之下，一个激进的法官更注重“正义”这个词，他可能会更多地关注他的本能感觉，即在他面前的案件需要什么样的正义结果，然后寻求合理化或证明他的决定。（当然，很少会有法官承认这样的做法。）

他可能会试图延伸一个特定的原则，使其能够适应他面前的事实。例如，替代责任的原则是让雇主为雇员的错误行为负责。在 *Cox v. Ministry of Justice* 案中，原告是一名监狱厨房的经理，当一名囚犯（在狱中做一些工作而获得象征性的工资）在搬运物资时不小心将一袋大米掉到她的背上，使她不幸受伤。她根据替代责任的原则，就该囚犯的行为起诉了司法部部长。

在下级法院，法官认为司法部没有责任，因为这里不存在雇主与雇员的关系。在上诉中，上诉法院（以及随后的最高法院）认为，司法部应承担替代责任，因为该囚犯执行的任务是监狱活动的一个组成部分。这样一来，替代责任的理论就被扩展到了这样一种情况，即不法行为人并不是严格意义上的雇员，而是处于一种被称为“类似于”雇员的情况。（有兴趣的读者可以参考 *Armes v. Nottingham CC* 案，以了解该理论更为激进的延伸。）

如果法官有这样的想法，他可以在遵循先例（遵循先例规则；见第 22 章）的范围内，改变法律或创造新的法律，以达到他认为公平的结果。他有很多工具可以使用，包括：

- 将法律框架里的要件转变为因素（第 16 章）；
- 给既定规则制定一个例外（第 17 章）；

disposal, including:

- changing requirements of a legal framework to factors (Chapter 16);
- creating an exception to the rule (Chapter 17);
- resorting to a peripheral objective in that area of law (Chapter 28);
- exercising judicial discretion (Chapter 30); or
- reversing the burden of proof (Chapter 35).

Of course, most of these measures are drastic ones and should be resorted to only circumspectly.

Judicial appetite for legal change varies. Conservative judges highlight the importance of consistency and predictability in the law. It may be added that the party on the losing end of a decision where the law changes may protest that the law has changed retrospectively. Legislation, in contrast, is prospective and not retrospective.

Activist judges place greater emphasis on ensuring that justice is done. To that end, they are more prepared to bend or change the law.

The tension between justice and law continues and remains an inevitable feature of the legal system.

- 诉诸该法律领域的辅助目标（第 28 章）；
- 行使司法裁量权（第 30 章）；或
- 倒置举证责任（第 35 章）。

当然，这些措施大多是极端的，只能谨慎地使用。

不同法官对法律变革的喜好各不相同。保守派法官强调法律一致性和可预测性的重要性。此外，在法律发生变化的情况下，败诉方可能会抗议法律发生了溯及性变化。相比之下，立法则是前瞻性的，而非溯及性的。

激进的法官则更强调确保正义得到伸张。为此，他们相对来说更不介意扭曲或改变法律。

正义与法律之间的张力持续存在，并且将一直是法律制度的一个不可避免的特征。

Chapter 40
Hindsight Bias

Everything makes sense in hindsight.

——Daniel Kahneman

When a person's act or decision is being scrutinised, the assessment should be done objectively and fairly. The action should be adjudged good or bad, proper or improper, by reference to the circumstances at the point of the action.

Unfortunately, human beings are prone to hindsight bias and outcome bias. After the event, it is so easy, and tempting, to be influenced by the outcome to conclude that the action was right or wrong.

For example, in determining whether a defendant whose action resulted in the injury to the plaintiff should be held liable, the proper course would be to look at his act and consider what was the appropriate standard of care and, if he was in breach, whether the breach caused the damage. Hindsight bias, in contrast, works backwards — B was injured, so A must have been negligent. The bias is even stronger if the damage or injury is severe. Hindsight, in effect, is equated

第 40 章
后见之明偏误

事后诸葛亮永远正确。

——丹尼尔·卡尼曼

当一个人的行为或决定受到审查时，评估应该是客观和公正的，应该根据行动当时的情况来判定行动的好坏，适当或不适当。

不幸的是，人类很容易产生事后的后见之明偏误和结果导向偏误。在事件发生后，人们很容易受到结果的影响而得出行动是正确或错误的结论。

例如，在确定被告是否应该为其行为导致原告受伤而承担责任时，正确的做法是审视他的行为，并考虑适当的注意标准是什么，如果他不符合这一标准，再看他的行为是否导致了损害。与此相反，后见之明偏误是倒过来看的——B 受伤了，所以 A 一定有疏忽。如果损害或伤害很严重，这种偏误就更强烈。这实际是将“事后诸葛亮”等同于先见之明，当然是十

with foresight. Which is very wrong.

Conversely, a positive outcome, even an excellent outcome, does not necessarily mean the quality of the decision-making was a good one. The person who wins a lottery is not a smart or expert investor; on the contrary, he was just lucky.

Whenever hindsight bias unduly influences a judge's conclusion of whether the defendant had breached his duty (be it in tort or in contract), the standard expected of the defendant is set unreasonably high. Judges are aware of the danger and sometimes stress the need to be mindful of it. However, from time to time, there are lapses and injustice results.

The doctrine of *res ipsa loquitur* (discussed in Chapter 35) is an interesting one to consider in this regard. The conventional approach in a negligence case is that the plaintiff has to prove breach as well as causation. However, according to the *res ipsa loquitur* doctrine, there is reasonable evidence of negligence if:

- the thing that caused the injury was in the defendant's control;
- such an accident would not ordinarily happen if care had been taken; and
- there is an absence of explanation from the defendant.

So, in a case where a scalpel is left in the patient's body, a court may hold the surgeon liable because "the thing speaks for itself".

If one scrutinises *res ipsa loquitur* decisions, one suspects that a fair number of them are really examples of hindsight bias — that the conclusion of guilt was highly influenced by the eventual outcome. Take a case where the judge is uncertain if the defendant was responsible for a fire that started in his premises. If, after hearing all the evidence (and also the defendant's explanation of a possible

分错误的。

相反，一个积极的结果，甚至一个优秀的结果，并不一定意味着决策的高明。赢得彩票的人并不是聪明或专业的投资者；相反，他只是运气好。

每当后见之明偏误影响法官决定被告是否违反了他的义务（无论是侵权行为还是合同）时，对被告的预期标准就被设定得过高。法官们意识到了这种危险，有时还强调要注意这种危险。然而，失误和不公正的结果依然时有发生。

在这一点上，“不言自明推定”原则（在第 35 章中讨论）是一个值得考虑的问题。过失案件中的传统做法是，原告必须证明违约行为和因果关系。然而，根据“不言自明推定”原则，以下情况被视为存在合理的过失证据：

- 造成伤害的事物是在被告的控制之下；
- 如果采取了谨慎措施，这种事故通常不会发生；以及
- 被告没有作出解释。

因此，在一个手术刀被留在病人体内的案件中，法院可以要求外科医生承担责任，因为“事情本身就说明了问题”。

如果仔细研究根据“不言自明推定”作出的判决，我们会怀疑其中相当多的判决实际上是“事后诸葛亮”式的——有责任的结论受到最终结果的高度影响。例如，法官不确定被告是否对其房舍内发生的火灾负责。如果在听取了所有的证据（也包括被告对此事与他无关的可能原因的解释）后，法官不能确

cause which does not implicate him), the judge is unsure if the defendant had been negligent, the correct legal outcome should be that the defendant is not liable; the case is not proven on a balance of probabilities. Yet, in several cases involving scenarios such as this, the court found the defendant liable. Perhaps hindsight basis was at work, probably unwittingly.

In the realm of contract law, *Fulton v. Globalia* provides a fascinating study into the relevance of hindsight bias. There, a charter party (contract for the charter of a ship) was wrongfully terminated and the plaintiff– shipowner sued the defendant–charterer for damages. The defendant cleverly asserted that the amount of damages should take into account the fact that because of the breach, the shipowners sold the ship at a far higher price than if they had held on to the end of the charter period and the sale of the ship amounted to an act of mitigation of losses. If this benefit is taken into account, the amount of the plaintiff 's claim would be negative.

A unanimous Court of Appeal, overturning the High Court decision in the plaintiff 's favour, decided that the benefit was to be taken into account and, hence, the plaintiff 's claim failed. The charter appealed to the Supreme Court. What should be the fair outcome, and upon what reasoning?

The Supreme Court unanimously overturned the Court of Appeal's decision and held that the benefit of the higher sale price should not be taken into account. The reasoning was that the sale was not an act of mitigation; rather, it was the shipowner's own business decision which was taken at its own risk. The charterer's breach did not cause the sale of the ship but simply provided the occasion for the shipowner to make a business decision. The sale of the ship and the attendant gain was a separate matter from the shipowner's claim for loss of

定被告是否有过失，那么，正确的法律结果应该是判决被告没有责任；从概率平衡角度看，该案件没有得到证明。然而，在几个涉及诸如此类情况的案件中，法院认定被告负有责任。这也许是不知不觉中后见之明偏误在起作用。

在合同法领域，*Fulton v. Globalia* 案为后见之明偏误的影响提供了一个精彩的例子。在该案中，一份租船合同被错误地终止了，原告船东起诉被告租船人要求赔偿。然而被告巧妙地主张，损害赔偿金的数额应考虑到这样一个事实：由于违约，船东以远高于整个租期内可得租金的价格出售了船舶，出售船舶相当于减轻损失。如果考虑到这一好处，原告的索赔金额将是负数。

上诉法院一致推翻了高等法院对原告有利的判决，决定将该获益考虑在内，因此判决驳回原告的索赔请求。船东向最高法院提出上诉。公平的结果应该是什么，应当基于什么理由？

最高法院一致推翻了上诉法院的决定，认为不应考虑较高售价的好处。其理由是，出售并不是一种止损行为；相反，这是船东自己的商业决定，其风险自负。租船人的违约行为并没有导致船舶的出售，只是为船东做出商业决定提供了机会。船舶的出售和随之而来的收益与船东的收入损失索赔是两回事。正如法院正确指出的那样，如果航运市场走向了另一个方向，船东就无法要求赔偿更大数额的损失。在我看来，无论是从公正的结果，还是从法律分析来看，最高法院的判决都是正确的。

earnings. As the court rightly pointed out, had the shipping market gone the other way, the shipowner would not have been able to claim for a greater loss. In my view, the Supreme Court's decision is correct, both in terms of a just outcome as well as legal analysis.

It may surprise readers that superior courts, even apex courts, can make wrong decisions. The case is a good reminder that hindsight bias can cloud logical reasoning and result in controversy and error.

读者也许会感到惊讶：上级法院，甚至是最高法院也可能会做出错误的决定。此案很好地提醒我们，后见之明偏误会蒙蔽逻辑推理，从而引发争议和错误。

Chapter 41
Imperfect World, Imperfect Laws

The law isn't justice. It's a very imperfect system.

——Raymond Chandler

The world is a very imperfect place, and this is a fact which each of us takes years and decades to fully appreciate and accept. Imperfection pervades all realms of human knowledge and activity. It is so in medicine, psychiatry, geology, engineering, technology, sociology, philosophy and all other disciplines. To err is human (and to forgive divine) .

Law is also imperfect, as we have observed many times throughout the length of this book. There are several reasons for the law being imperfect.

First, the world is a very complex and complicated place. The law seeks to do justice in every scenario. But each scenario has its own dynamics, stakeholders, problems and tensions. The lawmaker or, in the case of a dispute, the judge, needs to understand the complicated context in which the law seeks to proffer a view of what is right and what is wrong. Depending on the context,

第41章
不完美的世界，不完美的法律

法律并不是正义，而是一个非常不完美的系统。

——雷蒙德·钱德勒

世界非常不完美，关于这个事实我们每个人都需要花费数年甚至数十年时间才能完全理解和接受。不完美充斥着人类知识和活动的所有领域。医学、精神病学、地质学、工程学、技术学、社会学、哲学和所有其他学科都是如此。凡人皆舛误（唯有神见宥）。

正如我们在这本书的整个篇幅中多次观察到的，法律同样不完美。法律的不完美有几个原因。

第一，世界非常复杂。法律试图在所有情况下实现正义，但每个情况都有其自身的特殊环境、利益相关者、问题和矛盾关系。法律制定者或者（在发生争端时的）法官需要了解复杂的背景，以及在这种背景下，法律如何判断什么是对的，什么是错的。根据不同的背景，法律制定者必须了解医学、考古学、

the lawmaker has to understand medicine, archeology, climatology, physics, economics or whatever the situation involves. Often, the law is imperfect simply because the context is complex and imperfect.

Secondly, in this very diverse world, there are so many different interests in a given scenario and the varying interests are often competing and conflicting. The gain for an interest group is often the loss for another group. The law has the unenviable task of achieving an optimal balance of the interests of all the relevant groups. Depending on the circumstances, it may be necessary to prioritise the interest of one group over the other or the others, particularly where a binary outcome is required.

Thirdly, when deciding legal disputes, much turns on the ascertainment of the facts. This is an inherently difficult exercise. Frequently, the judge is unable to say who is telling the truth and who is lying. Further, the dispute may involve a relationship or situation which spans several years. Also, in many cases, causation can pose a real challenge; sometimes, nobody knows how the illness occurred or how the incident (such as a fire) eventuated. The imperfections in fact ascertainment may lead to imperfections in the administration of justice.

Fourthly, the complete realm of the law is vast and the legal issues that may arise are almost limitless. The law at any point of time is always a work in progress. There will be controversies, inconsistencies and gaps in the law. The lawmaker, whether parliament or judiciary, only has a finite amount of time, which will be expended on what is either more important or more urgent. And law will always lag behind the innovations, disruptions and other changes that take place on many fronts.

Finally, the lawmaker, like all professionals, is just a human being. The

气候学、物理学、经济学或任何涉及的情形。常常仅仅是因为背景的复杂和不完美而导致法律的不完美。

第二，在这个非常多样化的世界里，在特定的情况下会涉及许多不同的利益，而不同的利益往往相互竞争并发生冲突。一个利益集团的受益往往意味着另一个集团的损失。法律肩负着实现所有相关群体利益最佳平衡的艰巨任务。根据不同的情况，可能需要将一个群体的利益置于其他群体的利益之上，特别是在需要一个非黑即白的结果时更是这样。

第三，在决定法律纠纷时，很大程度上取决于对事实的确认。这项工作原本就非常困难。法官往往无法判断谁在说真话，谁在说谎。况且，争议可能涉及跨越数年的关系或事件。此外，在很多案件中，因果关系可能构成真正的挑战；有时，没人知道疾病是如何发生的，或事件（如火灾）是如何发生的。事实确认的不完善可能会导致司法公正的不完善。

第四，法律涉及的整个领域极其庞大，可能出现的法律问题几乎是无限的。法律工作在任何时候都是在持续进行。法律中会有争议、不一致和漏洞。立法者，无论是议会还是司法机构，都只有有限的时间，这些时间会被用于更重要或更紧急的事情。而法律总是会落后于方方面面的创新、破坏和其他变化。

第五，像所有的专业人士一样，立法者只是一个人。法律必须解决的背景因素可能很复杂，立法者必须尽力去理解，必要时还需要借助其他领域专家的帮助。他精通一般的法律，在一些法律领域有特殊的专长。他必须寻找出所有相关的法律和争议，并确定什么是解决当前争议的正确原则。他必须熟悉他所掌握的全部工具，并在面对争议和难题时，以最佳方式巧妙

contextual dynamic that the law has to address may be complex and he has to try his best to understand it, where necessary with the aid of domain experts. He has proficiency of law in general and special expertise in a few areas of law. He has to seek out all the relevant laws and issues and ascertain what are the correct principles for the matter at hand. He has to be familiar with the whole armoury of tools at his disposal and adroitly craft the law (where crafting is required) in the best possible way, and in the face of controversy and complexity.

Inevitably, there may be missteps in logic or in perceptions of the policy considerations. Further, he has his personal value subscriptions which consciously or subconsciously surface. As US Supreme Court justice Robert Jackson acknowledged: "We are not final because we are infallible, but we are infallible only because we are final." In a similar vein, Harold Kushner notes that "human beings are not meant to create perfection".

The tasks of administering law and making law are very difficult ones. The judge or lawmaker has substantial but finite intelligence and wisdom. In the final analysis, law is imperfect because the world is imperfect and ever-changing; also, the lawmaker is imperfect.

地制定法律（如果需要这样做的话）。

不可避免的是，人在逻辑上或对政策考虑的认识上可能有失误。此外，每个人都有自己的个人价值取向，而这些价值取向会自觉或不自觉地浮现出来。正如美国最高法院大法官罗伯特·杰克逊所承认的，“我们不是因为不犯错才成为终审法院，只是因为我们是终审法院所以才不犯错”。同样，哈罗德·库什纳指出，“人类本就不是来创造完美的”。

实施法律和制定法律的工作非常困难。法官或立法者拥有相当的，却也是有限的脑力和智慧。归根结底，法律是不完美的，因为世界是不完美并不断变化着的；同时，立法者也并不完美。

Final Words

I can see clearly now the rain is gone I can see all obstacles in my way.

——Johnny Nash

Indeed, the law is often complex and at times, incomprehensible. To laymen and, sometimes, even to lawyers. But complexity inhabits all substantive disciplines. In this sophisticated, diversified, fluid and chaotic world, the challenge of keeping peace and order, and of administering justice, cannot be an easy one.

For each of us, as we go about our daily lives within society and in the context of our work or business, myriad laws affect us, and often in serious and dramatic ways. We have no choice but to seek to understand the laws which are relevant to us so that we can comply and, where possible, leverage the position to protect our interests.

In this book, I propose four steps or ways to understand complex laws. The first is to appreciate the overall dynamics of crafting law. The starting point is to scrutinise the context of the matter at hand — the parties and stakeholders, the issues and the problems. The crafting of law essentially involves a consideration

写在最后的话

当雨过天晴，我便能看清所有挡在我面前的拦路虎。

——约翰·纳什

确实，法律往往复杂且有时难以理解。对于普通人，甚至有时对律师来说也是这样，但所有实实在在的学科都是复杂的。在这个复杂、多元、多变和混乱的世界中，应对维持和平与秩序并实现正义的挑战绝非易事。

对于我们每个人来说，在社会中生活或者工作的每一天，都会受到无数法律的影响，而且这种影响可能是强烈的，乃至戏剧性。我们别无选择，只能设法了解与我们相关的法律以便能够遵纪守法，并在可能的情况下利用这些法律来保护我们的权益。

在这本书中，我提出了理解复杂的法律的“四步法”。第一步是了解制定法律的整体机制。这首先需要仔细研究我们面对的事务的背景——当事人和利益相关者、涉及的问题和难点。制定法律本质上涉及考量背景、应用正义概念以及确定相关政策（见图 1）。

of the context, the application of notions of justice and an ascertainment of the relevant policies (see Fig. 1) .

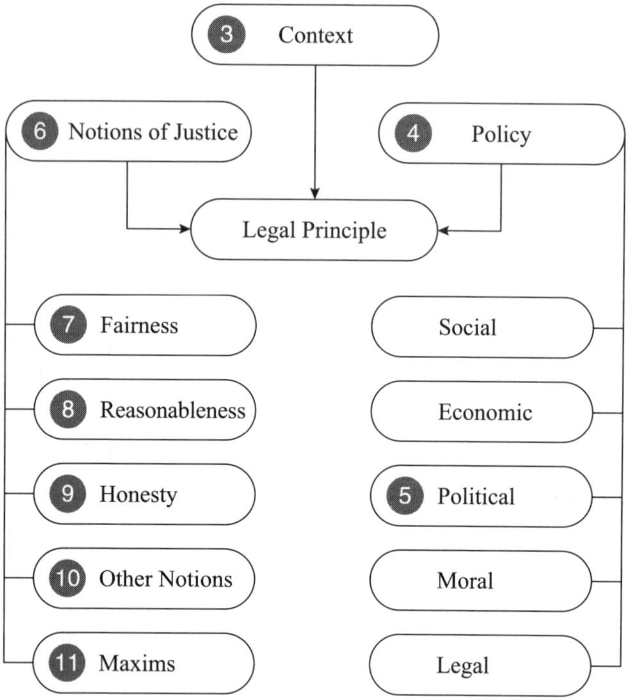

Fig. 1: Dynamics of Crafting Law
(numbers indicate the chapters in which the topic is covered)

With this broad approach in mind, one proceeds to configure a legal principle for the matter at hand. Every legal principle has its elements. The crafting of these elements entails a good use of linguistic tools. Often, the legal framework is complete only when exceptions and defences are included (see Fig. 2 on the previous page) .

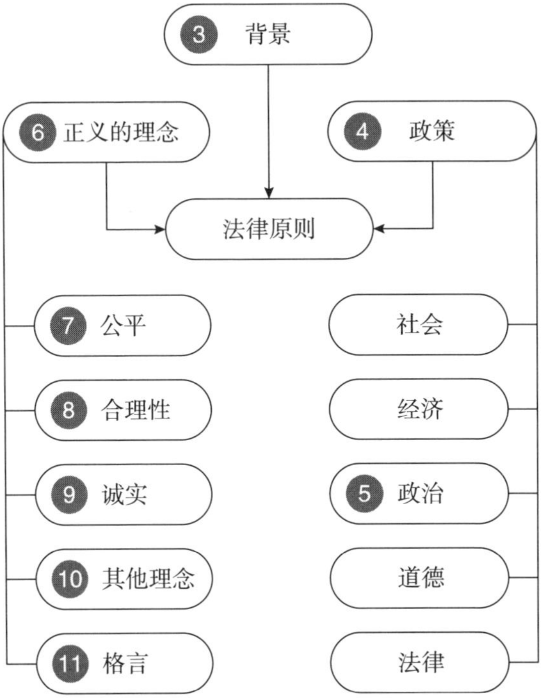

图 1：制定法律时考虑的因素
（数字代表讨论相关课题的章节号）

在掌握这个制定法律的一般步骤之后，我们开始根据手头需要解决的问题来设计具体的法律原则。每个法律原则都有其要件，确定这些要素需要很好地使用语言工具。通常情况下，完整的法律框架需要包括例外和抗辩事由（见图 2）。

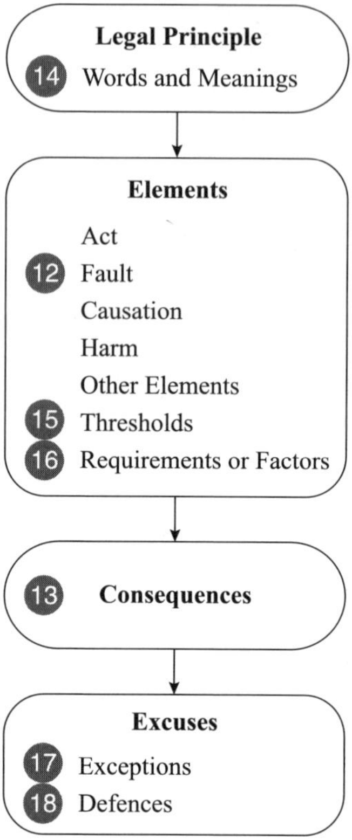

Fig. 2: Configuring a Legal principle
(numbers indicate the chapters in which the topic is covered)

In seeking to ascertain and understand the law, one encounters numerous complexities and controversies. There are many instances of and reasons for these difficulties (see Fig. 3), and we considered them in Part IV.

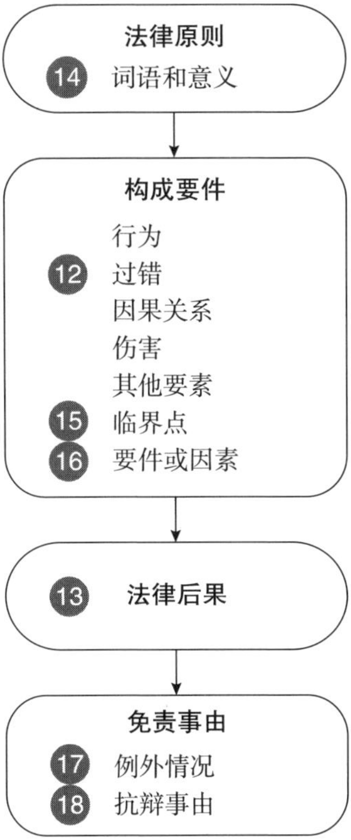

图 2：配置法律原则

（数字代表讨论相关课题的章节号）

在寻求确定和理解法律的过程中，人们会遇到许多复杂性和争议问题。这些问题有很多实例及其成因（见图 3），我们在第四部分进行了讨论。

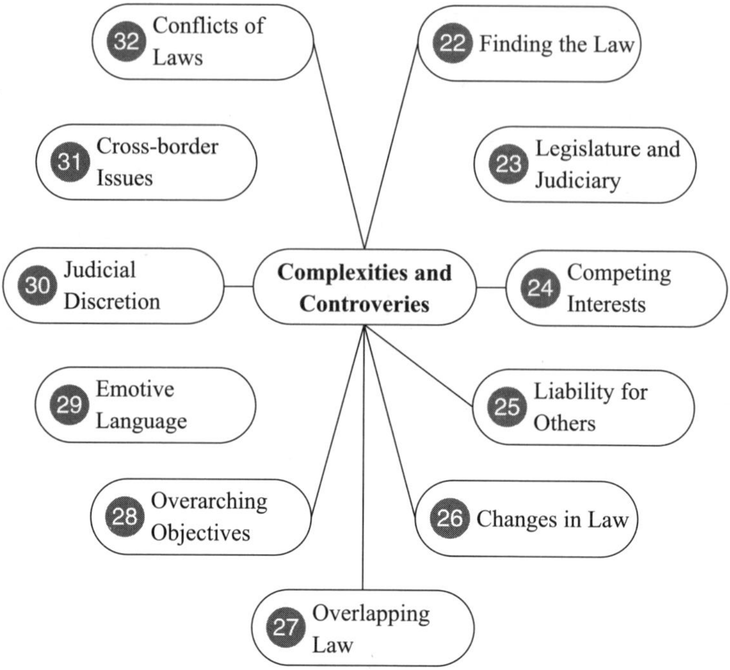

Fig. 3：Complexities and Controversies
（numbers indicate the chapters in which the topic is covered）

Relatedly，there are times when the law appears to be wrong or unfair or both. In Part V，we identified and analysed error and unfairness in law，so that we can understand law better（see Fig. 4）.

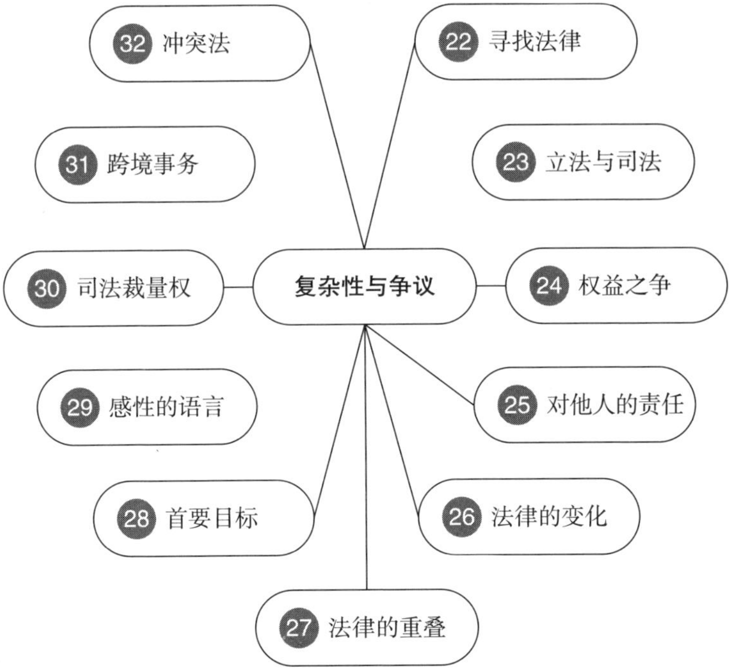

图 3：复杂性与争议
（数字代表讨论相关课题的章节号）

与此相关的是有时法律似乎是错误或不公平的。在第五部分，我们找出法律中的错误和不公平并加以分析，以便我们能够更好地理解法律（见图 4）。

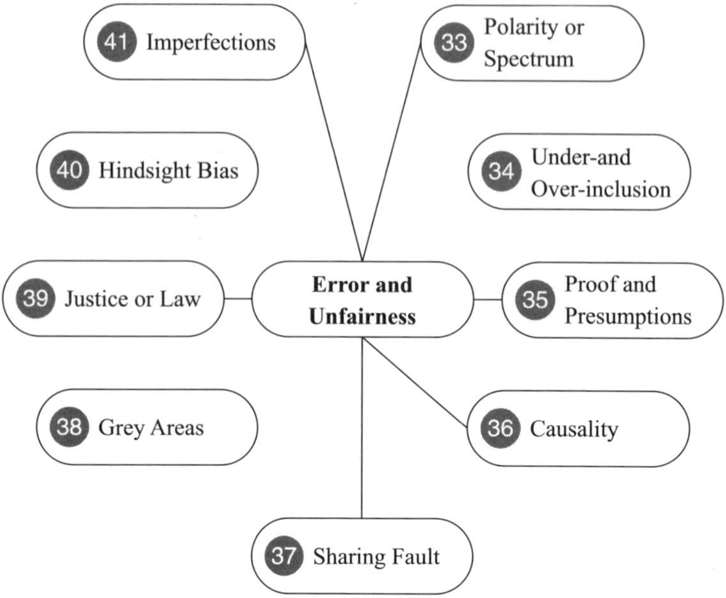

Fig. 4: Error and Unfairness

(numbers indicate the chapters in which the topic is covered)

The composite picture of the law is a very complicated one. As I look at law — the big picture, the individual areas of law and the specific legal principles in an area — my personal view is that there is a substantial amount of order, harmony and sense in the law.

However, the truth is that there is also a fair amount of controversy, obscurity and injustice within the law. And, in some parts and on some issues, the law is simply impenetrable to the layperson.

As I wrote the chapters, I was regularly reminded that my endeavour is an ambitious one, and that there is no single or simple way to explain complex law.

This book seeks to give you a clear view of the law. I hope you found it helpful.

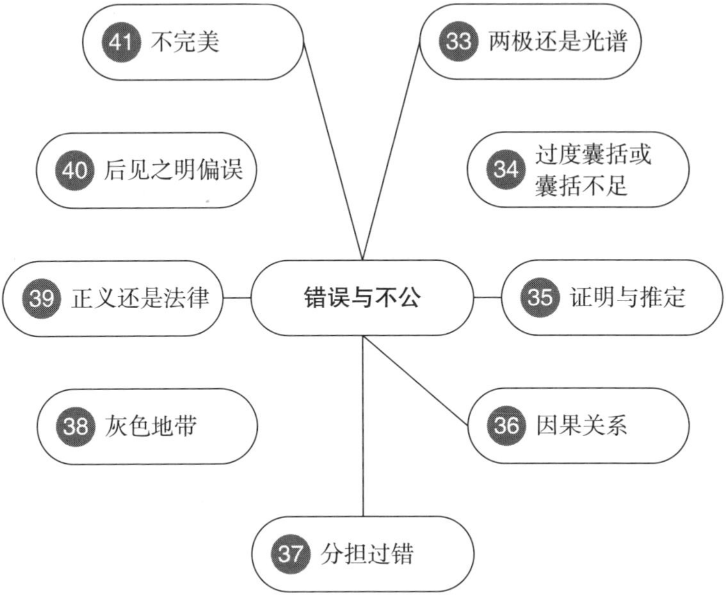

图 4：错误和不公平

（数字代表讨论相关课题的章节号）

综合起来看，法律显得特别复杂。当我审视法律时——无论是从整体、具体法律领域还是从某个领域的具体法律原则的角度看——我个人的观点是法律中包含了大量的秩序、谐调和理性。

然而事实上，在法律中也确实存在着相当多的争议、晦涩和不公正。在某些部分和某些具体问题上，法律对普通人来说就是无法理解的。

在我写下这本书的时候，我经常提醒自己，虽然我努力尝试，但是，想要解释复杂的法律，并无捷径可循。

本书旨在让你能够洞悉法律的门径。希望此书对你有所助益。

著作权合同登记号：图字 01-2022-3633 号

图书在版编目 (CIP) 数据

洞悉法门：理解法律的复杂性：汉英对照 /（新加坡）刘启扬著；张巍，翁磊，李嘉宝译 .—北京：中国法制出版社，2022.11

书名原文：A Clear View of the Law：Making Sense of Legal Complexity

ISBN 978-7-5216-2892-0

Ⅰ.①洞… Ⅱ.①刘… ②张… ③翁… ④李… Ⅲ.①法律—研究—汉、英 Ⅳ.① D9

中国版本图书馆 CIP 数据核字（2022）第 168514 号

策划 / 责任编辑：王雯汀　　封面设计：李　宁

洞悉法门：理解法律的复杂性：汉英对照

DONGXI FAMEN：LIJIE FALÜ DE FUZAXING：HAN-YING DUIZHAO

著者 /［新加坡］刘启扬

译者 / 张巍　翁磊　李嘉宝

经销 / 新华书店

印刷 / 三河市紫恒印装有限公司

开本 / 880 毫米 ×1230 毫米　32 开　　印张 / 12.5　字数 / 270 千

版次 / 2022 年 11 月第 1 版　　2022 年 11 月第 1 次印刷

中国法制出版社出版

书号 ISBN 978-7-5216-2892-0　　定价：65.00 元

北京市西城区西便门西里甲 16 号西便门办公区

邮政编码 100053　　传真：010-63141000

网址：http://www.zgfzs.com　　**编辑部电话：010-63141824**

市场营销部电话：010-63141612　　**印务部电话：010-63141606**

（如有印装质量问题，请与本社印务部联系。）